ARCHIVES

OF THE

STATE OF NEW JERSEY.

FIRST SERIES.

General Index.

This volume was prepared by authority of the State of New Jersey, at the request of the New Jersey Historical Society, and under the direction of the following Committee of that Society:

NATHANIEL NILES, *Chairman.*
WILLIAM NELSON,
GARRET D. W. VROOM,
FREDERICK W. RICORD,
WILLIAM S. STRYKER.

GENERAL INDEX

TO THE

DOCUMENTS

RELATING TO THE

COLONIAL HISTORY

OF THE

STATE OF NEW JERSEY.

FIRST SERIES, IN TEN VOLUMES.

PUBLISHED UNDER AND BY VIRTUE OF AN ACT ENTITLED
"AN ACT FOR THE BETTER PRESERVATION OF THE
EARLY RECORDS OF THE STATE OF NEW JER-
SEY," PASSED MARCH TWENTY-NINTH,
ONE THOUSAND EIGHT HUNDRED
AND SEVENTY-TWO.

PREPARED BY

FREDERICK W. RICORD.

CLEARFIELD

Originally published
Newark, New Jersey, 1888

Reprinted by Genealogical Publishing Co., Inc.
Baltimore, Maryland, 1994

Library of Congress Catalogue Card Number 94-76713

Reprinted for Clearfield Company by
Genealogical Publishing Company
Baltimore, Maryland, 2011

ISBN 978-0-8063-4874-2

Made in the United States of America

INDEX TO
NEW JERSEY COLONIAL DOCUMENTS.

Volumes I to X Inclusive.

Abbat, John, iii, 165.

Abbott, Mordecai, ii, 41-6, 65-73, 76, 79, 88, 90, 99.

Abercrombie, General, James, viii, Part II, 222—ix, 118—x, 25.

Abrahams, Cornellis, i, 49, 150.

Achter Cull, See Achter Kol.

Achter Kol, i, 14, 130, 141; Name applied to New Jersey, 124-147.

Adam, Alexander, ii, 332, 333.

Adam, Elizabeth, i, 186.

Adams, Fenwicke, i, 187.

Adams, John, i, 186, 227, 414—ii, 148.

Adams, John, x, 529, 664.

Adams, Joseph, ii, 384.

Adams, Mary, i, 186.

Adams, Samuel, x, 529.

Adderly, Henry, ii, 470.

Addison, Joseph, iv, 11; Announces to the Lords of Trade the King's satisfaction with Governor Hunter, 327; Referred to, 331, 338.

Adkinson, William, iv, 98.

Admiralty Courts, Establishment of, ix, 620, 621.

After Cull, See Achter Kol.

Aghter Col, See Achter Kol.

Aickman, William, i, 529.

Aikman, William, ii, 202.

Ainsley, William, See Aynesley, William.

Akarman, Sr., John, i, 289.

Akarman, Jr., John, i, 289.

Albania, Name given to New Jersey by Governor Nicolls, i, 47.

Albany, The Garrison at, i, 79.

Alberson, John, ii, 42-62, 66-74, 79.

Albertis, John, Ensign, ix, 187.

Aldricks, Evert, i, 269.

Alexander, Elizabeth, ix, 336.

Alexander, George, i, 522—ii, 187, 193; Disbursements by, on account of East Jersey, 204.

Alexander, James, i, 524—ii, 114.—Authorized to collect quit rents, iv, 241; Appointed Surveyor-General of West Jersey, 288; Referred to, 390; One of the Commissioners for running partition line, 394; Notice of, 399; Referred to, 406, 418, 419, 428, 453, 454.—Recommended for the Council, v, 34; Appointed a member of Council, 52; Letter from, to Ex-Governor Robert Hunter, 55; Letter to, from the Council of Proprietors of West Jersey, 67; Referred to, 102; Money paid to, 137, 147, 148, 151; Money received from, 138; Letters to, from Ex-Governor Robert Hunter, 179, 187; Commissioner to try pirates, 197; Letter from, to Cadwallader Colden, relating to Peter Sonmans, 202; Letter to, from Thomas Budd, relative to the appointment of a Surveyor-General, 211; Order of the West Jersey Council to, 212; Letter to, from John Burr, 212; Letter from, to Governor Burnet, respecting the relative authority of the Plantation Assemblys, 230; Letter to, from Cadwallader Colden, relative to a proposition from the Society for the Propagation of the Gospel in Foreign Parts, 237; Letter from, to Ex-Governor Hunter, referring to the death of Governor Burnet, and New Jersey affairs, 261; Memorial of, to Governor Montgomerie, relative to the West Jersey Surveyor-Generalship, 273; Answer to said memorial, 278; Letter to, from Thomas Penn, recommending Ferdinand John Paris as Agent for New Jersey, 293; Complained of, by Governor Cosby, 324; His removal from the Council recommended, 325; Letter from, to F. John Paris, relative to New Jersey affairs, 327; Referred to, 343, 345; Letter from, to Robert Hunter, relative to Governor Cosby, 359; Letter from, to Secretary Popple, on the same subject, 360; Letter from Governor Cosby, relating to, 395-402; Petitions, 404; Complaints against, laid before the Queen, 408; Letter to, from Robert Hunter Morris, 431; Referred to, 439; Signs petition, 443; Referred to, 454, 456, 468.—Letter from, to Peter Collinson, relating to his difficulties with Governor Cosby, vi, 71; Letter from, to Rodrigo Pacheco, 77; Referred to, 107, 109; Affidavit of, relative to the north partition point between New Jersey and New York, 145; Referred to, 294, 314, 315, 316, 317, 329, 355, 359, 360, 367-378, 395; Letter from, to the Lords of Trade, giving an account of the Provinces, 419; Letter to, from Ferdinand John Paris, 422; Letter from, to the Lords of Trade, at the request of President Hamilton, 446; Letter to, from Chief-Justice Morris, relative to New Jersey affairs, 471—vii, 5; Member of Governor Belcher's Council, 6; Letter to, from F. J. Paris, 12; Letter to, from Chief-Justice Morris, 17; Letter from, to David Ogden, referring to the rioters, 53; Letter from, to Joseph Murray, relative to the propriety of Governor sitting with the Council in their legislative capacity, 77; In Council, 86, 88; Letter to, from John Coxe, detailing some proceedings of the Gov-

ernor and Council, 97; Commends Sundry Officers, 102; Letter to, from R. H. Morris, relative to the appointment of Samuel Nevill as Judge, 107; Reports a draft of an address from the Council to the Governor, 110; Letter from, to Cadwallader Colden, relative to the riots, 113; Letters from, to Ferdinand John Paris, relative to the division line between New Jersey and New York, 119, 125, 131; To John Coxe, relative to the dissolving of the Assembly, 122; Reply thereto, 127; Address of, to the Speaker of the Council of New York, 141; Letter from, to F. J. Paris, relative to the division line between New York and New Jersey, 152; To John Coxe, relative to the riots, 154; Letters from, to F. J. Paris, relative to the New York and New Jersey line, 156, 167, 176; Letter from, to John Coxe, relative to the rioters, 161; To the Lords of Trade, 170; Attempts, with other members of the Council, to advise Governor Belcher, 183; Communication from, as a member of Council, to the same, 185; Addresses, with other Councilors, the King, relative to the riots, 189; Letter from, to F. J. Paris, relative to the riots, 197; To John Coxe, relative to the action of Governor Belcher, 204; Answer of, to the rioters, 233; Letter to, from F. J. Paris, relative to action against the rioters, 234; Signs, 237; Letter to, from the same, relative to Governor Belcher, 238; Letter from, to F. J. Paris, concerning Governor Belcher and the rioters, 251; Letter to, from F. J. Paris, relative to business before the Lords of Trade, 260; Letter from, to F. J. Paris, relative to the division line between New York and New Jersey, 262; Letter to, from F. J. Paris, relative to the conditions of the affairs of the Province in London, 271; Referred to, 284, 285, 287, 288; Letter from, to David Ogden, on the propriety of trying the rioters in Essex county, 288; Letter to, from F. J. Paris, relative to his proceedings in London, 294; From the same, in regard to the boundary between New York and New Jersey, 297; From the same, concerning the riots, 301, 304; Letters to, from F. J. Paris, concerning the pardoning of those accused of treason, and of the disturbances in New Jersey, 308, 310; Referred to, 323; Letter from, relating to the riots in Newark, 328; Letter from, to F. J. Paris, in relation to reuniting New Jersey to New York, 331; In Council, 335, 343; Letter to, from David Ogden, relative to the titles of the rioters, 343; Referred to, 347, 352, 353; Letter to, from F. J. Paris, respecting the junction of the Provinces of New York and New Jersey, 360; Letters to, from David Ogden, respecting the riot at Horseneck, 364, 368; Referred to, 403; Deposition of, concerning the riots, 413; Letter from, to David Ogden, relative to the trial of the rioters, 430; Letter from, to Governor Belcher, relative to the state of the Province, 452; Referred to, 462, 472, 473, 479, 507, 508, 511, 525, 527, 553, 554, 573; Letter from, to Robert Hunter Morris, relative to the action of the legislature, 626; To the same, relative to the Constitution of the Council of New Jersey, 644; To the same, in relation to

proceedings of Governor Belcher, 651.—Member of Council, viii, Part I, 16, 29, 61, 101, 103, 105, 107; Papers authenticated by, 135; Bond of indemnity, 200; Counsel for Swaartwoots, 208; Surveyor for East Jersey, 209; Referred to, 221, 232, 235, 236, 253, 254, 261; His declaration concerning Jarrat's surveying instruments, 263; Memorandum concerning line between New York and New Jersey, 267, 269; Sentiments of, respecting the East Jersey line, 275; Referred to, 290.—Referred to, viii, Part II, 23; Letter from, relative to the action of the Council of New York, respecting the boundary line, 89; Letter to, from Governor Belcher, 142; Referred to, 182; Death of, 214—ix, 342.

Alexander, John, i, 530.

Alexander, Joseph, iv, 215.

Alexander, Robert, iv, 215.

Alexander, Mary, viii, Part II, 228.

Alexander, William (Lord Stirling), Bond of indemnification to, from the Council of Proprietors of East Jersey, viii, Part I, 200.—Recommended as the successor of his father in the Council, viii, Part II, 214; Notice of, 214; In relation to the boundary difficulties, 243.—ix, 151; Petition of, with others, for payment of the purchase money for Long Island, granted to their ancestors, 226; Member of Council, 274; Named as one of the commissioners for trying pirates, 284; Letter from, relative to the Stamp Act, 509; Referred to, 582.—Land mortgaged by him to Mrs. Mary Verplank, x, 547; Member of Council, 561; Appointed a Colonel by the Provincial Congress, 662; Suspended from the Council, 676, 679; His arrest of Governor Franklin, 699, 702, 705.

Alford, Colonel John, Letters to, from Governor Belcher, vii, 91, 579—viii, Part I, 10; Subscribes to the College, 109.

Algure, William, Grand Juror in riot case, iii, 486, 487.

Algus, Markas, i, 269.

Aliens, Query as to their right to hold lands in America, ix, 382, 397.—Act relative to, x, 300, 324-329, 337; Instructions relative to 410, 411.

Allan, Jedediah, ii, 332, 362, 364.

Allen, Anthony, i, 288.

Allen, Caleb, ii, 397.

Allen, David, x, 718.

Allen (Allin), George, ii, 363, 396.—Affidavit of, in relation to Cornbury Fund, iii, 213; Referred to, 219.

Allen, James, Contributes to the supposed Cornbury Fund, iii, 212.—viii, Part I, 109.

Allen, Job, x, 717.

Allen, John, ii, 339, 397.—Grand Juror, iii, 486, 487, 496.—Recommended for the Council, v, 133—vi, 110.— Certificate of, vii, 560, 604.—Treasurer, viii, Part I, 66-75, 230, 231.

Allen, Joseph, ii, 42-62, 66-74, 99.

Allen, Matthew, i, 269—ii, 384.

Allen, Nathan. iii, 165.

Allen, Samuel, ii, 124, 339.

Allen, Thomas, ii, 470.

Allen, William, vii, 323, 377, 515.—Certificate of, 560—ix, 582, 591, 624, 631, 632.

Alling, John, ii, 326.

Allison, Richard, Letter to, from Daniel Cox, iv, 266, 274.; Dead, 274.

Allinson, Samuel, Appointed Surrogate, ix, 359.

Alliways' Creek, Lands sold at in England by John Fenwick, i, 414.

Allyn, Judeth, i, 307.

Almy, Christopher, i. 51.

Alricks (Alrichs). Peter, i, 72, 73, 75, 80; Permits from, to take up land, 113, 114; Letter from, to New York Council, 200, 203; Letter from, to John Fenwicke, 281.

Alsop, John, x, 530.

Alstin, John, iv, 190.

Alting, Samuel, v, 155.

Ambo Point, See Perth Amboy.

Amherst, Sir Jeffrey, Major General, ix, 161, 169, 170, 299, 339; Order from, to Captain Elias Dayton, 365; Referred to, 392, 393, 398, 399, 401; Vice-Admiral, 622.

Anderson, Abraham, vi, 416—vii, 212; Indicated, 458; Referred to, 478.

Anderson, Alexander, Lieutenant, ix, 185, 186.

Anderson, Enoch, vii, 546.

Anderson, James, viii, Part II, 163; On military requirements, 176.— Referred to, ix, 185.

Anderson, John, Recommended for Council, iv, 63, 153, 154, 169, 170; Attack upon, by Jacob Henderson. 156, 178, 179; Member of Council, 182, 253, 310, 334, 340, 363; Payments, 370, 372; Referred to, 373.—One of Governor Burnett's Council, v, 3; Suspended, 34, 35, 52; Money paid to, 143, 147; Commissioner to try pirates, 197; Signs Memorial, 301; Announces to the Duke of New Castle the death of Governor Cosby, and that he had assumed the government, 440; Signs petition, 443; Death of announced, 445; Referred to, 454, 455, 456, 467, 475, 482-488—vi, 455.—Congratulates Governor Belcher on his arrival, vii, 64; Leader of the rioters, 87; Referred to, 544—viii, Part II, 15, 163.

Anderson, William. Removed by Lord Cornbury from the Clerkship of the Assembly, iii, 227; Referred to, 261.

Anderson, Thomas, i, 414.

Andras, Andrew, i, 413.

Andress, Justa, i, 111.

Andress (Andries, Andrias, Anders, Andrus, Andriessen), Lawrence, i, 49, 66; Juror, 82; Member of Council, 89, 91, 92, 97, 110; Affairs with Council of New Netherlands, 125, 146.

Andrews, Ephraim, Petitions the Assembly in relation to the East Jersey records, iii, 220; Foreman of Grand Jury, 481.

Andrews, John, ix, 622.

Andries, Joakim, i, 50.

Andros, Edmund, i, 74; Answer to an application for a patent from Capt. Cantwell and Johannes Dehaes, 112; Order from, to repossess Jean Paul Jacquet of lands taken from him, 117; Order from, authorizing the court at New Castle to take care that the inhabitants be not disturbed in their possession by Major Fenwick or others, 118; Commission of, to be Governor of New York, 156; Notice of, 155; Letter to, from Sir Joseph Werden, 179; Letter from, to Capt. Cantwell, regarding Indian affairs, 179, 181; Conference between and the Indian Sachems of New Jersey, 182; Special warrant by, against John Fenwicke, 188; Letters from, to the authorities of New Castle, 189, 204; Letter to, from Sir John Werden, 230; Letter from, to Captain Billop, 270; Letter from, to the Commissioners for West Jersey, 271; Commission from, to Overseers at Salem, 284; Order to authorities at New Castle, to protect the inhabitants on the East Side of the River in the possession of their lands, 285; Letter from, to Governor Carteret, 292; Proclamation of, against Governor Carteret, 293; Letter to, from Governor Carteret, condemning his proceedings, 297; Visit of, to New Jersey, 299; Warrant from, to arrest Governor Carteret, 302; Account of his visit to New Jersey to meet the Assembly, 304; Letters from Governor Carteret, concerning, 314, 315; Communications to, from Town Officers, 333; Petition to, from William Pardon, 335; Letter to, from John Warren, 337; Letters to, from Sir John Werden, 345, 347; Proclamation against, from Governor Carteret, 346; Referred to, 353, 532, 536.—Letter from, to the Lords of Trade, announcing his arrival in New York. ii, 37.—Referred to, 231, 349, 417, 443—ix, 336—x, 516.

Andross, Lady, i, 305.

Anehoopoen, i. 1.

Anirell, Joseph, ii, 396.

Anson, Lord, ix, 16.

Antil (Anthill), Edward, ii, 32, 376, 408, 411, 416; Signs the Surrender of the Government, 456-460.—Asks that Andrew Hamilton be appointed Governor. 470—iii, 314, 315, 498.— Recommended for the Council, vi, 110, 232; Notice of, 233; Recommended by the Lords of Trade, 237; Member of Council, 367-378, 424—vii, 5; Member of Governor Belcher's Council, 6, 11, 98, 183, 188, 189, 280, 343, 455, 501.—Member of Council, ix, 274; Named as one of the commissioners for trying pirates, 283; Suspended from the Council, 299, 316; His removal therefrom, 335; Notice of, 336, 338.

Antill, John, ix, 339, 340.

Antill, Marquet, ix, 339.

Antle, Dr. Lewis, ix, 339.

Attorney-General, Salary of, ix, 620.

Appelgadt, Bartholemew, i, 142, 143.

Appelgadt, Thomas, i, 142, 143.

Apsley, Sir Allen, Letter to, from Sir John Werden, relative to customs, i, 353.

Archer, Edward, vii, 368, 371-374, 444, 446.

Archdale, John, Governor of Carolina, ii, 119.

Arents, Dr. Jacob, iii, 421, 447; Affidavit of, respecting the proceedings of Peter Sonmans, 451; Referred to, 456—Indicted, iv, 88, 293.— Naturalization of, v, 382.—Referred to, vi, 308, 309, 345—vii, 45.

Arents, Mary, iii, 452.

Arentsen, Claes, i, 49.

Arentsen, Lawrence, i, 49.

Arlington, Lord, Letter to, from Governor Nicolls, relative to the grants to Berkeley and Carteret, i, 46; Letter to Samuel Mavericke, relative to the same, 57.

Armstrong, John, ix, 117.

Arnold, Colonel Benedict, x, 608-610.

Arnold, Elizabeth, Indicted, iv, 88, 89.

Arthur Cull, See Achter Kol.

Ashaly, Robert, ii, 396.

Ashbrook, John, ii, 146.

Ashfield, Lewis Morris, Recommended to be a member of the Council, vii, 585, 586; Appointed a member of the Council, 590; Referred to, 609; Indicted, 612; Letter concerning him from Governor Belcher, 614; Refused admission to the Council by Governor Belcher, 617; Five affidavits relating to, 619-622; Governor Belcher in relation to, 623; Referred to, 626, 628; Affirmation of William Morris, relative to his conduct, 642; Referred to, 648.—Letter relative to, from Governor Belcher, viii, Part I, 8; Refused admission to the Council, 16, 17; Acquitted of, 36; Result of the trial of, 40; Message of Governor Belcher, relative to his admission to the Council, 101; Demands admission to the Council, 107; His non admission referred to the Lords of Trade, 111; Notes upon his trial by the Attorney-General, 112; Governor Belcher's course towards him disapproved by the Lords of Trade, 124; Admitted to the Council, 126.—Petitions as a Proprietor, viii, Part II, 228; Warrant to, 234—ix, 274; Named as one of the Commissioners for trying pirates, 283; Claims precedence in the Council, 430; Precedence denied to him, 447.—Dead, x, 131; Notice of, 131.

Ashfield, Richard, v, 125.—Recommended for the Council, 317, 319—vi, 110; Signs as a Proprietor, 137.—Referred to, x, 131.

Ashurt, Sir William, iv, 131.

Ashton, James, i, 88—ii, 396, 397.—Contributes to the supposed Cornbury Fund, iii, 213.

Ashton, John, i, 394.

Ashton, Joseph, ii, 363.

Askew, John, ii, 460.

Assembly of New Jersey, first called, i, 56; Proposed by Governor Andros, 296; Countermanded by Governor Carteret, 297; Deputies to, in 1680, 306; Proceedings of, under Andross, 307-312.—Speech of Governor Cornbury to, iii, 8; Reply to the same, 11; Speech of the same to the same, 165; Petition of, to the Queen relating to the difficulties attendant on Lord Cornbury's government, 171; remonstrance of, against certain evils to which Lord Cornbury was subjecting the Province, and his reply, 173, 180; Colonel Quarry's remarks concerning, 236, 237, 272; Address of, to Lord Cornbury in reply to his answer to their remonstrance, 242; Several members of, reported by Lord Cornbury as not qualified, 269; Proceedings of, objected to, by the Council, 285, 287; Minutes of, from the 5th to the 12th of May, 1708; Speech of the Governor to, 293; Reply of, to the same, 295; Speech to, by Governor Lovelace, 361; Reply to the same, 362; Address of, to Governor Lovelace in relation to an Address of the Lieutenant Governor and Council to the Queen, 367, 368; The Council in defence of their address to the Queen, 372; Address of, to Governor Lovelace, complaining of Peter Sonmans, 374; Address of, to the same, relative to Peter Fanconnier, 379; From the same to the same, expressing their want of confidence in the Council, 379; Addresses from, to the Queen, relative to the address of the Council complaining of the Assembly, 385; Answer of Peter Sonmans to their complaints, 416; Petition to, against Peter Sonmans by the Grand Inquest of Middlesex County, 445; Report of the Committee upon the said Petition, 447; Account of their proceedings given to the Lords of Trade by Lieutenant-Governor Ingoldesby, 467.—An intended meeting of, iv, 11; Place of meeting of, 16; Minutes of, 19; William Sandford expelled from, 22; Representation of, relating to the Administration of Governor Cornbury, 24; Complaint of, to Governor Hunter, against William Hall, one of the Council of New Jersey, 79; Memorial of, to Governor Hunter, relative to the perversion of justice in the Courts of Law, 87; Petition of several of the members of, to Lord Cornbury, 110; Address of, to the Queen, tendering their support, 134; Raised £5,000 for the expedition to Albany, 138; Dispute between it and the Council, 140; Letter from Governor Hunter relative to certain acts of, 221; Speech of Governor Hunter to, 249; Address of, to Governor Hunter, relating to the expelling of their Speaker, 250; Dissolving it on account of small pay, 264; Speech of Governor Hunter to, 267; Address of, to Governor Hunter, 268; Meeting of, at Chesterfield, 273; Acts of, transmitted by Governor Hunter, 292 ; Message and speech of Governor Hunter to, 364, 365.—Dissolved by Governor Burnet, v, 8; Governor Burnet's Speech to, 24; Address of, to Governor Burnet,

25; Governor Burnet's speech to, 26; Address of, to the King, 77; Report on several of the Acts of, 79; Respecting the manner of electing Representatives of, 83; Comments of Governor Burnet upon acts of, 104, 190: Comments of Governor Montgomerie on certain acts of, 247; Views of the same upon certain acts, relative to a separate Governor, 285; Remarks of Governor Cosby on certain acts of, 365; Act of, for making £40,000 in bills of credit, disapproved by Solicitor John Sharpe, 410; Reply of Richard Partridge to John Sharpe, 416.—Thanks of, to the King, for giving them a Governor separate from New York, vi, 58; Differences between, and the Council, 62-65; Settle a support for three years on Governor Morris, 68; Action of, in respect to raising troops, 101; Representation of, respecting the making of iron, 140; Two acts of, submitted for the opinion of Mr. Fane, 150; Speeches of Governor Morris to, and answers to the same, 178-190; Dissolved by the Governor, 190; Observations from the votes of, upon a bill for better regulating the militia, 201-204; Several acts of, rejected by the Council, with reasons therefor, 219; Proceedings of, relative to an act for ascertaining the fees to be taken by the several offices, 239; Minutes of, 246; Message of Governor Morris to, 251; Petition to, from the Essex County rioters, 348; Message to, from President Hamilton, 436; Message from, to President Hamilton, 438.— Addresses of, to Governor Belcher, vii, 25, 345; Petition of, to the King, relative to the condition of the Province, 351; Contention between it and the Council, 356; Letter from Governor to the Lords of Trade respecting the proceedings of, 361; Complaint against, for not paying the amount of salary due to Governor Morris, 401; Representation of, to the Lords of Trade, relative to arrears of salary due to the late Governor Morris, 459; Petition of, to the King, 462; Behaviour of, commented upon by the Lords of Trade, 551; Messages to, from Governor Belcher, 580, 583; Dissolved by Governor Belcher, 587; Messages to new session of, 591, 615, 625.—Messages to, from Governor Belcher, viii, Part I, 12, 21; Report of the Lords of Trade on some of the proceedings of, 28; Petition of, asking that the Governor be permitted to assent to a bill making current £60,000 in bills of credit, 183; Proceedings of, transmitted to the Lords of Trade, 287; Vote £15,000 for the support of Colonel Schuyler's regiment, viii, Part II, 11; Printed journals of, forwarded to the Lords of Trade, 12; Petition of, to the King, relative to the bill for making amount of £70,000 in bills of credit, 14; Unsatisfactory proceedings of, 24; Action of, upon various subjects, 26; Message to, from Governor Belcher, 93; Action of, thereupon, 94; Represenation of the Lords of Trade to the King, relative to the petition of, 100; Message to, from Governor Belcher, 119; Meeting of, at Elizabethtown, requested by Governor Belcher, 126; Messages to, from Governor Belcher, relative to military affairs, 128, 162; A meeting

of, to be called, 181; Message to, from Governor Belcher, 193, 198;
Summoned to meet, 249.—Prorogued by Governor Bernard, ix, 126;
Message from, to Governor, 129; Speech of the Governor to, 159;
Answer to the same, 162; Unanimity and dispatch of, commended
by Governor Bernard, 166; Speech of Governor Bernard to, 220;
Reply of, to the same, 222; The amicable proceedings of, 248; Action
of, in relation to raising additional troops, 260, 261; Address of,
to Governor Boone, 287; Answer to the same, 288; Two Acts of,
disapproved, 331; Bill before, for laying a duty on imported negroes,
345; Acts of, sent to the Lords of Trade, 383; Proceedings of
Governor Franklin with, in respect to the means of repelling the
hostilities of the Indians, 398; Certain acts of, relative to raising
levies, 428, 458; Act of, to render void Peter Gordon's lottery
repealed, 487; Address from, to the King, on the repeal of the Stamp
Act, 560; Votes of, transmitted to the Lords of Trade, 567, 568;
Pay of the Speaker of, 607; Fees of the Clerk of, 607; Fees of the
Sergeant-at-Arms of, 608; The King's displeasure with, for not
obeying the act of Parliament in regard to mutiny and desertion,
636; Alteration in the number of, forbidden, 637, 638.—Petition to
the King for relief from act of Parliament imposing a duty on them
for revenue purposes, x, 18; Proceedings of, in connection with the
passage of the bill for issuing £100,000 in currency, 60; The Lords
of Trade recommend that the act of, for issuing £100,000 be disallowed, 106; Act disallowed, 115: Speech of the Governor to, in
relation to the riots in Monmouth and Essex Counties, 172; Reply
of, to the same, 180; Displeasure of, at the disallowance of the Paper
Money Act, 200; Action of, in relation to supplies for the troops, etc.,
201; Message to, from the Governor, relative to supplies for the
troops, 203; Answer from, to the same, 204; Insolvent laws of, 236;
Refuse to provide for the King's troops, 237; Speech of Governor
Franklin to, 238; Answer of, 242; Message to, 243; Reply to, 251;
Rejoinder, 256; Supplies for the troops still refused by, 297, 304;
Dispute with the Governor in regard to the resignation of Mr. Ogden,
as a member of the House, 306; The position of the Governor in this
dispute approved by Secretary Hillsborough, 318; The matter referred
to Richard Jackson, one of his Majesty's Counsel-at-law, 319; Consent to pay the arrears due to the troops, and debt incurred during
the late war, 321; Order in Privy Council relative to acts of, concerning the recovery of debts from non-residents, 324-329; The
dispute in regard to Mr. Ogden's resignation as a member of, 334;
Dissolved by the Governor, 356; Report on the claim of, to order an
election for a member in the room of Mr. Ogden, 369; The Earl of
Hillsborough on the same subject, 374; Money granted by, for the
support of the King's troops, 378; Conduct of, satisfactory to the
Earl of Dartmouth, 388; Proceedings of, in reference to robbery of
the Treasury, 412, 414, 415; Message to, from the Governor, relative

to the resignation of the Treasurer, Stephen Skinner, 420; Two acts of, transmitted to the Earl of Dartmouth, 461; Report of Richard Jackson on thirty-three acts of, 508; Speech of the Governor to, 538; Address of, to the Governor, 543; Committee of, appointed to attend the Continental Congress, 546; Intended to appoint members to the Congress, 571; Speech of Governor Franklin to, 620; Address of, in reply thereto, 633; The Governor's rejoinder, 638; The proceedings of, 676; Notes of what Mr. Dickenson said before the House of, 689; Message from, in reply to the Governor, 697.

Assessors of Counties, Proclamation of, iv, 400.

Assheton, Robert, Member of the Pennsylvania Council, iv, 393.

Atkins, Sir Edward, i, 366; ii, 388.

Atkins, Sir Robert, i, 366; ii, 388.

Atkinson, James, ii, 148.

Atwood, Chief Justice, Letter from, to the Lords of Trade, ii, 428.

Auchmuty, Robert, x, 375, 377.

Auchmuty, Rev. Samuel, x, 313, 341.

Augustine, i, 221.

Aul, William, x, 531.

Austen, Joseph, Commissioner of Customs, ii, 168, 179.

Avery (Every) the Pirate, ii, 151, 223, 235, 358.

Aynsley (Ainsley, Aisleby, Ailesby), William, Appointed Chief Justice, viii, Part II, 190; Warrant to, 247.—Death of, ix, 124, 173; Referred to, 177, 214, 217, 232, 236.

Ayres, Jonathan, x, 531.

Ayres, Moses, vii, 422.

Ayscough, John, Letter from, to Robert Hunter Morris, relative to Provincial affairs, viii, Part I, 116.

B.

Bacon, John, ii, 380—iii, 165—iv, 215.

Bacon, Joseph, iv, 215.

Bacon, Nathaniel, The Virginia rebel, vii, 309, 311, 315.

Bacon, Samuel, iv, 215.

Bacon, William, iv, 215.

Bagley, Charles, i, 268.

Bahama Islands, Retreat for pirates, ii, 119, 358.

Bailey (Bailees), John, i, 15, 18, 504–506—ii, 125, 126.

Bainbridge, Edmund, vi, 455, 465.—Congratulates Governor Belcher, vii, 64; Arrested, 87; Referred to, 206, 220, 451; Indicted, 458; Referred to, 628.

Bainbridge (Bambridge), John, Recommended for the Council, iv, 217, 227, 375, 377.—Referred to, vii, 217, 231, 449, 451, 482.

Bainbridge (Bunbridge), Jr., John, vi, 455, 460, 463–469.

Bainfield, Mr., iv, 297, 300, 305, 374.

Baid, Peter, iv, 197; Recommended for Council, 377.—One of Governor Burnet's Council, v, 2, 3, 34; Money received from, on account of bills of credit, 134; Money paid to, 137, 139, 141, 147, 148; Grand Juror, 187; Commissioner to try pirates, 197; Signs memorial, 301; Dead, 375, 402; Referred to, 454.

Baker, Abraham, ii, 334, 397.

Baker, John, i, 18, 98, 122, 529—ii, 227—vi, 208, 351—vii, 457.

Baker, Lewis, i, 307.

Baldwin, Amos, vi, 351.

Baldwin, Benjamin, ii, 339.

Baldwin, Caleb, vi, 351—vii, 457.

Baldwin, David, vi, 351—vii, 457.

Baldwin, Senior, John, ii, 336.

Baldwin, Jon., x, 587, 588.

Baldwin, Moses, Newark rioter, vii, 179.

Baldwin, Nathan, vi, 351—vii, 457.

Baldwin, Nehemiah, vi, 245, 295, 401—vii, 210; Indicted, 457.

Baldwin, Samuel, vi, 294, 346, 350, 361, 367—vii, 64, 74, 208, 470.

Ball, Aaron, vi, 351.—Newark rioter, vii, 179, 403-405, 433, 434, 437, 438, 441, 442; Examination of, 443: Indicted, 458, 511-513.

Ball, Caleb, ii, 339.

Ball, Edward, ii, 336, 339.

Ball, Esekill, vi, 351—vii, 458.

Ball, Lewis, Autograph, v, 510.

Ball, Nathaniel, vi, 351—vii, 457.

Ball, Richard, iv, 299.

Ball, Robert, iv, 310.

Ball, Timothy, vi, 351—vii, 458.

Ballinger, Henry, iii, 164.

Baltimore, Lord, i, 420—ii, 124, 360.

Bambridge, Peter, vii, 628.

Bankrupts, Bill relating to, iv, 126.

Banks, Joseph, iv, 370.

Banks, Josiah, Ensign, ix. 185, 187.

Banyar, George, ix, 182.

Barber, Francis, i, 50, 83.

Barbarie, John, iv, 340, 408—v, 197—vii, 650—viii, Part I, 237—ix, 366.

Barbou, Edward, v, 187.

Barclay, David, An East Jersey Proprietor, i, 383, 341, 448, 460; Shipments by, to East Jersey, 464, 465, 466, 467, 499, 528.

Barclay, James, vii, 420.

Barclay, John, An East Jersey Proprietor, i, 446, 460, 465, 529.—ii, 2, Commissioned as Surveyor-General of East Jersey, 81; Notice of, 81; Signs as Proprietor, 113; Clerk, 271, 275, 317; Surrenders the Government of East Jersey, 387; Signs the surrender, 456-460; Objected to as a member of Council, 488.—Prohibited by Governor Cornbury

from receiving quit rents, iii, 132; Referred to, 253, 254; Complaint of, at the non-recognition of his commission as Receiver-General, 331; Arrest of, by advice of Peter Sonmans, 375, 420, 447, 451, 456, 457; Recommended for Council of Governor Hunter, 498—iv, 9, Letter from, relative to prepartions for the accommodations of Governor Hunter, 13; Statement of, respecting Peter Sonmans, 15; Referred to, 42, 74, 107; Clerk of Middlesex and Somerset Counties, 142; Referred to, 241; Salary as Clerk of the Assembly, 369; Deputy Secretary, 403; Deputy Register, 431.—Referred to, v, 57.

Barclay, Robert, Proprietor and Governor of East New Jersey, commissions Thomas Rudyard as Secretary and Register of East Jersey, i, 376; Commissions Samuel Groom as Receiver General of the same, 378; One of the twenty-four Proprietors of East Jersey, 383, 410, 412; Commissions Gawen Lawrie as Deputy Governor of East Jersey, 423; Signs as a Proprietor, 437; Named as a Proprietor, 441, 446, 448, 451, 454, 457, 459, 462; Interested in goods shipped to East Jersey, 467; Instructions from, relative to setting out of land in East Jersey, 470; Instructions from, to Governor Lawrie, 476; Named, etc., as Proprietor, 499, 500; Notice of, 502; Letter from, to Deputy Governor and Council of Proprietors in East Jersey, 506; Instructions from, and other Proprietors to Andrew Hamilton, 508; Referred to, 509, 517; Agreement as to the dividing line between East and West Jersey. 519; Referred to, 528; Letter from, and other Proprietors in England, to the Deputy Governor and Council in East Jersey, 541—ii, 22, 26; Agreement with Governor Cox in regard to the boundary line, 34; Named as a Proprietor, 187–193; Disbursements by, on account of East Jersey, 202; Signs as a Proprietor, 257, 263; Referred to, 389; Asks the appointment of Andew Hamilton as Governor, 470.

Barefoot, Brimstone, iv, 315.

Barentsen (Barents), Francis, i, 194, 196.

Bargoun, Peter, iii, 446.

Barker, Thomas, One of the East Jersey Proprietors, i, 383, 424, 433, 434, 437, 442, 446, 451, 454, 457, 460, 462, 474, 483, 484, 490, 499, 500, 504, 530—ii, 26, 171, 177, 186–193; Disbursements by, on account of East Jersey, 203; Signs instructions to Governor Basse, 213; As Proprietor, 257, 263, 376, 408, 411; Signs, 431; Referred to, 437; Signs the surrender of the Government, 456, 460; Recommends Andrew Hamilton for Governor, 470.—Referred to, iii, 313.

Barkstead, Joshua, ii, 377, 473—iv, 344, 345.

Barnes, Mr., vi, 388, 391.

Barnet, Ichabod B., x, 363, 364, 365, 368.

Baron, Machgyel, i, 268.

Baron, Michell, i, 191, 204, 284 414.

Barr, George C., x, 717.

Barracks, See Military Affairs.

Barrington. Lord, ix, 8, 14, 16, 17.

Bartleson, Andrew, i, 269.

Bartlett, Benjamin. ii, 41, 45, 48.

Bartlett, Thomas, iv, 80–85.

Barton, Joseph, Lieutenant, ix. 185.

Barton, Thomas. i, 269.

Barton, Thomas, Inspector of the Press, viii, Part II, 70.

Bartow, John, i, 510—iv, 174.

Bartow, Thomas, vi, 317, 353, 356, 440.—Clerk of the Assembly, vii, 89, 343—viii, Part II, 172.

Basse, Jeremiah, i, 509.—Commission to, from the West Jersey Society in England as their agent, ii, 91: Notice of, 91; Letter to, from the Proprietors of West Jersey in England, 97; Form of bond sent to him, to be entered into by the Proprietors of the several plantations in America, 141; Draft of commission to, as Governor of West Jersey, 143; Memorial of the Proprietors of East and West Jersey, asking his appointment as Governor, 149; Required by the Lords of Trade to give security before being appointed Governor, 150; Letters from, to Secretary Popple, in regard to pirates and piracies, and the security demanded of him as Governor, 150, 154–157; Letters to, from Secretary Popple, in answer to the above, 155, 162; Petition from, as a Proprietor, to the Lords Justices, 171; Announcement of his appointment as Governor of East Jersey, 176; Proclamation of, for the suppression of vice and immorality, 206; Instructions to, as Governor, 209; Letter from, to Secretary Popple, announcing his arrival in New Jersey, 214; Referred to, 217, Proclamation of, establishing Perth Amboy as a port, 227; Correspondence between, the Earl of Bellemont, relative to the delivery of two privates to the latter, 229; Referred to, 235; Letter to, from Secretary Popple, commending him for his zeal in suppressing piracy, 243; Referred to, 244; Complaints against, by the Earl of Bellemont, to the Lords of Trade, 241, 245; Note on, 246; Referred to, 247, 248, 252; Reflections upon his conduct by the town of Newark, 270; Proclamation of, against certain immigrants from Scotland, 272; Referred to, 280; Letter from, relative to pirates and illegal traders, 286; Proclamation of, against certain ships from Scotland, 297; Called to account by the West Jersey Society, 299; Letter from, relative to his administration of New Jersey affairs, 310; Petition relative to the ship Hester, 311; Referred to, 318, 320, 321; An account of the disturbances in East Jersey, 329; Letter from, to the Lords of Trade, 340; Referred to, 241, 242; Letters from, to the Lords of Trade, 343, 352; Referred to, 350, 351; Memorial from, to the Lords of Trade, asking for a consideration of the remonstrance of the inhabitants of East Jersey, 357; Referred to, 367, 378, 381, 382; Memorial of, to the Lords of Trade, relating to the Government of East Jersey, 391, 392; Referred to, 394, 398, 399, 400–404; Memorial from, to the

Lords of Trade, relative to the surrender of the Government, 418; Referred to, 423, 434, 435, 439, 442, 444, 473, 475; Nominated for Council, 487; Objected to, 488; Remarks of, concerning certain persons recommended for the Council, 502; Referred to, 502.— His appointment as Secretary of New Jersey opposed by Peter Sonmans, iii, 23; A true representation of the case of, 26; Accused of carrying the public records out of the province, 92, 127, 152, 253, 254, 325; His party's actions related by Lewis Morris, 275–277; His proceedings referred to 445; Certificate of, relative to Sonman's affairs, 458–460; Presides at the Court of Common Right, 479; Referred to, 489, 492, 493, 494—iv, 45, 46, 48; Addresses and depositions against, 71–74; Referred to, 76; Indicted for perjury and forgery, 88; Answer of, to a representation of George Willock's against him, 90, 97; Referred to, 123, 124; Obnoxious to Governor Hunter, 139; Letter to, from Governor Hunter, relative to commissions for the Supreme Court Judges, 139; To, from the same, relative to swearing officers, 141; Letter from, to Governor Hunter, relative to surveys, 142; Complained of by Thomas Gardiner, 144; Letter from, to Governor Hunter, relative to Thomas Gardiner, 148; Announces to Governor Hunter the election of a new Council by the Proprietors of West Jersey, 151; Salary, 172, 185, 368, 369, 370; Referred to, 209, 237, 238, 259, 260, 301—v, 58, 135, 137, 138, 143.

Basset, Arnold, viii, Part I, 225, 226.

Bateman, John, x, 613.

Bates, Alexander, x, 717.

Bates, Thomas, iv, 42.

Bath, Earl of, i, 366.

Battersley, Nicholas, ii, 41–6, 65–73, 79.

Baton, Michael, Deposition of, i, 274.

Batsey, Robert, vi, 169.

Bawta, Weart, ii, 327.

Baxter, Major G., i, 518.

Bayard, John, vi, 144.

Bayard, Nicholas, i, 131, 142, 143, 517, 518—ii, 106, 237—x, 169, 170, 189.

Bayard, William, ix, 451–453, 456, 463; Writes to Governor Franklin relative to Captain Kennedy's complaint, 467; Referred to, 470; Letter to, from Governor Franklin, relative to Captain Kennedy's complaint, 471; Deposition of, in the same matter, 472.—Recommended for the Council of New Jersey, x, 131, 140; Claims of, to common lands in Bergen Township, 153; Petition of, in relation to said claims, 168; Referred to, 189, 190.

Bayley, Charles, i, 414.

Baylies, John, vi, 207, 208, 211.

Baynton, Peter, Named for the Council, vi, 107, 109; Deceased, 237.

Beadle, Daniel, vii, 426, 428.

Beadle, Jacob, vii, 423, 426.

Beadle, Michael, vii, 427.

Beaks, Edmund, iv, 42—vii, 637.

Beasley, Michael, Examination of, relative to the sloop St. Migel, vi, 388.

Beatty, Col. Erkuries, ix, 7.

Beatty, Gen. John, ix, 6.

Beaver Skins, Duties upon, ix, 405.

Beckman, Gerardus, iii, 64—iv, 340, 408.

Bedford, Duke of, Letter to, from Governor Belcher, relative to commerce
    with the French, vii, 134; Letter to, from the same, transmitting
    Acts of the Assembly, 137; Address to, from members of the New
    Jersey Council, relative to the riots, 191; Letter to, from Governor
    Belcher, relative to the affairs of New Jersey, 289; Letter to, from
    Governor Clinton, 531: Letter to, from Governor Belcher, relative to
    New Jersey affairs, 598.

Bedford, Jonas, Lieutenant, ix, 185.

Bedford, Joseph, x, 718.

Bedford, Steven, ii, 396.

Beekman, Gerard, viii, Part I, 237.

Beere, Jonathan, ii, 148, 380.

Belcher, Andrew, Letter to, from his father, Governor Belcher, viii, Part
    II, 196—ix, 622.

Belcher, Counsellor, Opinions of, as to bills of credit being made legal
    tenders in New Jersey, viii, Part II. 87.

Belcher & Foye, Letter to, from Governor Belcher, viii, Part I, 108.

Belcher, Jonathan, His appointment as Governor of New Jersey, first re-
    ferred to, vi, 363, 423, 434; Petition to the King, relative to salary,
    443; Petition of, to be absent from his Government for three months,
    450; Report of the Lords of Trade on said petition, 453.—Notice of,
    vii, 1; Commission for, to be Governor of New Jersey, 2; Instruc-
    tions to, 4, 7; Proceedings of the Council on the arrival of, 11; Ad-
    dresses to, and replies from, on his arrival, 13–17; Referred to, 18;
    Address of, to the Council and Assembly of New Jersey, 19; Auto-
    graph of, 22; Answers of the Council and the Assembly to his ad-
    dress, 23–29; Letter from to the Lords of Trade announcing his
    arrival in the Province, 29; Letter from, to Rev. Mr. Bradbury, 54:
    Letter from, to Governor Clinton, 55; To committee of the West
    Jersey Society, 57; To Mr. Craddock, describing his residence at
    Burlington, 58: To Richard Partridge, about private affairs, 59; To
    Secretary Willard, 61: Congratulatory address to, from a committee
    of the disffaected, 63: Letter from, to Col. Winslow, relative to the
    rioters, 65; To Mr. Justice Budd, 67; Message of, to the Council and
    Assembly of New Jersey, 67; Petition to, from alleged rioters, 71:
    Letter from, to Richard Partridge, 75; To Mr Oliver, 75; Referred
    to, 77; Address of the Council to, 81; Letter from, to Col. Alford,
    91; Letter from, in favor of Col. Peter Schuyler, and other New Jer-
    sey officers, 93; Message of, to the Council and Assembly, relative to

the expedition to Crown Point, 94; Letter of Congratulation to, from the Lords of Trade, 96.—Letter from, to Richard Partridge, vii, 100; Message to the Assembly, 103; Prorogues the Legislature, 104; Letter from, to Richard Partridge, relative to the action of the Legislature, 106; Addresses of the Council, 110; Reply thereto, 112; Letter from, to Rev. Aaron Burr, relative to the new college, 115; To James Alexander, relative to the expedition against Crown Point, 117; To Rev. Mr. Pemberton, relative to the college, 118; Referred to, 121; Letter from, to James Logan, relative to a charter for the college, 124; Referred to, 126; Letter from, to Anthony Palmer, President of the Pennsylvania Council, 130; Reply thereto, 131; His consideration for the Quakers, 133; Letter from, to the Duke of Bedford, relative to the commerce with the French, 134; To Governor Shirley, relative to a conference with the Indians, 135; To the Duke of Bedford, transmitting Acts of the Assembly, 137; To the Lords of Trade, relative to Acts of the Assembly, 140: To the committee of the West Jersey Society, relative to appointing agents in the Province, 145, 150; Message from, to the Council and Assembly of New Jersey, 149; Referred to, 168; He rejects the advice of his Council, 183; Referred to, 203; His actions criticized by James Alexander, 204; Referred to, 219; His proceedings commented upon by F. J. Paris, 238; Letter from, to the Lords of Trade, answering certain queries, 243; From the same, to the same, relative to certain acts passed in New Jersey, 246; From the same, to the same, relative to the riots, 249; Letter from J. Alexander and R. H. Morris, relative to the same, 251; Referred to, 271; Letter from, to the Duke of Bedford, relative to the affairs of the Province, and the complaints against him, 289; Letter from, to the Lords of Trade, relative to the riots, 293; Message from, to the Legislature, 332; Address of the House of Assembly to, 345; Letter from, to the Lords of Trade, relative to the contention between the Council and the Assembly, 356; Letter from, to the Lords of Trade, respecting the proceedings of the Assembly, 361; Letter from, to the Secretary of State, inclosing affidavits, showing the state of the Provinces, 369; Transmits to the Lords of Trade accounts of ships entered and cleared at the ports of Burlington and Perth Amboy, 381; Proclamation upon the occasion of two riots in New Jersey, 382; Referred to, 401, 414; Letter to, from members of the Council, relative to the state of the Province, 452; Referred to, 483, 517, 523; Letter from, to the Lords of Trade, relative to the suspension of John Coxe, 540; Letter to, from Thomas Cadwalader, 544; From T. Severns, 546; Letter to, from the Lords of Trade, relative to the behaviour of the Assembly, 551; Seized with a palsy, 5 3; Letter from, to Richard Partridge, relative to the proceedings of the Legislature, 553; Letter from, to the Duke of Bedford, relative to pig and bar iron, 554; To the same, relative to the proceedings of the Assembly, 555; To the Lords of Trade, relative to the

same, 556; Certificates and papers relating to mills, etc., for rolling iron in the Province of New Jersey, 558; Proclamation of, relative to an act to encourage the importation of iron, 561; Letter from, relative to the complaints against him, 571; Letter from, to R. Partridge, relative to New Jersey affairs, 573; Recommends William Morris for the Council, 575, 577; To Col. Alford, in regard to college building, 579; Message from, to the Council and Assembly, 580, 583; His renominations for the Council objected to by the Lords of Trade, 585; To the Duke of Bedford, relative to dissolving the Assembly, 587; Message of, to the Council and Assembly, 591; Letter from, to Richard Partridge, 592; To the Earl of Halifax, relative to complaints against him, 594; To Governor Clinton, relative to a proposed conference with the Indians, 596; To the Massachusetts Commissioners, to treat with the Indians, 597; To the Duke of Bedford, relative to New Jersey affairs, 598; To Richard Partridge, relative to William Morris and Samuel Smith, 600; To the Lords of Trade, relative to the same, 607; To Lord Hardwicke, relative to the same, 611; To Richard Partridge, relative to Lewis M. Ashfield, 614; Message from, to the Council and Assembly, 615; Refuses to admit L. M. Ashfield to the Council, 617; Letter from, to Rev. Aaron Burr, relative to the college, 618; To the Lords of Trade, relative to L. M. Ashfield, 623; Message from, to the Assembly, relative to irregular proceedings, 625; Additional instructions to, 631–634; Message of, to the Council, 634; Changes his residence, 640; Transmits eight acts of the Legislature to the Secretary of State. 646; J. Alexander in relation to the proceedings of, 651.—Letter from, to Benjamin Franklin, relative to an electrical apparatus, viii, Part I, 7; To Lord Halifax, relative to Lewis M. Ashfield, 8; To Col. Brattle, relative to the electrical cure, etc., 9; To Col. John Alford, relative to the College, 10; To Mr. Walley, relative to the same, 11; Messages from, to the Legislature of New Jersey, 12, 21; Letter from, to his nephew, Mr. Foye, 22; To William Morris, relative to a library at Trenton, 32; To Richard Partridge, relative to Lewis M. Ashfield, 36; To Andrew Johnston, relative to the imprisonment of Simon Wyckoff, 37; To Samuel Nevill, relative to the riot at Perth Amboy, 38; Letter to, from Samuel Nevill, relative to the trial of Lewis M. Ashfield, 40; Letter relative to Wyckoff and Waller, 45; Letter from, to the Lords of Trade, relative to the riot at Perth Amboy, 52; To Richard Partridge, relative to the same, 52, 61; To the Lords of Trade, relative to the same, 60; To R. Partridge, relative to James Alexander, 61; Transmits the accounts of various officers to the Lords of Trade, 65; Letter from, to George Whitefield, on religious subjects, 84; To Lady Huntingdon, 87; To President Burr, on his marriage, 89; To Mr. Shippen, relative to the College, 94; To Lord Hardwicke, relative to orders from the King, 95; To the Earl of Granville, asking for continued confidence, 97; To Lord Halifax,

relative to the affairs of the Province, 99; Message to the Council, relative to L. M. Ashfield, 101; Letter from, to the Lords of Trade, urging the transmission of orders from the King, 102; Extracts from letter to Partridge, concerning R. H. Morris, 102; Speech before the Council, 103; Denies L. M. Ashfield admission to the Council, 107; Letter from, relative to manufactures, 108; To Col. Alford, thanking him for a subscription to the College, 109; To the Lords of Trade, relative to his not admitting Mr. Ashfield to the Council, 111; To the same, on the revision of the laws, 118; His course toward Mr. Ashfield disapproved by the Lords of Trade, 124; Letter from, to the Lords of Trade, relative to Messages of the Legislature, 125; He admits Mr. Ashfield to the Council, 126; Requested by the Lords of Trade to give aid to the missionaries in New Jersey, 140; Letter from, to the Lords of Trade, transmitting documents, 151; Circular letter to, from the Lords of Trade, 156; Instructions to, from the Lords of Trade, 188; Letter to Lords of Trade, relative to disputes between the people of New York and New Jersey for want of a dividing line, 190; Memorial of the Proprietors of East Jersey to, 202; Transmits proceedings of Council and Assembly to the Lords of Trade, 287; Letter to, from Sir Thomas Robinson, 292; Letter to, from the Lords of Trade, relative to the defence against the French, 294; Requests the aid of Richard Partridge, in favor of Cortland Skinner as Attorney-General, 298.—Letter from, to Colonel Schuyler, relative to the additional support for his regiment, viii, Part II, 11; To Sir Thomas Robinson, relative to the Assembly, 24; To the Lords of Trade, relative to the same, 26; Transmits, to the same, papers relative to the boundary question, 30, 72; Also bill for making current £70,000 in bills of credit, 36; Letter from, to Sir Thomas Robinson, relative to affairs in the Province, 76; Answers certain questions relative to the present condition of New Jersey, 78; Message of, to the Assembly, 93; Transmits paper, to the Lords of Trade, 102, 112; Letter from, to Sir Thomas Robinson, relative to military matters, 105; Letter from, to Lieutenant-Governor Morris, 116; To General Braddock, 117; To Secretary Read, relative to the defeat of General Braddock, 117; Congratulates Lieutenant-Governor Pownall on his appointment, 118; Message from, to the Council and Assembly, relative to military matters, 119; Letter to Governor Dinwiddie, on the same subject, 122; Reply of Lords of Trade to several of his letters, 124; Desires the Council and Assembly to meet him at Elizabethtown, 126; Letter to Governor DeLancy, relative to embargoes, 127; Message from, to Council and Assembly, relative to military affairs, 128; Letter from, to Mr. Oliver, relative to the condition of the forces on the frontier, 131; To Sir John St. Clair, on the necessity of driving the French from America, 133; To Richard Partridge, relative to the appointment of a Lieutenant-Governor, 135; To Sir Thomas Robinson, relative to raising additional troops, 135; Congratulates Mr. Pownall on his appointment, 139; Letter from, to

Commissioner Yard, on supplies for the troops, 140; Complimentary letter from, to Governor Hardy, 141; To the same, relative to the boundary line, 142; To James Alexander, 142; To Governor Dinwiddie, relative to the movement of the troops, 143; To Rev. George Whitefield, relative to the erection of Nassau Hall, 146; To Sir Thomas Robinson, relative to military affairs, 148; To Colonel Allen, relative to the invasion of the French, 156; Proclamation of, to the Colonels of militia, directing them to muster their troops, 157; Letter from, to Governor Morris, relative to the threatened approach of the French and Indians, 158; To Lieutenant-Governor Pownall relative to the movement of the troops, 160; To Governor Morris, relative to military affairs, 161; Message from, to the Council and Assembly, 162; Letter from, to Lieutenant-Governor Morris, relative to the enemy, 165; To Rev. Aaron Burr, relative to the College, 166; To Governor Hopkins, relative to a convention of Commissioners, 167; To General Shirley, relative to military affairs, 168; To Mr. Pownall, requesting him to attend the convention of Governors in New York, 170; To Lieutenant-Governor Dinwiddie, relative to military affairs, 172; Directs the Colonels of regiments to muster their troops and march to the Delaware river, 174; Letter from, to his nephew, P. Oliver, 175; To Colonel Anderson, relative to military requirements, 176; Directions of, to Colonel Andrew Johnston, 178; To Colonel Joseph Tuttle, relative to the defence of the frontier, 179; To Colonel Schuyler, relative to marching to Minisink, 180; To Governor Morris, relative to military affairs, 181; Directs a meeting of the Assembly to be called, 181; Proclamation of, relative to the defence of Morris and Sussex counties, 182; Letter to General Shirley, relative to councils of war at Oswego, 182; To Governor Hardy, relative to division line and building of block houses, 183; Answers of, to queries from the Lords of Trade, 185; Letter to the same, relative to New Jersey affairs, 187; To Lord Hardwicke, relative to the necessity of capturing Canada, 188; To Richard Partridge, relative to the appointment of Chief-Justice Aislely (Aynsley), 190; To Secretary Read, relative to the imprisonment of Indians in Pennsylvania, 191; Message of, to the Council and Assembly, 193; Letter to Governor Shirley, 194; To Mr. Walley, referring to Rev. Mr. Whitefield, 195; To his son, Andrew, 196; To Richard Partridge, 197; To Consul Dean, relative to the College, 197; Message to the Assembly, 198; Letter from, to Lord Halifax, relative to Attorney-General Skinner, 200; Message to Assembly, asking for an augmentation of the forces in New Jersey, 201; Letter from, to General Shirley, commenting on the last campaign, 203; Letter to, from the Lords of Trade, commending the services of New Jersey, 206; Announces to the Lords of Trade, the death of James Alexander, and recommends his son William as his successor in the Council, 214; To depute Lieutenant-Governor Pownall to attend meetings of the Governors, 215; Referred

to, 217; Expresses to the Lords of Trade, his gratification that the course of New Jersey is approved of, 219; Comments on the recent proceedings of the Government, 220; Letter to the Lords of Trade, concerning the boundary and inclosing petition of Proprietors, 224, Nominates Samuel Woodruff for the Council, 236; Proclamation, relating to the exportation of provisions, 237; Summons Council and Assembly to meet, 249; Letter to the Earl of Holderness, relative to the embargo on grain, and to imprisonment of two captains of privateers, 254; To the Lords of Trade, relative to the boundary line, 256; Death of, 257, 259–270.—Referred to, ix, 119, 134, 157, 206, 270, 367—x, 131.

Belestre, ———, x, 610, 611.

Bell, Henry, ii, 397.

Bellamy, Rev. Joseph, ix, 258.

Bellomont, Earl of, ii, 114; Letter to, from the Lords of Trade, relative to ports in New Jersey, 201; Letter to, from the Lords of Trade, relative to the same, 216; Proclamation of, against the establishment of courts in New Jersey, 218; Letter from, to the Lords of the Treasury, inclosing said proclamation, 221; Letter from, to the Lords of Trade, relative to his proclamation, 222; Correspondence between, and Governor Basse, relative to the delivery of two privates to the former, 229; Letter from, to the Lords of Trade, 234; Letter from, to the Lords of the Admiralty, relative to taking two supposed pirates out of the hands of Governor Basse, 236; Referred to, 239; Letters from to the Lords of Trade, complaining of Governor Basse, 241, 245; Referred to, 244, 247, 252; His seizure of the ship Hester, 255; Letter from, to the Lords of Trade, 271; Referred to, 286, 291; Letter to, from the Lords of Trade, relative to New Jersey matters, 302; Referred to, 312, 321; Letter from, to the Lords of the Treasury, relative to the ship Hester, 341; Report to, on the harbor of New York, 354; Letter to, from the Lords of Trade, relative to the boundary between New York and New Jersey, 367; Referred to, 434—iii, 115, 493.

Beman, David, x, 717.

Beman, Josiah, x, 718.

Benckes, Jacob, i, 122.

Benedyck, Thomas, i, 15—vi, 207.

Bennet, H., iii, 302.

Bennet (Banet), Jeremiah, ii, 327, 396.

Bennet, John, ii, 456–460, 470.

Bennet, Peter, i, 183.

Bennett, Joseph, A West Jersey Proprietor, iii, 95, 498.

Bennit, Arie, ii, 325, 332.

Benson, Thomas, i, 269.

Benthall, Walter, An East Jersey Proprietor, i, 442, 454, 457, 462, 474, 482, 483, 490, 504, 530—ii, 26, 164, 165, 171, 177, 186–193, 198; Dis-

bursements by, on account of East Jersey, 203; Signs instructions to Governor Basse, 213; As Proprietor, 257, 263, 376, 4C8, 411—iii, 314.

Bergen, Oath of Allegiance at, 1665-1668, i, 48; Order prohibiting the exercise of authority in, not sanctioned by the Governor, 92; Relations with the Council of New Netherlands, 123, 125, 127, 129, 135, 140, 145, 146, 151, 320; Schoolmaster and Precentor to be supported, 141.—Inhabitants of, ask for trees to construct stockades, iii, 149.

Bergen County, Taxes, iv, 368, 369; Fees of representatives, 370.—Common lands of, ix, 451, 454, 459-475, 478.—Act relating to the common lands in, x, 152; Petition of William Bayard in relation to his claims to said lands, 168; Lords of Trade recommend the disallowance of the act relative to the common lands in, 188; Act disallowed in the Privy Council, 196.

Berkeley and Carteret, Lease to, from the Duke of York, for New Jersey, i, 8; Release to the same, for the same, 10; Commission of Philip Carteret, as Governor of New Jersey, 20; Instructions to Governor Carteret, 21; Commission to Robert Vauquillin as Surveyor-General, 26; Seal of, 27; Concessions and agreements to and with all who shall settle and plant in New Jersey, 28; Address to, from the New Jersey Council, 94; Declaration from, of the true intent and meaning of their concessions, 99, 101; Letter from, to the Governor and Council of New Jersey, relative to the injuries done by William Meaker to William Pardon, 104; Grant from, to the Officers and Freeholders of Woodbridge, and to Samuel Moore, 104; Directions from, to the Governor and Council of New Jersey, and agreement to build a prison and send over guns, ammunition, etc., 105; Letter from, to Deputy-Governor Berry, relative to the disturbances in the Province, 108; Letter from, to the pretended representatives of Elizabethtown, Newark and New Piscataway, 109.

Berkeley, Lord, ii, 126, 388, 421.

Berkeley, Maurice, i, 25.

Berkeley, Sir John, Notice of, i, 25.

Berkstead, Joshua, i, 414.

Bernard, Francis, Approved of as Governor of New Jersey, ix, 21; Notice of, 21; Commission of, 23; Instructions to, 40, 77; Gives to the Lords of Trade an account of his arrival in his Government, 116; Visits different parts of his Government, and informs the Lords of Trade respecting the invasions of the Indians, 120; Gives an account of the death of Chief-Justice Ainsley, 124; Message of, to the Minisink Indians, 125; Prorogues the Assembly, and reports vacancies in the Council, 126; Receives message from the Assembly, 129; Observations of, respecting bills of credit, and the necessity of special instructions empowering him to pass acts of Assembly relative thereto, 131; Represents to the Lords of Trade the necessity of raising money to continue the war, 137; Gives an account of the conferences held

with the Indians at Easton, 139; Answer to several of his communications, from the Lords of Trade, 152; Instructions to, relative to bills of credit, 156; Speech of, to the Legislature, 159; Answer to the same, 162; Address of, to the Legislature, March 15th, 1759, 163; Commends to Secretary Pitt, the unanimity and dispatch of the Assembly, 166; Informs the Lords of Trade that the Assembly had passed a bill for raising 1,000 men, and a bill for their support, 168; Observations of, upon the money bills, 170; Informs the Lords of Trade that the New Jersey regiment had arrived in Albany, and that he had laid out a town for the Indians in Burlington County, 174; Informs the Lords of Trade, concerning the pretensions of Robert Hunter Morris to the office of Chief-Justice of New Jersey, 176; Is appointed Governor of Massachusetts, 188; Thanks the Lords of Trade for this appointment, and sends to them Mr. Morris's patent, 209; Gives an account to the Lords of Trade, of the proceedings of the Supreme Court in relation to the claims of Mr. Morris, 212; Speech of, to the Assembly, 219; Reply to the same, 222; Comments of, on the bill for raising troops in the Province, 224; Referred to, 232, 233, 236, 239, 248, 270, 343; List of papers from, relating to the Stamp Act, 527–530; Vice-Admiral, 622.—Referred to, x, 114.

Bernard, Fran., Captain, ix, 186.

Berrien, John, ix, 463; Writes to Governor Franklin, relative to Captain Kennedy's complaint, 470.—Referred to, x, 357.

Berry, Henry, x, 718.

Berry, John, i, 66, 76; President of the Special Court held at Elizabethtown, February, 1672, 81; Member of Council, 89; Letter to, as Deputy-Governor, from Charles II, relative to the authority of the Lords Proprietors, 107; Letter to, from the Lords Proprietors, relative to the turbulent spirits in the Province, 108; Grant from, as Deputy-Governor, to James Bollen, 110; Note on, 110; Orders from, to the inhabitants of several towns to take out their warrants, 119; Note on, 122; Affairs with the Council of New Netherlands, 125, 131, 145, 149, 150; To swear in officers, 177; Commissioned by Governor Carteret to be his successor, 295; Referred to, 301, 303, 499—ii, 327, 486, 502.

Besborough, Lord, ix, 249.

Beswick, Francis, i, 270.

Betten, Daniel, iv, 188.

Betts, Richard, i, 150.

Beulah, Ship, x, 562–569.

Beune, Aty, ii, 396.

Beversham, William, i, 183.

Beys, Henricus, iv, 174.

Biard, John, x, 717.

Bibby, Richard, ii, 461.

Bickley, Abraham, Proposed for the Council, iii, 51.

Bickley, May, iii, 354.—Indicted, iv, 88; Attorney, 92, 97, 103.
Bickly, Mrs., Contributes to the supposed Cornbury Fund, iii, 213.
Biddle, E., x, 529.
Biddle, William, i, 268—ii, 148, 380.—An agent of the West Jersey Proprietors, iii, 221.—Referred to, ix, 4.
Biddles or Pensbury Island, v, 42, 44.
Biglow, Aaron, x, 718.
Biglow, Daniel, x, 718.
Biglow, Jabez, x, 718.
Bigelow, Jon, x, 717.
Biglow, Josiah, x, 718.
Biles, Benjamin, vii, 606—viii, Part II, 234.
Biles, William, iii, 165.
Billing, Edward, i, 158—iv, 127.
Billop, Christopher, i, 195, 196, 197, 201, 202, 203; Letter to, from Governor Andros, 270; Referred to, 281, 476, 485—ii, 417—iv, 344, 345.
Billop, Joseph, Escheator-General, iv, 129, 132.
Bills of Credit, Acts relating to, v, 3, 84, 94; Scheme for issuing and sinking £40,000 of, 98; Opinion of the Lords of Trade respecting, 120; Interest on canvassed by Governor Burnet, 129, 163, 165; Governor Montgomerie's views respecting the payment of interest money for incidental expenses, 249-260; Answer to the same, from the Lords of Trade, 266; Reference to, 305, 365; Reasons of John Sharpe, Solicitor, for the non-approval of an act of the New Jersey Assembly for making £40,000 in bills of credit, 410; Reply of Richard Partridge, to the reasons of John Sharpe, 416—Assent of Governor Morris to, how given, vi, 22; Scheme of Captain John Thomlinson, relating to, 111-116; Report of the Lords of Trade, relative to, 122; Letter from Governor Morris, relative to, 131-137; Observations upon, in the Governor's message, 259-263; Order in Council, relative to the emission of £40,000 in bills of credit, 361; Representation of the Lords of Trade respecting, 433. See also Paper Money.
Bingley, William, i, 530—ii, 187-193, 198; Disbursements by, on account of East Jersey, 204; Signs name, 213, 257—Grand Juror, iii, 486, 487.
Bird, John, vii, 182.
Bird, William, vii, 377.
Bishop, John, Sr., i, 66, 67; Juror, 82; Member of Council, 89, 91, 93, 97, 110, 134—ii, 226, 255, 270, 315-317, 373, 386, 488, 541—iii, 454, 479, 482, 484, 485—iv, 10, 190.
Bishop, John, Jr., i, 50, 307.
Bishop, Noah, iv, 188.
Bishop of London, Desires that marriage licenses may be directed only to a Protestant minister of the Gospel, ix, 504, 520.
Bispham, Joshua, vii, 99—viii, Part I, 73.—Inspector of the press, viii, Part II, 70, 234.
Black, William, i, 269, 288.

Blackall, John, ii, 461.

Blackamore, Mr., iv, 225.

Blackfields, Peter, iii, 358—iv, 42, 45.

Blackwood, Robert, i, 529.—Disbursements by, on account of East Jersey, ii, 204.

Blackwood, Samuel, x, 351.

Blair, Samuel, x, 717.

Blakeney, Colonel, vi, 103.

Blakiston, N., On the irregularities in the Province of New Jersey, ii, 462.

Blanchard, John, x, 588.

Bland, Richard, x, 530.

Blane, William, Affidavit of, against Lewis M. Ashfield, vii, 621.

Bloemmaert, Samuel, Patent to, for the east side of Delaware river, now Cape May County, i, 1.

Blond, Gabriel, Surrogate, ix, 359.

Bloomfield (Blumfield), John, i, 82, 177.—Petitions the Assembly in relation to the East Jersey records, iii, 220; Grand Juror on Woodbridge riot, 486, 487.

Bloomfield, Moses, x, 345.

Blumfield, Thomas, i, 50—iii, 446.

Board of Trade. See Lords of Trade.

Boddington, James, ii, 42-61, 65-73, 76, 79, 95, 99, 276, 302, 470.

Bodine, Jacob, Indicted, vi, 456, 465—vii, 458.

Boelen, Abram, v, 153.

Boerum, S., x, 530.

Boes, Captain Nicolaes, i, 122.

Bogert, Jan., ii, 326.

Boinell (Bonnell), Isaac, ii, 129, 334.

Boinel (Bonnell, Bunnell), Nathaniel, ii, 129, 334.

Bollen, James, i, 108; Grant of land to, 110; Ordered to give up to the Dutch authorities records and papers belonging to the late Province of New Jersey, 131; Appointed to swear in officers, 177; Letter to, from Governor Carteret, 316; Referred to, 350; Secretary to the Council, 355 to 365—ii, 363, 364, 397—iii, 485.

Borngat, Roeloff, ii, 326.

Bond, Benjamin, ii, 396.

Bond, Captain, iv, 89.

Bond, Elijah, vii, 544.

Bond, Joseph, i, 50.

Bond, Robert, i, 50, 81, 82, 128—vii, 425.

Bondet, Daniel, iv, 174.

Bonham, Jeremiah, x, 667.

Bonnel, Abraham, Lieutenant, ix, 185.

Bonnell, Isaac, ii, 327.

Bonnel, Jacob, Ensign, ix, 187.

Bonnell, Joseph, iv, 253—v, 142, 144, 147, 149, 150.—Speaker of the

House of Assembly, vi, 59; Vote on the Militia Act, 202, 203; Affidavits before, 427–432.—Dead, vii, 253, 259.

Bonnet, Joseph, v, 155.

Bonney, Joseph, viii, Part I, 104.

Booker, John, Signs surrender of the Government, ii, 456–460; Recommends Andrew Hamilton for Governor, 470.

Bools, Thomas, ii, 113.

Boone, Charles, Asks permission of the Lords for his brother, Governor Boone, to visit England, ix, 263.

Boone, Thomas, Appointed Governor of New Jersey, ix, 188, 189; Commission for, 190; Instructions to, 193, 194; Commission to, as Vice-Admiral, 195; Acknowledges his appointment, 205; Referred to, 211; Sets out for his Government in New Jersey, 218; Arrival of, 234; Notice of, 234; Informed by Mr. Morris, of the dispute between him and Mr. Jones for the office of Chief-Justice, 235; Transmits Mr. Morris's letter to the Lords of Trade, 238; Writes to Secretary Pitt, in regard to the imputed illegal trade in New Jersey, 240; Informs the Lords of Trade of the amicable proceedings of the Assembly, 248; Writes, relative to the defective Post arrangements in the Province, 249; Letter to, from President Colden, relative to the northern boundary dispute, 253; Informs the Lords of Trade as to what had been done in raising additional troops, 260; Informs Secretary Pitt as to the same, 261; Desires to visit England, 263; Referred to, 265; Transmits to the Lords of Trade acts of the Assembly, 270; Address of the Assembly to, 287; Answer of, to the same, 288; Informs the Lords of Trade of the passage of an act for continuing a part of the New Jersey regiments, and of the suspension of Mr. Antill from the Council, 299; Gives an account to the same of the seizure of a vessel engaged in illicit trade, 300; Congratulations from, on the intended marriage of the King, 304; To the Lords of Trade, relative to his leave of absence, 305; Referred to, 307, 335.

Borden, Benjamin, ii, 363, 396.

Borden, James, ii, 396—vii, 542.

Borden, Jean, Contributes to the supposed Cornbury Fund, iii, 214; Moneys paid by, to the Receiver-General, 351, 352.

Borden, Joseph, x, 427.

Borden, Richard, ii, 363—vii, 542, 543; Affidavit of, against John Coxe, 547.

Bore, Joshua, i, 288.

Borten, John, i, 270.

Boscawen, Admiral, viii, Part II, 123, 135, 163, 254.

Boston Port Act, x, 457, 460, 532.

Bostwick, Rev. David, Informs Rev. Joseph Bellamy of the death of Rev. Samuel Davies, fourth President of the College of New Jersey, ix, 258.

Boud, Adlord, iii, 223.

Boude, Grimston, Affidavit of, against Lewis Morris and George Willocks, iii, 477.

Boudinot, Elias, x, 345, 430, 467, 575.

Boundary Line between East and West Jersey—Instructions to Governor
Lawrie, relative to, i, 428; Minutes of New York Council, relative to,
517; Agreement between the Governors to submit it to arbitration,
519; Obligation of the authorities of West Jersey to abide by the determination of the arbitrators, 522; Award of John Reid and William
Emley, respecting it, 523.—Commissioners appointed by the East
Jersey Proprietors to confer with the Governor of West Jersey, relative thereto, ii, 1; Narrative of Governor Coxe, relative thereto, 10;
Letter without signature, to the Proprietors in England, relative to,
18; Minutes of the West Jersey Proprietors, relative to running it in
accordance with the award of Reid and Emley, 24; Agreement between the Governors in regard to, 34.—Letters from James Logan,
relative to, iv, 377, 388; Instructions to John Harrison, from the
Commissioners on, 391; Caveat of Daniel Coxe, relating thereto,
441; Proceedings of the Council of the West Jersey Proprietors, relating thereto, 452.—Representations from the Lords of Trade to the
King, relative to, v, 213; Order in Council aproving the act respecting, 243.—Instructions from John Hamilton and Andrew Johnston,
to John Lawrence, relative to, vi, 154; Commissioners appointed to
run, 352.

Boundary Line between New York and New Jersey—Agreement relative
to the powers of the surveyors of the lines of the three Governments,
i, 517; Instructions from the Council, at New York, to their surveyor,
relative thereto, 518; Position of the 41st degree of north latitude on
Hudsons river, 520; Certificate of Governor Morris, relative thereto,
521.—Letter from Governor Hamilton, to Governor Fletcher, respecting, ii, 105; Letter from the Lords of Trade concerning, 367.—Memorial from Peter Fauconnier, recommending the adjustment of, iii,
388.—Proper persons to be empowered to run it, iv, 365; Appointment of Commissioners, 383; Tripartite indenture, 394; Petition of
Allane Jarratt, respecting, 403; Report of New York Council on his
petition, 406; Memorial of the Proprietors of New Jersey, relative to,
408; Petition of the inhabitants of New York, relating thereto, 433;
Letter from Lewis Morris, to the Lords of Trade, relating thereto,
439; Letter from the same, to Peter Schuyler, relating thereto, 446;
Proceedings of the Council of West Jersey Proprietors, relating
thereto, 452.—Memorial of the Proprietors, relative to, vi, 138; Address to Governor Morris, relative to, 144; Affidavit of James Alexander, relative to, 145; Letter from Governor Morris, relative to,
162; Report of Robert Hunter Morris, concerning, 168; Memorial of
the East Jersey Proprietors, respecting, 216.—Letters relative to,
from James Alexander, vii, 119, 125, 152; Address relative to, 142;
Letter from F. J. Paris, relative to, 156; Letter from Governor
Clinton, relative to, 159; Speech of Colonel Lewis Morris, in the
New York Assembly, relative to, 163; Letters from, F. J. Paris,

relative to, 167, 176; Petition of F. J. Paris to the Lords of Trade, relative to, 226; Letter from J. Alexander and R. F. Morris, relative to, 262; From F. J. Paris, relative to, 297.—Opinion on, by the Lords of Trade, viii. Part I, 128; Letter from Robert Charles, relating to, 135; Argument that the forks of Delaware are the true limits of New Jersey on the North, 139; Question referring to, answered, 141; Representation of the Lords of Trade, relative to the repeal of the act of 1747, concerning, 144; Letter from Ferdinand J. Paris, relative to, 152; Reply to the same, 157; Petition of the Proprietors of East Jersey, relative to the Boundary Act of 1747, 160; Disputes concerning, 190, 192; Memorial of Proprietors of East Jersey, concerning, 202, 232; Documents relating to, 233–286; Letters from Governor DeLancey, to the Lords of Trade, relative to, 288, 297. —Disturbances arising from the non-adjustment of, viii, Part II, 13, 20, 27, 28; Papers relative to, transmitted to the Lords of Trade, 30–35, 72; Letter from Lieutenant-Governor DeLancey, referring to, 74; The action of the Council of New York, in respect to, 89; Communication from the Lords of Trade, relative to, 108; Proceedings of the Privy Council, relative to, 114; A commission to arrange, recommended by the Lords of Trade, 129; Governor Belcher, in relation to, 183, 187; Governor Hardy, in relation to, 207; Commission for settling, 212; Petition of the Proprietors of East Jersey, relative to, 224–228; Memorandum, relative to the Commissioner for, 242; William Alexander, in relation to, 243; Governor Belcher, in relation to, 256.—Arrests of trespassers in Sussex County, New Jersey, by order of the New York Council, ix, 178; Petition of Philip Swartwout, relative to, 250; Letter from President Colden, relative to, 253; Act of the Assembly, relative to, 389; Commissioners to settle, 390, 447, 581, 588, 622, 623, 630.—Statement of the claims of New York, x, 119; Surveyor of, appointed by Governor Colden of New York, 194; Observations of Governor Franklin upon, 386, 407; Letter from Governor Tryon, relative to, 393; Approved by the King, 416; Report of the surveyors of, 501.

Boundary Line between New York and Massachusetts Bay, x, 660.

Boune, James, ii, 396.

Boune, William, ii. 332.

Bourden, Ben, i, 413.

Bout-town, Lands at, sold by John Fenwick, i, 413.

Bouts, Richard, ii, 460.

Bowde (Boud), Adlord, ii, 50.

Bowen, David, x, 531.

Bowers, Captain, i, 300.

Bowler, Garrat, ii, 363, 397.

Bowman, George, Indicted, vii, 458.

Bowman, Thomas, Indicted, vii, 458.

Bowne (Brown), Andrew, ii, 270; Letter from, relating to the disorders

in New Jersey, 327; Note on, 329; Objected to, as Governor of East Jersey, 385; Signs petition, 369; Referred to, 401, 416, 423; Recommended for Council, 429, 486, 487; Referred to, 439, 445, 446; Appointed member of the Council, 507.—Referred to, iii, 1; Commissioner of New Jersey, 64; Referred to, 75, 76, 155, 156; Contributes to the supposed Cornbury Fund. 212; Appointed a member of the Council, 317; Death of, mentioned. 340, 341; Referred to, 463, 479, 482.—Member of Governor Hunter's Council, iv, 2; Referred to, 76.

Bowne, James, ii, 327.

Bowne (Bound, Bown, Boun), John, i, 44, 51, 88, 143, 305, 307, 309, 333, 355, 364—ii, 486.—Collecting money supposed to be for Lord Cornbury, iii, 199–219; Expelled from the Assembly, 227, 277; Proposed as a member of the Council by Governor Cornbury. 341.

Bown, John, Removed from the Judgeship in Monmouth County, iv, 129; Recommended for Council, 133; Signed, 310.

Bowne, Obadiah, ii. 363, 397.—Contributes to the supposed Cornbury Fund. iii, 212, 214—iv, 111.

Bowne, William, ii, 397.

Bowyer, i, 414.

Boyle, Solomon, Affidavit of relation to the riots, vii, 419, 426.

Boyse. John. ii, 396.

Brackett, John, Senr., i, 50.

Bradbury, Rev. Mr., Letter to, from Governor Belcher, vii, 54.

Braddock, General, Edward, viii, Part II, 104, 111, 113, 116; Letter to, from Governor Belcher. 117; Reported defeat of, 117, 118, 119; Referred to, 148, 183, 209, 221.

Bradford, William, Clerk of the Assembly, iv, 74, 80, 81, 123; Salary, 185, 363; Signs as Clerk, 251; Payments for printing, 369, 371.—Referred to, v, 34, 139, 141—viii, Part I, 106; Part II, 232.

Bradish, Hannah, x, 614.

Bradley, Attorney-General, Letter to Captain Roddam, relative to the killing of Elizabeth Stebbins, vii, 534.

Bradstreet, Captain John, Letter from, to Governor Belcher, viii, Part II. 113.

Bradstreet, Colonel, ix. 365.

Bradway (Broadway), Edward, i, 118, 268, 283, 284, 292, 414.

Brae. Judge, x, 272.

Praedy, Hydrek, Clark, i, 320.

Brahm, Dee, See De Brahm.

Braim, Benjamin, iii, 314.

Brainard, Rev. David, vi, 406, 407—vii, 598—ix, 355.

Brainard. John. vii, 598—viii, Part I, 140—ix, 175, 355—x, 345.

Brainerd, Jr.. Hezekiah, ix, 355.

Braine, James, An East Jersey Proprietor, i, 384, 424, 433, 434, 437, 442, 474, 482, 483, 490, 504, 530—ii, 26, 204—iii, 314.

Bramen, John, ii, 48.

Bramma, Benjamin, ii, 146.

Brandreth, Timothy, ii, 146.

Bransart, Thomas, iv, 310.

Brattle, Col., viii, Part I, 9.

Bray, John, ii, 327, 328; Presented by Monmouth Grand Jury, 332, 363; Fined for contempt of Court, 363; Signed petition, 396—Contributes to Cornbury Fund, iii, 212.

Brearley, David, x, 512.

Breasted, William, vii, 421.

Breese, Samuel, x, 600.

Breum, Joseph, ii, 339.

Brian, Thomas, iii, 164.

Brick, John, vii, 99—viii, Part I, 73.

Brick, Joshua, x, 531.

Bridge, Chris, iv, 174.

Bridger, John, Surveyor-General of his Majesty's Woods, iii, 122.

Bridges, John, ii, 42-62, 66-74, 76, 79, 84, 186-194, 199, 258, 276, 300, 302, 376, 408, 411; Signs surrender of the government, 456-460; Recommends Andrew Hamilton for Governor, 470.—A Proprietor, iii, 38, 51, 82, 95, 302, 314, 498—iv, 141.

Bridges, Dr., iii, 209, 216, 217, 277.

Bridges, Rev. Thomas, Letter to, from the West Jersey Society, ii, 94; Letter to, from Daniel Coxe, 96.

Bridgewater, Earl of, One of the Lords of Trade, ii, 132, 136, 185, 201, 268.

Brierley (Brearly), David, Congratulates Governor Belcher on his arrival, vii, 64; Rescued from prison, 86; Referred to, 206, 219; Indicted, 458; Referred to, 483, 628.

Brierly, John, vii, 628.

Brightwen, William, i, 288.

Brindly, Luke, i, 288.

Brinley, William, vii, 257.

Brinson, Daniel, i. 289.

Bristed (Brested), William, vi, 429, 430-432.

Broadwell, Josiah, viii, Part II, 165.

Brockholes, Capt. Anthony, i, 186, 196, 349; Letter from, to Governor Carteret, 350; Note on, 352; Referred to, 353, 458.

Bromfield, Thomas, ii, 42-62, 66-74, 79, 470—iii, 498.

Bromhall, Richard, ii, 42-46, 65-74, 79.

Brookes, Timothy, ii, 384.

Brookes, William, ii, 42-62, 66-74, 79.

Brooksbank, Joseph, ii, 42-46, 65-73, 78, 276, 302, 376, 408, 411, 470—iii, 38, 82, 95, 302, 314.

Brooksbank, Stamp, vii, 326.

Brotherton, A town laid our for the Indians, ix, 175; Referred to, 357.

Brown, Abraham, i, 51—iii, 485—iv, 309.

Browne, Daniel, ii, 339.

Brown, George, iii, 486—iv, 9—x, 352.

Brown, Isaac, ix, 640.

Browne, John, ii, 46, 327—iii, 376, 393, 394, 401, 422-428, 447, 452, 453—
iv, 9, 98, 99, 371—vii, 32—x, 303,717.

Brown, Jr., John, vi, 351—vii, 457.

Browne, Joseph, ii, 148.

Brown, Morris, vi. 351.

Brown, Moses, vii, 457.

Brown, Philip, ix. 5.

Brown, Preserve, v, 187.

Brown, Thomas, x, 531.

Brown, William, ii, 129, 325, 334, 396.

Browne, Andrew, ii, 326.

Browne, Nicholas, i, 51, 134—iii, 485—iv, 310.

Browe, Zebedee, vi, 351—vii, 457.

Bruen, Obadiah, vii, 32.

Brumson, Barefoot, iv, 89.

Bryant, Anthony, i, 111.

Bryant, Captain William, viii, Part I, 116.

Buck, John, x, 531.

Buckhalson, Francis, ii. 396.

Buckley, Richard, ix, 591.

Budd, James, ii, 50.

Bull, John, Petition of, with others, for grants of land, i, 289—x, 367.

Budd (Bad le), Thomas, i, 268, 414, 419—ii, 18, 19, 65, 99—iii, 158—v,
211.

Budd, Justice. Letter to, from Governor Belcher, vii, 67.

Budden, Captain, ix, 524.

Bude, William, ii, 384.

Buffington, Richard, i. 269.

Bulark, John, iv, 310.

Bule, Mr., iv, 159.

Bulkley, Charles, ix, 590, 594.

Bull, or Boel, ——, x, 664.

Bunel, Hommuel, ii, 396.

Bunell, John, ii, 336.

Bunn, Matthew, i, 66.

Bunn, Miles, iv, 189.

Bunnell, Isaac, Grand Juror for Essex County, iii, 496.

Bunnell (Bonell), Nathaniel, i, 50, 65.

Bunting, William, iv, 371.

Burchan, Robert, i, 196.

Burnet, I., Surveyor-General of Customs, iv, 49, 78, 124, 139.

Burden, Benjamin, iii, 483, 484.

Burdon's Island, v, 42, 44.

Burgess, Captain, ii, 291, 292.

Burges, Isaac, i, 413.

Burke, Francis, x, 711.

Burkhurst, Admiral, i, 152.

Burkmaster, Edward, ii, 290.

Burlington (Bridlington), Road between Perth Amboy and, i, 428.—Instructions relative to the port of, ii, 178; Riots at, 379, 402; Propritors wish it recognized as a port, 405; Markets at, 406.—Transportation between and Perth Amboy, iii, 177, 186, 250; Referred to, 11, 16, 67, 167, 184, 221, 227, 239, 264, 274, 279—iv, 11, 12, 14, 16, 22, 57, 67, 73, 74, 76, 88, 95, 97, 128, 129, 142, 157, 167, 172, 184, 221, 224, 225, 227, 239, 240, 261, 264, 273, 274, 276, 277; Small-pox at, 264; Surveyor-General's office, 289.—Referred to. v, 11, 12, 40, 45, 58, 59, 73, 77, 83, 133.—Described, vi, 108.—Governor Belcher's opinion of, vii, 65, 92.—Removal of the seat of government from, to Perth Amboy, x, 457, 468.

Burlington County, Population of in 1699. ii, 305.—Taxes of, iv, 368, 369, 370.—Money received from Collector of, v, 132—viii. Part I, 66, 67, 68, 73, 74.—Instructions to the Assemblymen of, in regard to the liabilities of the Eastern Treasurer, x, 417.

Burlington Island, Description of, v, 38, 42, 44.—Caveat, relative to, x, 515.

Burnet, John, ii, 187-193, 198, 213, 257, 263—vi, 416—viii, Part I, 200; Part II, 228.

Burnett, Obadiah, ii, 42-62, 66-74, 79. 194, 199, 300, 302; Signs the Surrender of the government, 456-460; Recommends Andrew Hamilton for Governor, 470.—Proprietor, iii, 38; Sonmans' Commission, 314.

Burnet, Robert, An East New Jersey Proprietor, i, 425, 433, 434, 437, 442, 446, 448. 451, 454, 457, 462; Interested in goods shipped to East Jersey, 467; Signs as Proprietor, 474, 482, 483, 513; Referred to, 529, 530.—Named as a Proprietor, ii, 26, 32, 187-193; Disbursements by, on account of East Jersey, 203; Name to instructions to Governor Basse, 213; As Proprietor. 257, 263; Surrenders the government of East Jersey, 387; Signs the surrender of the government, 456-460.

Burnet, William, iv, 12: Commission of, as Governor of New York and New Jersey, transmitted by the Lords of Trade. 447. — Instructions to, as Governor of New Jersey, v, 1; Notice of, 1; Additional instruction to, 3; Letter to, from the Lords of Trade. relative to Secretary Smith's fees, 4; Letter from, to the Lords of Trade, relative to the New Jersey Assembly, 8; Instruction to, relative to the clergy of the Church of England, 23; Letter from, to the Lords of Trade, relative to New Jersey affairs. 32: Referred to, 40; Instruction to, relative to the acts regulating trade and navigation, 46; Letter to, from the Lords of Trade, relative to

vacancies in the New Jersey Council, 51; Transmits to the Lords of Trade. sundry acts of the New Jersey Assembly, 53; Letter from, to Lord Carteret. relative to gold and silver mines in New Jersey, 64; Notice of, 70; Letter to, from the Lords of Trade, 70; Instructions to, relative to private acts. 71; Referred to, 72, 73; Letter from, to the Lords of Trade, relative to paper money, 75; Instruction to, relative to the election of Representatives to the Assembly, 84; Letter from, to the Lords of Trade, relative to certain acts passed by the Assembly of New Jersey, 86; Announces the death of Chief Justice Trent, 97; Referred to. 101; Letter from, to the Lords of Trade. relative to New Jersey Affairs, 104; To the same, relative to certain returns to be made, 117; Letter to. from the Lords of Trade, relative to gold and silver mines in New Jersey, 120; Instructions to, relative to the suspension of sentences, 122; Proclamation of, against any authority by Peter Sonmans, as Receiver of Quit Rents, 124; Letters from, to the Duke of Newcastle, 129, 130: Letter from, to the Lords of Trade, 131; Letter to, from the Lords of Trade, relative to Paper Money of New Jersey, 156; Instruction to. relative to appeals, 157; Instructions to, relative to vice and immorality, 159; Letter from, to Secretary Popple, 163; Letter from, to the Lords of Trade, relative to the application of interest money, 165; Referred to, 179; Letter from, to the Lords of Trade, transmitting documents, 181; Referred to, 199, 200, 207; Letter to, from James Alexander, respecting the relative authority of the Plantation Assemblage, 230; Death of, 261; Referred to, 287, 344, 360, 374, 484—vi, 71—viii, Part I, 208.

Burr, Rev Aaron, Letter to, from Governor Belcher, relative to the new College, vii, 115, 618; Referred to, 119.—President of the new College, viii, Part I. 9, 11, 85: Letter to, on his marriage, from Governor Belcher, 89; Letter to, from the same, relative to the College, Part II, 166—x, 240.

Burr, Henry, iii, 164.

Burr, John, v, 211; Letter from, to James Alexander, 212.

Burrow, John, A West Jersey Proprietor, iii, 95.

Burwell, Samuel, ii, 333, 334.

Burwell (Burrell), Theophilus, vi, 351, 455, 465, 467—vii, 403-405, 433; Examination of, relative to Essex County riots, 434; Referred to, 437, 441, 444; Indicted. 458; Referred to, 511, 513.

Burwell, Zachary, Jr., ii, 357.

Bushroods, Thomas, i, 223.

Bussott, John, i, 128.

Bustall (Bustill), Samuel, iv, 261; Letter from, against Governor Hunter, 262; Referred to, 267; Signs, 344—v, 187, 277, 279, 281, 282.

Butcher, John, i, 269.

Butterworth. Moses, ii. 362, 371.

Byerly, Thomas, Recommended for the Council, iv, 62, 153, 154; Re-

ferred to, by Rev. Jacob Henderson, 157; Recommended for the Council. 160, 171, 182; Member of Council, 253, 326, 334, 340, 363; Payments to, 370, 372 —One of Governor Burnet's Council, v, 3, 34; Place in Council filled, 52, 71.—Referred to, vii, 645.

Byles Island, v, 41, 44.

Byllinge (Billing, Billinge), Edward, i, 158, 185; Quintipartite deed to, from Sir George Carteret. 205; Instructions from, and others, to their Commissioners in West Jersey, 219; His interest in the Province presented to his creditors, 232; Name signed to Concessions, etc., to settlers in West Jersey, 268; Memoranda as to his claim, 223; Grant to him and others, from the Duke of York, 324; An East Jersey Proprietor, 384, 442; Letter to, from Charles II, 458; Name signed, 504; Agreement as to the dividing line between East and West Jersey, 51); Referred to, 530.—Notice of, ii, 4; Referred to, 6, 8, 10, 12, 13, 14, 16, 22, 41, 46, 49, 62, 64, 65, 66; Disbursements by, on account of East Jersey, 202; Referred to, 388, 422—iii, 158, 413—vii, 350.

Byllynge, Loveday, ii. 48.

C.

Cadwalader, Thomas, vii, 542; Letter from, to Governor Belcher, 544.

Cage, Thomas, ii, 461.

Caiger, ———, x, 113.

Caldwell, James, x, 345.

Callingor, Henry, ii. 148.

Callwell, Allen, iv, 9.

Camberling, William, x, 273.

Cameron, Ewen, i, 529.

Camp, Joseph. vii, 405, 444, 512.

Camp, Nathaniel, vi, 346, 350, 361, 367, 395, 396, 413—vii, 49, 50, 64, 74, 415.

Camp, Samuel, ii, 336.

Campbel, Archibald, ii, 186-193, 198, 213.

Campbell, Hume, viii, Part I, 145, 155.

Campbell, John, An East Jersey Proprietor, i, 460, 499, 522, 528.—Commissioned to confer, relative to the boundary line between the Provinces, ii, 1 —Desires to report. 24 – iv, 9, 142—ix, 325.

Campbell, Lord Neill, Governor of East Jersey, i, 509, 522, 529; Appoints Andrew Hamilton Deputy Governor, 541.—Referred to, ii, 10, 18, 19, 27, 32—iii, 115.

Campbell, Lord William, ix, 621.

Canada, Expedition to, iv, 133—vi, 370, 371—vii, 341, 354, 383—viii, Part I, 70, 79; Part ii, 188—ix, iii, 149, 183.

Canaghqueison, Chief of Oneidas, x, 56.

Cand, Joseph, ii, 396.

Candler, John, iv. 215.

Cane, Major, x, 670, 671.

Cannan, Patrick, ii, 332.

Cantwell, Capt. Edmund, Lands sold to, by the Indians, i, 111; Grant to, from Governor Carteret, 111; Letters to, from Governor Andros, regarding Indian affairs, 179, 181; Warrent to, to arrest John Fenwicke, 18?; Declaration of, in regard to Fenwicke, 193; Estate of William Tom, 196; High Sheriff, 201; Deposition of, 274.

Cantwell, William, i, 268.

Cape May County, First grant of, i, 1.—Population of in 1699, ii, 305.—Taxes, iv, 368, 369—v, 132, 133.—Money received from collector of, viii, Part I, 66, 67, 68; From Commissions, 71; Interest from, 73, 74.—Justices of, x, 207, 213, 215-219, 275-297.

Car, Sir Robert, ix, 229.

Cardiff, James, x, 717.

Cardry, John, x, 717.

Carey, John, Answers objections made to his acting as Attorney-General in the courts of Salem and Cumberland Counties, x, 362; On Committee, 471.

Carkesse, Charles, Letter from, relative to the exportation of copper ore from New Jersey to Holland, v, 7—In relation to a glass house, vi, 98.

Carle, Jacob, vii, 421.

Carle, Mr., iv, 267.

Carolina, Illegal trading with, ii, 119.

Carpenter, Samuel, ii, 120.

Carpenters Island, v, 43, 44, 45.

Carr, Captain, i, 74, 76; Letter to, from Governor Lovelace, reproving him for neglect of duty in regard to the Indian murders at Matiniconck island, 79.

Carrington, Jonathan, x, 717.

Carrington, John, ii, 31.

Carrol, John, x, 710.

Carter, Barnabas, ii, 334, 396.

Carter, Nicholas, i, 50, 65, 82, 84.

Carter, Samuel, ii, 129; Proceedings against him for contempt in the Essex County Court, 313; Signs remonstrance, 327; Proceedings against him continued, 333, 334, 339; Signs petition, 395.—Grand Juror, iii, 496.

Carteret, Sir George, Notice of, i, 25; Letter from Charles II, concerning obedience to the government of, 153; Warrant to prepare a patent to, for East Jersey, 160; Release to, from the Duke of York, for the same, 163; Directions and instructions from, to the Governor, Council and inhabitants of East Jersey, 167; Explanation by, of the concessions made by the Lords Proprieters, 173.—Referred to, ii, 14, 231 .

Carteret, Sir George (grandson of the original Proprietor), Release to, from the Duke of York, for East New Jersey, i, 337.

Carteret, James, i, 72, 75; Declaration and protestation of the Governor and Council against, 89; Letter from the New Jersey Council, to the Governor, concerning, 91; Complaint against, by the Council of New Jersey, 91; Referred to, 153, 334.

Carteret, Lady Elizabeth, i, 346, 349: Letter to, from Governor Carteret, 353; Lease from, to the first twelve Proprietors of East Jersey, 366—ii, 388.

Carteret, Lord, Letter to, from Governor Burnet, relative to gold and silver mines in New Jersey, v, 64.

Carteret, Philip, Commission of, as Governor of New Jersey, i, 20; Instructions to, from the Lords Proprietors, 21; Letter from, to those purposing a settlement on the Delaware, 51; Letter from, to the Indian Sachem, Oraton, relative to the Newark tract, 55; Proclamation of, calling the first Assembly, 56; Seal of, 60: Warrant of, for requiring the surrender of a paper signed by the inhabitants of Middletown, against the laws, 61; Letter from, to Surveyor-General Vauquillan, relative to the Lords Proprietors lands about Woodbridge, Amboy and Piscataway, 62: Order from, enlarging the authority of the court at Woodbridge, 62; Letter from, to the people of Woodbridge, relative to persons admitted to vote at town meetings, who had not lands surveyed and patented, 63; Present at a Special Court at Elizabethtown, 65, 76; Order for a Special Court at Elizabethtown, 81; Confirms certain privileges to Middletown and Shrewsbury, 88; Order of, prohibiting the exercise of any authority in Bergen, not sanctioned by him, 92; Grant of land to Edmund Cantwell and Johannes Dehaes, 111; Grant from, to Lucas Pictor to purchase land from the Indians, 115; Inventory of his estate ordered by the Dutch Council, 130; Directions, instructions, etc., to, by Sir George Carteret, 167; Number of his family on his arrival in New Jersey, in 1665, 183; Paying the Indians for the land, 184; Letter to, from Governor Andros, 292; Proclamation of Governor Andros, against, 293; Letter from, to Governor Andros, in reply to his of March 8th, 294; Commission from, to John Berry, to be his successor, 295; Letter from, to Governor Andros, countermanding orders for a General Assembly, 297; Warrant from Governor Andros to arrest, 302; Account of his trial, 303; Letter from, to the Proprietor, narrating the proceedings of Governor Andros, 314; Letter from, to James Bollen, 316; Proclamation from, against the authority of Governor Andros, 346; Letter from, to the Governor of New York and his Council, 349; Letter from, to Captain Anthony Brockholls, 350; Proclamation of, to the inhabitants of Staten Island, 350; Letter to, from Captain Anthony Brockholls, 351; Letter to Lady Elizabeth Carteret, 353. —Copy of a license to purchase of the Indians, vi, 339.—Referred to, vii, 33—ix, 456.

Cartwither, Caleb, i, 50.

Cartwright. Captain James, i, 121.

Cartwright, Solomon, viii, Part II. 13.

Carty. John, viii, Part II, 230—x, 358, 450.

Casabon, Jan. Eversen, i, 49.

Caspar, A German, Manufacturer of glass, viii, Part I, 110.

Caswell, Richard, x, 530.

Catherwood, Mr., viii, Part I, 94, 117, 123. 154, 159.

Census, of New Jersey, in 1726, v, 164; Of the different Colonies, vi, 89;
Of New Jersey, 1737-38, and in 1745, 242-244.

Chadwick, James, Commissioner of Customs, ii, 131.

Chamberlayne, John, iv, 158.

Chamberlayne, William, Affidavits of, x, 3, 7.

Chambers, John. i, 510—v, 404—ix, 283.

Chambers, Robert, vii. 426, 427.

Chambers, Mr , viii, Part I, 122, 123.

Champance, Mr., iv, 257.

Champion, John, i, 288.

Champion, Matthew, iv, 253, 370—v, 137.

Champneys (Chamneys. Chamnis), Edward, i, 186, 227, 283, 414.

Chandler, John. vii, 439; Affidavit of, relative to the riots, 440.

Chandler, Rev. Thomas B., x, 311, 313.

Changerora, Land at, i, 474, 478, 498—ii, 32, 33.

Chaplin, John, ii, 396.

Chapman, John, vi, 147—viii, Part I, 207.

Charles, An Indian king, iv, 282.

Charles II, Patent to James, Duke of York, for tract of land in New England, including New Jersey, i, 3; Letter from, to Captain John
Berry, Deputy-Governor. confirming the laws and government estab-
lished in New Jersey by the Lords Proprietors, 107; Letter from,
concerning obedience to the Government of Sir George Carteret, 153;
Letter from, to the Governor and Council of East Jersey, 438; Letter
from, to Edward Byllyngs, 458.

Charles, Robert. Letter from, to Governor Clinton, relative to boundaries
between New York and New Jersey, viii, Part I, 135; Referred to,
145—viii, Part II, 244, 245.

Charles, Mr., Agent for New York, vii, 121, 168, 299, 300.

Chase, Samuel. x, 530.

Chaunders, Thomas, i, 414.

Cheescock's Patent, viii, Part I, 209, 223, 275.

Cheeseman, Olim, ii, 364.

Cheesman, William, vi, 465.

Cheete, George, i, 51.

Chesman, William, Sr., ii, 395.

Chesman, William, ii, 396.

Chettwood, William, Sheriff of Essex County, vii, 178, 210.

Chetwood, John, x, 467.

Chew, Samuel, Excommunicated by the Quakers, vi, 173.

Child, John, President of the West Jersey Society, Autograph, vii, 327.

Childe, John, Autograph, v, 510.

Cholmendelay, Robert, ix, 289.

Christany-Neck, Lands at, sold by John Fenwicke, i, 413.

Chubs, Charles, ii, 396.

Church of England in New York and New Jersey—Representation of, by Rev. Jacob Henderson, Missionary, iv, 155; Remarks on Mr. Henderson's representation of the state of the Church, 161; Letter from the clergy of New York and New Jersey, to Rev. Jacob Henderson, disapproving of his course toward the Council of New Jersey, 173.— Instructions to Governor Burnet, relative to the clergy of, v, 23.

Church, Dr. Benjamin, x, 669, 670; Letter from, intercepted and delivered to General Washington, 671, 674.

Churchill, Sir John, 324.

Clackford, Daniel, iv, 10.

Claese, Gerrebrant, ii, 326.

Claes, Jacob, i, 50.

Claesen, Dirck, i, 146.

Clarendon, Lord, Letter from, with enclosure, to the Secretary of State, relative to the Council of New Jersey, 501.

Claridge, Samuel, i, 530.

Clark, Abraham, Jr., Clerk of the Assembly, viii, Part II, 72, 94.

Clark, Benjamin, iv, 253, 370—v, 139.

Clark, Charles, vii, 606.

Clark, Daniel, vii, 420.

Clark, Elisha, vii, 368, 375, 446.

Clark (Clerke), Ephraim, ii, 129, 315, 326, 339, 396—iii, 496.

Clarke, George, iv, 119; Notice of, 119; Salary, 185; Recommended for the Council, 217; Certificate of, 285; Salary, 368.—Announces the death of Governor Cosby, v, 438; Referred to, 462, 511—vi, 65-68, 73-78, 168—vii, 77, 78, 646—viii, Part I, 210, 266—ix, 283.

Clarke, Herman, i, 270.

Clarke, James, ix, 180, 181—x, 367.

Clarke (Clerk), John, ii, 129, 326, 334, 339, 396—iii, 165.

Clark, Joseph, iii, 485.

Clarke, Joshua, ii, 129, 396.

Clarke, Richard, ii, 326, 339, 397—iii, 496.

Clarke, Samuel, ii, 129, 131, 168, 178, 254, 326, 334, 339, 397—iii, 496.

Clarke (Clerk), Thomas, ii, 334, 396—iv, 344, 345—x, 351.

Clark, Walter, i, 44.

Clark, William, i, 289, 394.

Clarkson, James, iv, 189.

Claten, Jan., ii, 326.

Clawson, Aaron, vii, 371-374.

Clawson, Jonathan, x, 588.

Clawson (Clausen), Thomas, vi, 417, 465, 469—vii, 215, 447-451, 458, 478.

Clawson, William, iv, 189.

Claypool, James, i, 416.

Clayton, Asher, Affidavit of, relative to the supposed Cornbury Fund, iii, 214.

Clayton, David, ii, 396—vii, 620.

Clayton (Cleayton), John, ii, 326, 396—iii, 215.

Clayton, Robert, Commissioner of Customs, ii, 131.

Clayton, William, Sr., i, 288.

Clayton (Cleayton), William, vii, 606—viii, Part I, 74.

Clayton (Cleayton), Zebulon, ii, 363—iv, 310.

Cleayton, Arthur, iv, 310, 313.

Cleft, Samuel, i, 289.

Clements, Jacob, iv, 310.

Clement, Samuel, viii, Part II, 233.

Clergy of the Church of England, In New York and New Jersey desire a Bishop, x, 309.

Clerk, George, iv, 340.

Clevenger, John, ii, 327.

Clinton, Charles, Surveyor, viii, Part I, 209.

Clinton, George, Governor of New York, Letter to, from Governor Morris, relative to the boundary line, vi, 162; Referred to, 168, 169; Communication from, to the Council of New Jersey, relative to the Indians, 369; Letter from, to Colonel Schuyler, of the New Jersey forces, 441; Referred to, 448; Letter from, to the Duke of New Castle, relative to the payment of the troops, 451—vii, 18; Letter to, from Governor Belcher, 55; Letter from, to the Lords of Trade, relative to the New York and New Jersey division line. 1: 9; Referred to, 240, 310, 392; Letters from, to the Duke of Bedford, relative to the accidental killing of a maid by a shot from the ship Greyhound, 531, 536; To meet the Indian tribes called the Six Nations, 582; Letter to, from Governor Belcher, relative to a proposed conference with the Indians, 596.—Letters from, to Robert Hunter Morris, viii. Part I, 92, 116, 120; Taking money for an office. 94; Letter to, from Robert Charles, relative to the boundary line, 135; Referred to, 191, 213.

Clinton, James, x, 502.

Clowes, William, iv, 309.

Coates, Christopher, Secretary of the Province of New Jersey, ix, 257 —x, 1.

Cochran, Richard, x. 352.

Cock, Lance, i, 182, 183.

Cock, Lasse, i, 394.

Cock, Peter, i, 183.

Cocker, Emmanuel, vii, 281.

Cockerill, Thomas, Letter from, to Secretary Popple, relative to the death of Lord Lovelace, and the preparations for a Canadian expedition, iii, 466; Notice of, 467.—Referred to, iv, 46.

Cocks (Cox), Isaac, ii, 42-61, 65-73, 78—iii, 498.

Codington. Thomas, ii. 486.

Coe, Daniel, Ensign, ix, 187.

Cofting, J., ii, 257.

Cohansey. Lands at, sold by John Fenwick, i, 413, 414.—A port, ii, 405.

Coined Money, vi, 53-55; Proclamation of Governor Morris, relating to, 117.

Coker, Thomas, Commission of, to be Collector of Customs at Perth Amboy, ii, 130; Referred to, 238.

Colden, Alexander, ix, 340.

Colden, Cadwallader, v, 197, 202; Letter from, relative to a library for New York and neighboring Colonies, 237: Notice of, 242.—Letter to, from James Alexander, relative to the riots, vii, 113; Affidavit before, 419; Letter from, to Robert Hunter Morris, 552.—Referred to, ix, 246, 250; Letter from, relative to the northern boundary dispute, 253; Commissioner for trying pirates, 283; Referred to, 308, 325, 340; In relation to a stamp duty in the Colonies, 500, 511.—Commissions surveyors of the boundary line, x, 194; Referred to, 535, 571.

Cole, Cornelius, ix, 180, 181.

Cole, Jacob, i, 51.

Cole, John, ii, 397.

Cole, Jos., ii, 396.

Cole, Samuel, v, 133, 137.

Cole, Mr., ii, 239.

Colier, John, i, 117, 190.

College of New Jersey, Establishment of. under Governor Belcher, vii, 116; Letter from Governor Belcher, relative to, 118; Letter from the same, relative to a charter for, 124; Little encouragement to build a house for, 146, 580; Letter from Governor Belcher, relating to, 618. —Prospects of, viii, Part I, 10, 11, 94, 109; viii, Part II, 166, 197.

Collier, John, ix, 621.

Collings, Francis, One of the Council of the Proprietors, iii, 221.

Collins, Francis, i, 268—v, 135, 141.

Collins, Isaac, x, 358, 730.

Collinsen, Peter, Letter to, from James Alexander, vi, 71; Notice of, 71; Referred to, 77, 78.

Collyer, C., i, 299.

Collyer, Joseph, Signs the surrender of the Government, ii, 456-460; Asks that Andrew Hamilton be appointed Governor, 470.—Signs as Proprietor, iii, 95.

Colnam, Mr., vii, 447.

Coloham, John, ii, 50.

Colonies and Plantations, Order in Privy Council for the improved government of, viii, Part I. 23; Instructions to the Governors of, 27, 35; Circular letters to the same, 63, 156; Instructions to Governors of, relative to appeals in cases of error, 188; Instructions from the King, relative to the general security of, 194.—A plan for the defence of, viii, Part II, 1; Circular letter to the Governors of, urging enlistments in four new regiments, 17; A similar letter, 92; Number of white inhabitants in, 132; Governors of, informed of the establishment of packet boats, 146; Division of a certain appropriation of Parliament, among, 205; Circular letter to the Governors of, relative to the Earl of Loudoun, 209; On the state of defence of, 216; Additional instructions to the Governors of, 218; Governors of, urged to raise more troops, 241; Instructed not to lay any further embargo on corn or other grain, 248.—Circular letter to, inclosing proclamation for a general thanksgiving, ix, 183; Proclamation of George III, as King, sent to, 242; Warrants to, for using the old seals, 243; Instructions to the Governors of, relating to alterations in the prayers for the royal family, 244; New seals for, 247; Instructions to the Receivers-General of, 289–299; Instructions to the Governors of, relative to alterations in the prayers for the royal family, 303, 376; Instructions to the Governors of, relative to interference with the Indians, and to commissions granted to judges and other officers, 321-330; Circular letter to the Governors of, relative to recruiting the regular regiments in America, 330; Bill for trial and punishment of persons guilty of murder within the Admiralty limits of, 352; Instructions to the Governors of, in regard to fees taken in the several offices of government, 440; Governors of, informed that certain stamp duties would be charged in the, 448; Disturbances in, on account of the Stamp Act, 499-503; List of papers relating to the Stamp Act, from Governors of, 527; Report of the annual expense of, and the debts incurred by, as they stood at the end of the late war, 533; Governors of, notified of a bill before Parliament for the repeal of the Stamp Act, 549, 550; Persons who have incurred penalties under the Stamp Act, to be indemnified, 553; Governors of, required to give an account to the Lords of Trade of the several manufactures carried on in, 563; Instructions to Governors, relative to correspondence, 566; Circular letter to, relative to Indian affairs, 569; Governors of, requested to give an exact estimate of annual expenses of their respective governments, and mode of imposing quit-rents, and of granting lands, 573; Seals of, approved, 618; Salaries of Governors, Judges and other officers in, 619, 620; Establishment of Admiralty Courts in, 621; Governors of, forbidden to alter the number of the Assembly, 637.—Circular letter to Governors of, from the Earl of Hillsborough, x, 10; Warned against the Massachusetts Assembly circular, 14; Union of, to take steps to assert their constitutional liberty, advocated by the house of Burgesses, of Virginia, 21; Gov-

ernors of, admonished by the King, for passing acts contrary to an act of Parliament. 41; Governors of, cautioned relative to letters received from his Majesty's Secretary, 57; Instructions to the Governors of, relative to bills for raising money by lottery, 104, 108; Governors of, informed that the King has no design to tax America for purpose of revenue, 109; Circular letter to, relative to certain duties, 191; Order in, restraining the Governors of, from assenting to laws which make the property of persons who have never resided within the Colonies liable to be attached for debts due from such persons, 324–329; The appointment of agents of, in England, 330; Instructions to the Governors of, relating to an alteration in the prayers for the royal family, 331; Governors of, authorized as Chancellors to issue commissions for the care and custody of idiots and lunatics, 370; Instruction to the Governors of, relative to the grant of lands, 402; Instructions relative to the naturalization of aliens, divorces, and titles to lands, 410, 411; Circular letter to the Governors of, relative to disturbances in, 431; Circular letter to the Governors of, relative to the arresting and securing arms and ammunition imported from England, 497; Plan of a proposed union between Great Britain and, 504; The King determines to withstand every attempt to weaken his authority over, 513; Governors of, directed to prevent the choice of deputies to the Continental Congress, 534; Letter to the Governors of, from Earl of Dartmouth, expressing hopes of a restoration of the public tranquility, 553, and incloses a resolution adopted by Parliament, 555–557.

Colve, Captain Anthony, Member of the Council of New Netherlands, i, 122, 126, 127; Order of, as Governor of New Netherlands, to elect two persons of the true Protestant Christian Religion to be magistrates at Shrewsbury, N J., 134; Order to John Ogden relative to seizing the goods of Governor Carteret, 138; Proclamation for a day of humiliation and thanksgiving, 139; Order of, to John Ogden, relative to three pieces of ordnance, 141; Present at Council Meetings, 142, 149.

Commissioners of the Customs, Memorial to, from Edward Randolph, on illegal trade in the Proprieties, ii, 116; Letter from, to the Commissioner of the Treasury, on the Customs in New Jersey, 165; Letter from, to Mr. Randolph, relative to the establishment of the Ports of Perth Amboy and Burlington, 178: Customs to be paid in New York by all vessels trading in Hudson's river, 200; Documents relative to the Ports of New Jersey, referred to them, 247; Their report relative to the settlement of a Port at Perth Amboy, 252; Letter to, from Collector at Perth Amboy, relative to goods seized by him and rescued, 291.—Report of, on the memorial of John Keble, iii, 329.

Commissioners of Trade, etc. See Lords of Trade.

Commissioners of the Treasury. See Lords of the Treasury.

Committees of Correspondence, x, 458, 468; Letter from that of New Jersey to Benjamin Franklin, inquiring as to the proceedings of Parliament, 472; Letter from, that of Boston, to the Committee of Monmouth County, 498.

Compton, Cornelius, Presented by Monmouth Grand Jury, ii, 332.

Compton, John, Grand Juror on Woodbridge riot, 486, 487.

Comptom, Richard, 397.

Concessions and Agreements of the Lords Proprietors, of East Jersey, i, 28; Declaration of their true intent, 99, 101, 173; Of West Jersey, 241.

Concord, Proceedings of the King's troops at, x, 590.

Condit (Condict), John, vi, 294, 316, 346, 350, 361, 367—vii, 64, 74, 435.

Condict, Jotham, vi, 351.

Conduit, Jotham, vii, 457.

Cone, John, x, 718.

Cone, Nathan, x, 718.

Congar, Joseph, x, 717.

Congress of members of the several Houses of Assembly proposed, x, 457, 464.

Connecticut, Report of Solicitor-General Trevor on the Charter, ii, 100; Illegal trading in, 122, 361; Commissions for, iii, 64.—Quota of, for the defense of New York, viii, Part I, 194, 195—An act for punishing inimical persons, x, 686.

Conner, Daniel, Affidavit against Lewis Morris Ashfield, vii, 621—viii, Part I, 41.

Conneroson, John, ii, 327.

Constable's oath on taking charge of a Jury, i, 70.

Continental Congress, Members of the several Houses of Assembly proposed to meet as, x, 437, 464; Convention to nominate delegates to, 469; Information in regard to the first session of, Philadelphia given by Governor Franklin to the Earl of Dartmouth, 473; The King's anxiety concerning it, 496; Petition of the members of, to the King, 522; Committees formed in accordance with the recommendation, 530, 533; Earl of Dartmouth trys to prevent the choice of deputies to, 534; The same relative to the proceedings of, 535; Committee appointed by the New Jersey Assembly to attend, and instruct delegates to, 546; Resolutions of, in favor of non-exportation, 597; Appoint a fast-day, 598; Resolutions of, paroling Major Skeene, 649; War declared by, 652; Governors not to send despatches by his majesty's ship of war, 656; Three millions of dollars raised by, 670; France will come to the assistance of, 676; Authorizes the freighting of vessels to foreign ports, to make exchanges of produce for gunpowder and military stores, 684; Articles of Confederation and Perpetual Union entered into by delegates in, 692, 697 ; Action of sustained by the inhabitants of Pequanock, in Morris County, 716.

Conttrack, Abraham, ix, 117.

Conway, Secretary, Writes to Governor Franklin relative to the petition
of owners of islands in the Delaware. ix, 492; Authorizes Governor
Franklin to call out the land and naval forces, 501; Circular letter
from, 549, 550.

Coock, Arthur, i, 508.

Cook, Benjamin, Presented by Monmouth County Grand Jury, ii, 332,
363; Signs petition, 397.

Cook, Francis, vii, 282, 374.

Cook, John, iv, 215.

Cook, Michael, vi, 346, 350, 361, 367.

Cook, Rev. Mr., x, 341.

Cook. Samuel, v, 141.

Cook, Stephen, Contributes to the supposed Cornbury Fund, iii, 212.

Cook, William, vi, 202, 203—vii, 99—viii, Part II, 233.

Cooper, Daniel, Affidavit of, in regard to the riots in New Jersey, vii,
275; Referred to, 420.

Cooper, John, ii. 270, 339—iv, 142—v, 155.

Cooper, Joseph, ii, 148—v, 132, 134, 136, 139, 140—vi, 202—vii, 89, 99.

Cooper, Rev. Dr., x, 312, 341.

Cooper, Samuel, vii, 420.

Cooper, Thomas, An East Jersey Proprietor, i, 366, 374, 383, 412, 424,
433, 434, 437, 442, 446, 451, 454, 457, 463, 474, 482, 483, 490, 530—
ii, 26, 149, 177, 186-193, 198; Disbursements by, on account of East
Jersey, 204: Signs name, 213, 257, 263, 376, 408, 411; Signs the
surrender of the Government, 456-460—Referred to, iii, 313.

Cooper. William, ii, 148.

Copper ore, Exportation of, from New Jersey to Holland, v, 7, 9, 267;
Petition against laying a duty on, 376; Letter from Richard
Partridge relative to export duty on, 406.

Coram, Thomas, Memorial of, to the Lords of Trade, relative to the production of hemp and iron, iv, 286—v, 308.

Corbin, Richard, Named as one of the Commissioners for running the
boundaries between New Jersey and New York, ix, 390, 447.

Corden, Benjamin, ii, 397.

Corden, Richard, ii, 396.

Corey, Joseph, Newark rioter, vii, 179.

Corle, Benjamin, viii, Part i, 51.

Cornbury, Lord, ii, 114; Asks for an extension of his authority to appoint
Militia officers in New Jersey, 411; Commissioned to proclaim Queen
Anne in New Jersey, 450; Referred to, 464; Letter from, to the Lords
of Trade, relative to his proclaiming the Queen in New Jersey, 482;
Note on, 483; Named as Governor of New Jersey, 486; Commissioned
to be Governor, 489; Referred to, 503; Instructions to, as Governor
of New Jersey, from the Queen, 506; Letter from, to the Lords of
Trade, 536; Letter to, from the Queen, relative to the Governor's
salary, 537; Announcement to, of the death of Governor Andrew

Hamilton, 540; Letter to, from the Lords of Trade, relative to the defence of New York, 541; Letter to, from the Lords of Trade, 542; Note on, 543.—Letter from, to the Lords of Trade, announcing his entrance upon the duties of Governor of New Jersey, iii, 1; Speech of, to the General Assembly of New Jersey, 8; Reply to the same, 11; Letter from, to the Lords of Trade, relative to the business of the Assembly, 12; Letter from, to the Lords of Trade, relative to New Jersey affairs, 28; Referred to, 52; Letters from, to the Lords of Trade, 54, 65; Letter to, from Lieutenant-Governor Ingoldsby, 67; Reply to the same, rebuking him, 68; Letter from, to the Lords of Trade, relative to New Jersey affairs, 68; Petition of the West Jersey Proprietors, relative to his proceedings, 81; Complaints against him by the same, to the Lords of Trade, 85; Additional instruction to, 96; Letter to, from the Lords of Trade, 99; Letter from, to the Lords of Trade, relative to New Jersey affairs, 103; Letter from, to Secretary Hedges, relative to the same, 106; Complained of to the Lords of Trade, by Lieutenant-Governor Ingoldsby, 109; Letter from, to Secretary Hedges, on New Jersey affairs, 112; Observations of the Lords of Trade, on the memorial of the West Jersey Proprietors against, 117; Letter from, to the Lords of Trade, relative to his new instructions. etc., 119; Letter to, from the Lords of Trade, relative to complaints against him, 124; Answer of William Sloper, agent of Lord Cornbury, to said complaints, 123; Salary of, 144; Letter to, from the Lords of Trade, 148; Letter from, to the inhabitants of Bergen, asking for trees to construct stockades, 149; Affidavit of George Ingoldsby, relative to his arbitrary proceedings, 150; Similar affidavit by John Hamilton, 154; Letter from, to the Lords of Trade, relative to proceedings in New Jersey, 154; Letter from, to the Council of New Jersey, commanding them to show by what authority they pretend to be a Council of the Proprietors, 158; Letter from, to the Lords of Trade, 159; Petition to, from the Proprietors and purchasers of West Jersey, 164; Speech of, to the Assembly, 165; Additional instructions to, as to the administration of the Government in case of his death, 169; Petition of the Assembly of New Jersey, to the Queen, in relation to the difficulties of his Government, 171; Remonstrance of the Assembly against certain evils to which he was subjecting the Province, and his reply, 173, 180; Certain question by, answered by the West Jersey Proprietors, 220; Letter from, to the Lords of Trade, relative to New Jersey affairs, 224; The answer of the Assembly to his reply to their remonstrance. 242; Letter from, to the Lords of Trade, relative to the affairs of New Jersey, 267; Referred to, 274, 282; Letter from, to the Lords of Trade, transmitting an address of the Council, objecting to the proceedings of the Assembly, 285; Speech of, to the Assembly, 293; Reply thereto, 295; Referred to, 324, 326, 327, 331; Letter from, to the Lords of Trade, relative to immigration from New York into New Jersey, 333; To

the same, relative to New Jersey affairs, 334; Nominations by, for the Council of New Jersey, 349; Referred to, 355, 356, 360; Denounced by the Lieutenant-Governor and Council of New Jersey, to the Queen, 365; Referred to, 336; Memorial to, from Peter Fauconnier, recommending the adjustment of the line between New York and New Jersey, 388; Referred to, 395, 398, 405, 409, 410, 420, 425, 423, 433, 431.—Representation relative to the administration of, iv, 24, 76; His action in relation to the indictments against Peter Sonmans and others, 97; Letter from, to the Lords of Trade, relative to certain acts of New Jersey Assembly, 199.—Acts of, referred to, vii, 342.

Cornelinson. Garret, Indicted, vii, 458.

Cornelious, Lanse. i, 269.

Cornelise, John, i, 268.

Cornelison, Garret, vi, 456.

Cornelison, Mathews, ii, 327.

Cornellissen. Ider, i, 49.

Cornfield, Ephraim, vi, 351.

Cornwallis, General, ix, 8, 14, 16.

Corsen, Joseph, x, 210.

Cortlandt, i, 310.

Cory, John, ii, 129.

Coryell, George, Lieutenant, ix, 185, 187.

Cosby, William, v, 306; Appointed Governor of New York and New Jersey, 320; Letters from, to the Duke of Newcastle, 320, 322; Notice of, 322; Letter from, relating to the removal of James Alexander from the Council, 325; Letters from, to the Duke of Newcastle, complaining of Lewis Morris, 329, 344; Instruction to, admitting John Peagram to be a member of Council, 347; Comments upon his proceedings by Lewis Morris, 349; The same by James Alexander, 359, 360; Letter from, to the Lords of Trade, respecting certain Acts of the New Jersey Assembly, 364; Reasons of, for removing Lewis Morris from the Chief Justiceship, 366; Recommends John Schuyler for the Council, 374; Letter from, to the Lords of Trade, relative to James Alexander and Lewis Morris, 395; Recommends several changes in the Council, 402; Death of, announced, 435, 438, 440, 447; Referred to, 454, 456, 462, 472, 493—vi, 66, 71, 73-77—vii, 7—viii, Part I, 76—x, 226.

Cose, Charles. iv, 14.

Cotterall, Eleazer, ii, 326, 364.

Cottnam, Abraham, vii, 613—viii, Part I, 40.

Cotton, Thomas, x, 7.

Coucklin, Ben , i, 50.

Cough. William, x, 717.

Coulter, James, x, 717.

Council of New Jersey, Proclamation relative to Middletown and Shrews-

bury i, 58; Declaration of, against James Carteret, 89; Letter from, relative to the same, 91; Commissioned Samuel Moore to represent them in England, 93; Address of, to the Lords Proprietors, 94; Letter to, from Charles II, confirming the authority of Berkely and Carteret, 107; Order requiring the taking out of patents, 119.—Order of, on complaint of John Barclay, iii, 332; Address of, to the Queen, 364; Comments of the Assembly on said Address, 368; Address of, to Lord Lovelace, 372; Proceedings of, on complaints against George Willock and Lewis Morris, 482.—Address of, to Governor Hunter, iv, 17; Dispute among the members of, 61, 118; Changes in, suggested 149; Vacancies in, 227, 363, 374; Fees of, paid, 369, 372.—Minutes of, v, 34, 463.—Address of, to the King, thanking him for a separate Governor, vi, 58.—Difference between, and the Assembly, 62-65; Members of, suspended and discharged, 105, 106; Reasons of, for rejecting several Acts, 219; Recommendations for, 232; Minutes of, 367, 378, 424, 435.—Speech of Governor Belcher to, vii, 19; Answer to the same, 23; Address of, to Governor Belcher, relative to the riots, 81; Proceedings of, relative to the same, 86, 88; Altercations between, and the Governor, 93; Recommend sundry offices, 102; Address of, to the Governor, 110; Conference of, with the Governor, 183; Communication from, to Governor Belcher, 185; Address from, to the King, on the condition of the Province, 189; Address of, to the Duke of Bedford, relative to the action of the Assembly, 191; Letter from, relative to the riots, etc., 236; Proceedings of, relative to the arrears due the family of the late Governor Morris, 335; Certificate of certain members of, relative to Governor Belcher, 455; Memorial of, relative to the riots, 537; Minutes of, 541; Vacancies in, 611—Message to, from Governor Belcher, viii, Part I, 12; Richard Partridge in relation to the state of, 18; Message to, from Governor Belcher, 21; Governor Belcher, relative to the proceedings of, 60; Rebuked by Governor Belcher, 101; Minutes of, 103-107; Memorial to, from the proprietors of the Eastern and Western divisions, 244.— Messages to, from Governor Belcher, viii, Part I, 119, 128, 162, 193; Meeting of, desired by the Governor, 126; Summoned by the Governor, 243; Queries submitted by, to the Attorney General, 264.—Address of, to Lieutenant-Governor Pownall, ix, 4; Vacancies in, 126, 388; Minutes of, 509; Congratulate the Governor on the repeal of the Stamp Act, 562; Fees of the Clerk of, 597. —Minutes of, relative to charges against Sheriff Thomas Kinney, x, 419; Speech of Governor Franklin to, 538; Reply to the same, 541; Addressed again by the Governor, 542; Names of the members of, for 1775, 561. *See also* NEW JERSEY.

Council of New York, Minutes, relating to Indian murder at Matiniconk Island, i, 72, 76; Relating to John Fenwicke, 186; Letter from, relating to the same, 196; Order from, relating to same, 197; Minutes, relating to John Fenwicke, granting patents in New Jersey, 235;

Minutes, relating to the settlement of the passengers of the ship
" Kent." 239; Order of, against John Fenwicke, 278; Minutes, in
relation to, 283; Proceedings of, in relation to representatives from
the towns in New Jersey, 296, 319, 322; Minutes of, relative to the
line between East and West Jersey, 517, 518—ii. 106; Minutes of, relating to Amboy, 237; Letter from three of the members of, relating
to the condition of the Jerseys, 368.—Report of, on Jarratt's petition
relating to the boundary line, iv, 406; Petition of, relating to the
survey of the line, 433.—Petition of Allan Jarratt, viii. Part I, 233;
Reply thereto, 235; Petition to, from the inhabitants of New York,
233.—Action of, relative to the boundary line, viii, Part II, 89.—Order of, for the arrest of Sussex County men, ix, 178.

Council. Privy, Order of, respecting quo warrantos against New Jersey
and Delaware, i, 501.—Order of, directing the payment of all duties
to the Governor of New York, by vessels trading in Hudson River,
ii, 200; Order of, referring to the Lords of Trade a petition from the
Proprietors of East Jersey, 254; Order of, referring the petition of
West Jersey for the appointment of Andrew Hamilton as Governor,
to the Lords of Trade, 275; Order of, enclosing to the Lords of Trade
the Attorney-General's draft of the surrender of the government of
East and West Jersey, 450; Order of, that the surrender of the government aforesaid, be enrolled in the Court of Chancery, 461; Order
of referring to the Lords of Trade a petition from Peter Sonmans
and William Dockwra, against Andrew Hamilton, 465; Order of, referring to the same, a petition of the Proprietors that Hamilton be
appointed Governor, 468.—Order of, relative to the petition of Sonmans and Dockwra, concerning Staten Island. iii, 61; Order of, re-
voking Col, Ingoldesby's commission as Lieutenant-Governor of New
York, and appointing him one of the Council of New Jersey, 145;
Order of restoring Lewis Morris to the Council of New Jersey, 349.—
Order in, relating to the payment of a certain sum of money by
Thomas Gordon, iv, 217; Order of, appointing three New Jersey
Councillors, 331; Order of, referring to the Lords of Trade a petition
against allowing Quakers to affirm, 341.—Order in. relative to islands
in the Delaware. v, 23; Order in, relative to the suspension of sentences 122; Order in, relative to ecclesiastical jurisdictions in the
Plantations, 126; Order of, respecting the division line between East
and West Jersey, 243; Order of, appointing John Peagram a member
of Council, 347; Order of, declaring the reasons for removing Chief-
Justice Morris insufficient, 437; Order of, relative to Richard Partridge's petition for a separate Governor for New Jersey, 448.—Order
in, relative to the petition of the inhabitants of Elizabethtown, respecting their controversies with the Proprietors of East Jersey, vi,
205; Order in, relative to a bill for the emission of £40,000 in bills
of credit, 361; Order in, upon a petition of Jonathan Belcher, relative to salary, 443; Order of, relative to a petition of Jonathan

Belcher, for permission to be absent from his government for three months, 449.—Order in, approving of the appointment of Richard Salter to be of the Council of New Jersey, vii, 175; Petition, relative to the riots referred to the Lords of Trade by, 241; Order of, referring the petition of the Assembly of New Jersey, 461; Representation to, from, the Lords of Trade, on the State of the Province, 466; Memorial of, relative to the riots, 537; Appoints David Ogden a member of the Council, 588; Appoints Lewis Ashfield, to a seat therein, 590.—Order in, for the improved government of the Colonies, viii, Part I, 23; Order in, to His Majesty's Governors, 35; Order in, relative to the riotous proceedings in New Jersey, 53.—Order in, relative to rank of officers serving with the Provincial forces of North America, viii, Part II, 29; Proceedings of, relative to the boundary dispute between New York and New Jersey, 114.—Order in, relative to a bill for emitting £60,000 in bills of credit, ix, 11; Order in, approving the appointment of Francis Bernard as Governor, 21; Order in, approving the appointment of Charles Read and John Smith as members of the New Jersey Council, 151; Order in, approving the appointment of Thomas Boone as Governor of New Jersey, 189; Order in, continuing Christopher Coates and Joseph Warrell as Secretary and Attorney-General of New Jersey, 257; Order in, approving the appointment of Josiah Hardy as Governor of New Jersey, 259, 262; Approves the instruction for, 285; Order in, relative to patents for land on the Mohawk River, 308; Order in, relative to granting lands and Judges' Commissions, 324; Order in, approving of Samuel Smith and John Ladd, to be of the Council in New Jersey, 394; Order in, relative to Commissioner for settling the boundary line between New York and New Jersey, 588, 630; Approves of fourteen seals for the several Colonies of America, 618.—Order in, repealing an act relative to supplying the Barracks, and admonishing the Governors of the Colonies, x, 41; Order in, appointing Richard Stockton a member of the New Jersey Council, 59; Order in, disallowing act for making current £100,000 in bills of credit, 115, 196; Order in, relative to the grant of lands, 402; Recommends salaries more suitable to the civil officers, and the building of houses for the Governor, 549; Order in, for the Lord High Admiral to proceed to seize all ships taken from the Colony of New Jersey and other Colonies, 711.

Council of Proprietors of East Jersey. See East Jersey.

Council of Proprietors of West Jersey. See West Jersey.

Counties, Complaints that they are not equally divided, iv, 68; Taxes of, 368, 369; Assessors of neglectful, 400.

Courts of New Jersey, General, convened by the Governor and Council, i, 176.—Of Admiralty, memorial relating to, ii, 133; Wishes of Proprietors respecting, 407; Circular respecting, 539.

Courts, Variety of, iii, 4; Modifications, 72; Proceedings against Lewis

Morris in the Court of Common Rights, 479; Against Isaac Whitehead, 480; Court of General Quarter Sessions for Essex County, 495.—
Complained of, by the General Assembly, iv, 39; Supreme Court
objected to as constituted, 69; Court of Chancery demanded, 70;
Governor authorized to establish courts, 114; Two Judges appointed,
139; Displacements in the Supreme Court by Governor Hunter, 150;
Court of Chancery to be opened by proclamation, 150; State of, in
New Jersey, 166; Plantation Courts, 349—Instruction to Governors,
relative to appeals in cases of error, viii, Part I, 188; Governor's
power to establish, ix, 28, 29, 55; Minutes of the Supreme Court on
the claims of Mr. Morris to the office of Chief Justice, 214-218; Court
of Chancery, 297; Tenure of the Commissions of Judges, 308, 321–
329; Act of the Assembly relative to, 331; Ordinance for holding the
Supreme Court for the Province of New Jersey, 434; Instruments
used in, that will bear the highest Stamp duty, 480; Act regulating
the practice of the law, 491; Effects of the Stamp Act upon the business of, 506; Fees of the Justices of the Supreme Court, 593; Fees
of the Prerogative office, 595; Fees of the Clerk of the Supreme
Court, 596; Fees of the Attorney-General, 598; Sheriff's fees, 599;
Fees of Justices, 600; Fees of the Court of Common Pleas, 600;
Fees of the Clerk of the Sessions and Common Pleas, 601; Fees of
the Clerk of Assize, 602; Surveyors' fees, 603; Jury's fees, 603;
Constables' fees, 604; Cryer's fees, 604; Coroner's fees, 604; Practi-
tioners' fees, 605; Fees in the Court of Chancery, 609; Salaries of
Judges, 620; Admiralty Courts, 621.—Opinion of Richard Stockton
as to the authority of the Governor in the Court of Chancery, x, 155-
168; Ordinance in relation to the Court of Chancery, 184; Act, rela-
tive to the practice of the law in New Jersey, 199; Said act dis-
allowed, 213; Enumerated, 441.
Courts, Newcastle, Proceedings of, against John Fenwicke, i, 274.
Courts, New York, Proceedings of, against John Fenwicke, i, 236, 238;
Against Governor Carteret, 303.
Court, Herman, i, 49.
Coustrier, 315.
Cowescomen, i, 16, 18.
Coxe (Cox), Daniel, i, 530.—Letter from, to the Council of Proprietors of
West Jersey, ii, 4; Narrative of, relating to the division line between
East and West Jersey, 10; Signature of, 17; Agreement with Gover-
nor Barclay in regard to the boundary line, 34; Release from, of
West Jersey, to the West Jersey Society, 41; Notice of, 41; Release
of West Jersey, 41–63; Grant of the government of West Jersey
from, to the West Jersey Society, 64–72; Referred to, 87, 88, 89, 90,
94; Letter from, to Rev. Thomas Bredges, 96; Petition of, to the
Lords Commissioners of the Treasury, 164, 165; Disbursements by,
on account of East Jersey, 204; Referred to, 265, 486, 502.—Objections to his becoming a member of the Council, iii, 35; His answer

to the same, 39, 42; Recommended for the Council, 78, 340; Memorial of, with others, to the Lords of Trade relative to New Jersey affairs, 82; Proposed for the Council by the Lords of Trade, 115; Notice of, 116; Appointed a member of the Council, 125; Referred to, 130, 132, 155, 160; In Council, 290; Objected to as a member of the Council, 301; Appointed a member of Lord Lovelace's Council, 317, 328, 329; Signs addresses, 367, 373, 415, 473; The Proprietors ask that he may be left out of Governor Hunter's Council, 497; Member of Governor Hunter's Council, iv, 2, 19; Referred to, 14, 41, 42, 48; His removal from the Council recommended by Governor Hunter, 61, 141; Referred to, 142, 144, 145, 148, 149; His removal from the Council urged by Governor Hunter, 149; Elected a member of the West Jersey Council, 152, 153; Referred to, by Rev. Jacob Henderson, 157; Further reference to, 164, 169, 175, 182; Remonstrances against the reappointment of Governor Hunter, 198, 203; Referred to, 207, 209, 210, 211, 213, 216, 230, 233; Two Quaker speeches relating to, 243, 246; Referred to, 251, 255, 258, 263, 265; Letters from to Mr. Allisen, 266, 274; Referred to, 293, 294, 301, 313, 315, 318, 323, 324, 328, 336; Caveat of, relating to the partition line between East and West Jersey, 444—v, 19; Describes Burlington Island, 38, 43; Member of Council, 211.

Cox, Jr., Daniel, ii, 376, 408, 410.
Coxe, Daniel (the first), x, 225.
Coxe, Daniel (the second), x, 225.
Coxe, Daniel (the third), x, 225.
Coxe, Daniel (the fourth), x, 226.
Coxe, Daniel (the fifth),—Recommended for the Council, x, 225, 232; Appointed such, 273, 274, 306; In Council, 351; Letter from to Cortlandt Skinner, in which he expresses his fears of the *Lex Talionis*, 654.
Cox, Doctor Daniel, iii, 37, 116, 223.
Cox, Isaac, See Cocks.
Cox, John, ii, 363, 366, 396.
Coxe, John, vi, 139; Recommended for the Council, 233, 238, 424; Referred to, 467, 470, 472, 473.—vii, 5; Member of Governor Belcher's Council, 6, 86, 88; Letter from, to James Alexander, detailing some proceedings of the Governor and Council, 97; Commends sundry officers, 102; Letter to, from James Alexander, relative to dissolving the Assembly, 122; Reply to the same, 127; Letter to, from James Alexander, relative to the riots, 154; Letter from, to James Alexander, relative to the Governor's health, and proposed meetings of the Legislature, 158; Letter to, from James Alexander, relative to the rioters, 161; Letter to, from the same, relative to the action of Governor Belcher, 204; Signs, 237; Referred to, 450; Suspended from Council, 540; Affidavits and proceedings against, 541–550; Referred to, 575; Removed from his seat in the Council, 589; Referred to, 594, 602.

Cox, Joseph, Contributes to the supposed Cornbury Fund, iii, 212.

Coxe, Rebecca, ii, 41–63.

Cox, Samuel, iv, 198, 216, 318.

Cox, Thomas, An East Jersey Proprietor, i, 425, 433, 434, 437, 442, 451, 460, 462, 474, 482, 483, 490, 499, 500, 504, 529, 530—ii, 26, 49, 326, 396.

Coxe, William, vii, 543—ix, 187; Distributor of stamps, 497; Referred to, 515–517, 519.

Cozzens, Mr., ii, 246.

Craddock, Mr., Letter to, from Governor Belcher, describing his home at Burlington, vii, 58.

Crafford, John, ii, 146.

Craft, John, Diary of, relative to Governor Franklin's arrest, x, 710.

Cragge, Andrew, ii, 325, 397.

Cramer, John, ii, 327, 397—iv, 147.

Cramer, William, i, 50, 86.

Crane (Craine), Azariah, vi, 351—vii, 457.

Crane (Craine), Daniel, ii, 129, 334, 339—iii, 496.

Crane, Daniel, Jr., vi, 351—vii, 457.

Crane, Gamaliel, vi, 245—vii, 457.

Crane, Jasper, i, 128—ii, 336—iv, 111.

Crane (Craine), Jeremiah, ii, 129, 326, 334, 339—iii, 496.

Crane, Job, vi, 245—vii, 457.

Crane (Craine), John, ii, 334, 336—iii, 201—vi, 246, 251.

Crane, Nehemiah, vii, 179.

Crane, Phineas, Ensign, ix, 187.

Crane, Stephen, i, 50—ii, 325.

Crane (Craine), Stephen, vii, 233, 238, 651—viii, Part I, 105—x, 458, 467, 471, 530, 546, 576.

Crane, William, vi, 245—vii, 457.

Cranfield, Ephriam, vii, 458.

Craven, Thomas, iv, 215.

Craven, Peter, iv, 215.

Crawford, General, ix, 277, 278.

Crawley, Charles, x, 717.

Crawley, John, ix, 321.

Cremer, Thomas, i, 366.

Cresap, Michael, x, 495, 496.

Crew, Thomas, i, 366.

Crew, Thomas L., ii, 388.

Cripps, John, i, 288—ii, 24, 25.

Crisp, Stephen, iii, 413.

Crofts, William, i, 394.

Croghan, Colonel George, Deputy agent for Indian affairs, ix, 521.— Notice of, x, 112.

Cromarty, Earl of, iii, 315.

Crook, John, viii, Part I, 267.

Crooke, Charles W., x, 502.

Crosley, Henry, ii, 396.

Cross, John, vi, 429, 432.

Cross, Parson, vii, 154.

Crowe, Abraham, v, 187.

Crowell, Samuel, vi, 245—vii, 457.

Crowell, Yelverton, ii, 316.

Crown Point, Message of Governor Belcher, relative to the expedition to, vii, 94; Letter from the same, relative to, 117.

Cryer, Thomas, ix, 318, 321.

Cumberland County, Proceedings of the inhabitants of, in accordance with the recommendation of Congress, x, 530.

Cumin, Benjamin, iv, 10.

Cumin, George, iv, 9.

Curle (Corle), Benjamin, Grand Juror, on Woodbridge riot, iii, 486, 487.

Currency, See Paper Money and Bills of Credit.

Curtis, John, ii, 313, 314, 320, 333—iii, 495.

Curtis, Robert, ii, 41, 61, 65, 73, 79.

Curyslet, John, iv, 9.

Cushing, Thomas, x, 529.

Customs, See Commissioners of.

Cutter, Richard, iv, 10.

Cuttleback, William, ix, 178, 179, 250.

Cuttler, William, iv, 310, 313.

Cuykendall, Solomon, ix, 180, 181.

Cuyler, Henry, x, 137.

D.

Da Grodt, Piene, ii, 327.

Dagworthy, Captain John, v, 317—vi, 425—vii, 102.

Daily, James, x, 717.

Dalrimple, Joseph, Affidavit of, respecting the Newark riots, vi, 427; Referred to, 430, 431.—Dispossessed, vii, 154, 216, 420, 422, 426, 427.

Dangerfield, John, i, 369.

Daniel, Benajah, x, 717.

Daniel, Richard, i, 269.

Daniel, Thomas, x, 531.

Daniel, William, i, 269.

Daniell, Widow, i, 414.

Darby, William, ii, 326.

Dare, William, Contributes to the supposed Cornbury Fund, iii, 215, 216; Referred to, 355, 356—iv, 80.

Darvall, Doctor, i, 317.

Dartmouth, Earl of, One of the Lords of Trade, ii, 489, 503, 540—iii, 96,

100, 129, 146, 147, 149.—Letter to, as Secretary of State, from Governor Hunter, iv, 10.

Dartmouth, Earl of, x, 355; Writes to Governor Franklin, in regard to the plundering and burning of the Gaspée, 375; Expresses his satisfaction with the conduct of the Assembly, 388; In relation to the petition of the Presbyterian clergy, 404, 407 ; Reply of, to Chief-Justice Smyth, 404; In relation to the support of the King's Government in New Jersey, 408; In relation to the boundary line, and the Lottery Act, 416; In relation to the removal of the Treasurer of East Jersey, 456; To Governor Franklin, relative to the removal of the seat of Government, 468; To the same, expressing the King's anxiety concerning the Continental Congress, 496; Compliments to Governor Franklin, 501; Announces the King's determination to resist the Colonies, 513; Directs the Colonial Governors to prevent the choice of deputies to the Continental Congress, 534; In relation to the proceeding of the same, 535; Expresses hopes of a restoration of the public tranquility, 553; Transmits a resolution adopted by Parliament, 555; In relation to the act for striking £100,000 in bills of credit, etc., 557; Relative to the Commander-in-chief of the forces in America, 586; In regard to the Congress, and the skirmish near Boston, 642; Announces the King's determination to crush the rebellion, 645; Approves Governor Franklin's speech to the Assembly, 651; Notifies the Governors not to send dispatches by his Majesty's ships of war, 656; Sends to all the Governors of the Colonies, except Massachusetts and North Carolina, the King's speech, 667.

Dasal, William, ii, 326.

Dashwood, ———, x, 701.

Davenport, Francis, ii, 148, 380; Recommended to be one of the Council, 417, 429; Objected to, 488; Remarks concerning, 502; Appointed member of the Council, 507.—One of Governor Cornbury's Council, iii, 2, 64, 155, 160; Appointed a member of Governor Lovelace's Council, 317; His removal from Council recommended by Governor Cornbury, 340; Death of, mentioned, 341; Referred to, 463—iv, 2.

Davenport, Humphrey, x, 718.

Davies, Rev. Samuel, President of the College of New Jersey, Death of, ix, 258.

Davis, Deborah, ix, 251.

Davis, Elijah, vii, 439; Affidavit of, relative to the riots, 441.

Davis, Hugh, x, 717.

Davis, Jonathan, Jr., vi, 351—vii, 457.

Davis, John, ii, 470—x, 717.

Davis, Nathaniel, vi. 430, 431—vii, 421, 426.

Davis, Nicholas, i, 44.

Davis, Richard, ii, 326, 363, 366, 397.

Davis, Richard, Jr., ii, 397.

Davis, Samuel, i, 152.

Davis, Solomon, vi, 165—viii, Part I, 212.

Davis, Thomas, ii, 326—iv, 186, 188.

Davkin, Richard, ii, 148.

Dawson, Anna, i, 369.

Day, Amos, vi, 351—vii, 458.

Day, John, ii, 148—iii, 165.

Day, Joseph, vii, 50, 413, 415, 435, 444.

Day, Paul, ii, 337—vi, 351—vii, 457.

Day, Theunis, x, 251.

Day, Thomas, vi, 351—vii, 457.

Day, Thomas, Jr., vi, 351—vii, 458.

Day, William, ii, 327.

Dayton, Captain Elias, ix, 185-187; Letter to, from Sir Jeffrey Amherst, relative to the troops at Elizabethtown, 365.

Dayton, Jacob, ii, 146.

Deacon, George, i, 268, 283, 381—ii, 148, 380; Recommended for Council, 417, 429; Objected to, 488; Remarks upon, 502; Appointed, 507.— One of Governor Cornbury's Council, iii, 2, 64, 155, 340; One of the Council of the Proprietors, 221; Did not approve of Lord Cornbury's answer to the remonstrance of the Assembly, 225; Proposed as a member of Lord Lovelace's Council, 299; Appointed as such, 317.— Member of Governor Hunter's Council, iv, 2, 120, 128, 132, 133; Referred to, by Rev. Jacob Henderson, 157; Further reference to, 164, 326, 331, 334, 363; Payments to, 369, 372; Referred to, 373, 374, 377—viii, Part II, 151.

Dead, John Dickinson, i, 50.

Dean, Consul, Letter to, from Governor Belcher, relative to the College, viii, Part II, 197.

Dean, William, iv, 310.

Deane, Silas, x, 530.

Deare, John, Letter from, to Chief-Justice Morris, informing him of the riots at Perth Amboy, vi, 463; High Sheriff, 465.

Deare, Jonathan, x, 711, 719.

Deare, William, Affidavit of, relative to the riot at Perth Amboy, vi, 467. Sheriff, viii, Part I, 39, 44, 45, 48; Deposition of, 50.

De Berdt, Dennis, x; 114, 681.

De Berdt, Esther, x, 6.

De Bow, John, x, 717.

De Brahm, William, ix, 582, 591, 624, 631, 632.

Decker, Peter, viii, Part I, 227, 283; Affidavit of, against Thomas Dekey, 286.

De Cow, Isaac, Justice of the Peace, iv, 276, 281, 283—v, 277—viii, Part I, 70—x, 512,

De Cow, Joseph, vii, 638.

Dedras, Wander, ii, 327.

De Grey, William, ix, 629.

De Grodt, Jan, ii, 327.

Dehart, Cornelius, vi, 455, 465—vii, 64, 458.

Dehart, Daniel, ii, 129.

Dehart, Jacob, To agree with printer for printing bills of credit, viii, Part II, 71, 229.

Dehaes, Johannes, Land sold to, by the Indians, i, 111; Grant to, from Governor Carteret, 111; Ordered to arrest John Fenwicke, 191.

Dehart, John, x, 471, 530, 546, 575, 576, 680; Resigns his seat in Congress, 682.

Dekey, Jack, viii, Part I, 283.

Dekey, Jacobus, viii, Part I, 227.

Dekey, James, viii, Part I, 283.

Dekey (Dikey), Thomas, vi, 149.—Colonel of militia of Orange Co., N. Y., his abusive treatment of Daniel Harrison, viii, Part I, 214; His threats to tenants of Proprietors of East Jersey, 220; Beats and robs Richard Gardner and John Herring, 227; Referred to, 268-270; Further threats of, 272; Affidavits against, 282, 285, 286; His affidavit, relative to laying out a highway through Minesink, 299; Seeks protection of James Alexander, viii, Part II, 23; Referred to, 34.

De Lancey, James, v, 329, 333, 334, 344; Appointed Chief Justice in the room of Lewis Morris, 351, 374; Referred to, 397, 398—vi, 149, 169. —Correspondence with Captain Robert Roddam, vii, 528-537—viii, Part I, 122; Picture of him drawn by Governor Clinton, 122; Letters from, to the Lords of Trade, relative to the boundary line, 192, 288; Referred to, 232; Letter to, from the Lords of Trade, relative to the boundary line, 297.—Referred to, viii, Part II, 31; Letter from, referring to the boundary question, 74; Letter to, from Governor Belcher, relative to embargoes, 127; Referred to, 254—ix, 178, 250, 255.

De Lancey, Oliver, ix, 283.

Delancy, Stephen, ii, 291—ix, 641.

De la Prairie, i, 76.

Delavall, Thomas, i, 72, 283.

Delaware, Captain, i, 196.

Delaware, Lower counties of, ii, 360.

Delaware River, Oath of allegiance taken by the inhabitants upon, i, 51; Letter from Governor Carteret to those proposing settlements upon, 51; Petition of John Werden for lands on, 289; Islands in, to whom belonging, 347, 348; Quo warranto against the proprietors upon, 501; Northerly branch of, 517.—Islands in the, v, 6; Opinion of the Attorney and Solicitor-General respecting the ownership of, 15-18; Representation of the Lords of Trade respecting, 18; Order in Council relative to, 28; List of islands in the, 41.—Forks of, are the true limits of New Jersey on the north, viii, Part I, 139, 278.— Owners of islands in, petition to be annexed to New Jersey, ix, 488, 492.

De la Warr, Lord; Appointed Governor of New York and New Jersey, v, 490; Resigns, 491.—Referred to, vi, 2, 70.

Delrample, Sir John, 529.

De Maresque, i, 317.

Demarest, David, vi, 202.

Denham, David, iii, 446.

Denna, John, i, 269.

Dennes, John; Grand Juror on Woodbridge riot, iii, 486.

Dennis, Anthony, x, 502.

Dennis, Benjamin, x, 600.

Dennis, Charles, iv, 215.

Dennis, Jacob, Surrogate, ix, 360.

Dennis, John, x, 422, 471.

Dennis, Jonathan, Jr., iv, 215.

Dennis (Denes), Joseph, iv, 215, 309.

Dennis, Philis, iv, 190.

Dennis, Samuel, i, 82; Appointment by the Council of New Netherlands as a civil officer, and his acts as such, 128, 134; Elected Clerk at Woodbridge, 320; Warrant for the arrest of, 321; Clerk to the Deputies, 354, 365—ii, 240, 255, 270, 315, 317, 332, 362, 364, 373, 386; Recommended to be one of the Council, 417; Objected to, 488.—Affidavit in support of the Assembly's remonstrance, iii, 200; Referred to, 202, 203; Petitions the Assembly in relation to the East Jersey Records, 220; Referred to, 479, 482, 483, 484, 485—iv, 186, 188, 215.

Dennison, Robert, vii, 32.

Denny, William, Letter to, from President Reading, ix, 110; Notice of, 110; Referred to, 141.

De Noyelles, John, x, 194.

Denton, Daniel, i, 15, 18, 147, 149, 504-506—iv, 207.

Denton, Nathaniel, i, 15—vi, 207.

De Peyster, Col., ii, 342.

De Peyster, Abraham, iv, 340, 408.—Superseded as one of the New York Council, v, 70.—Signs, viii, Part I, 237.

Desbarres, ——, x, 518-520, 600, 661.

Dessmarest, David, ii, 326.

Desmarest, Jan, ii, 326.

Des Marest, Joan, ii, 326.

Des Marest, Samuel, ii, 326.

Devenish, Barnard, i, 269.

Dewilde, John, ii, 397.

Dewitt, Barent, vi, 455, 465—vii, 458.

De Yonge, Gerrts, ii, 326.

Dick, Captain William, v, 324.

Dickinson, John, x, 529, 574, 678; Notes of what he said before the Assembly of New Jersey, 689.

Dickinson, Jonathan, Member of the Pennsylvania Council, iv, 393.

Dickinson, Rev. Jonathan, vii, 116.

Dickson, Anthony, i, 269, 414.

Die, John, iv, 10.

Diedewecker, Hans, i, 306.

Diedrect, Hans, i, 49, 66, 82, 177.

Dinwiddie, Robert, On the Trade of the British Empire in America, vi, 83.
—Governor of Virginia, viii, Part II, 121; Letters to, from Governor Belcher, relative to military proceedings, 122, 143, 172.

Disbanded Courtier, Character of a, viii, Part I, 120.

Division Line, See Boundary Line.

Divorces, x, 410, 411.

Doane, Jonathan, Surrogate, ix, 360.

Dobie, John, ii, 35.

Dockminique, Paul, See Docminique. Paul.

Dockwra, William, Notice of, i, 378; An East Jersey Proprietor, 424, 433, 434, 437, 442, 446, 448, 451, 454, 457, 462; Interested in goods shipped to East Jersey, 464, 465, 467; Signs as Proprietor and as proxy, 474, 482, 483; Letter from, to Governor Lawrie, 486; Signs, etc., as Proprietor, 490, 499; Appointed agent for the Proprietors residing in Europe, 506; Signs as a Proprietor, 513; Letter from Proprietors in England to the Governor and Council of East Jersey, 514; Referred to, 527, 529; Revocation of all Governor Lawrie's powers in East Jersey, 531; Signs for Proprietors, 542.— Anonymous letter addressed to, relative to the division line between East and West Jersey, ii, 18; Letter to, from Andrew Hamilton, 27; Certificate as Secretary and Register, 39; Signature of, 83; Signs as agent of Proprietors, 84; Letter from, to Governor Hamilton, 101; Referred to, 113, 217; Petition from, as one of the Proprietors, to the Commissioners of the Treasury, 164, 165; The same to Lords Justices, 171; Named as a Proprietor, 186–193, 198; Disbursements by, on account of East Jersey, 205; Signs instructions, 213; Signs petition as Secretary, etc., 249; Signs as Proprietor, 257; As Secretary, 266; Letter to, from Secretary Popple, relative to the testing of the Proprietors' claims to the port of Perth Amboy at Westminster, 266; Signs as Secretary, etc., 297; Letter to, from Secretary Popple, inquiring as to the operation of the act against fraud in East and West Jersey, 306; His answer to the same, 306; Signs as Secretary, etc., 310; Referred to, 322; Letter to, from Secretary Popple, 340: Letter from, to Secretary Popple, relative to the state of the Jerseys, 343; Letter to, from the same, asking for the transmission of the proposed surrender of the Government of East Jersey, 353; Signs as Proprietor, 408; Referred to, 416; Signs, 431; Objections of, to the appointment of Andrew Hamilton as Governor of New Jersey, 432; His objections replied to by Lewis Morris, 442; Referred to, 448; Signs the surrender of the Government, 456, 460; Petition of, to the Queen, 466; Memorial from, to the Lords of Trade, transmitting objections

to Andrew Hamilton as Governor of New Jersey, 470; His papers transmitted to Sir Thomas Lane, 473; Reply of the Proprietors to his complaints against Mr. Hamilton, 475.—Referred to, iii, 36; His answer to the objections made to the appointment of Daniel Cox and Peter Sonmans as members of the Council, 39; His petition relative to the title to Staten Island referred to the Lords of Trade, 61; Memorial of, with others, to the Lords of Trade, relative to New Jersey affairs, 82; Memorial from, to the same, proposing Peter Sonmans to be one of the Council, 101; Reference to said memorial, 125; Signs as Secretary and Register, 133; Referred to, 141, 312–315; Memorial from, to the Lords of Trade, transmitting documents relative to Lewis Morris, George Willocks and others, 475—iv, 115 ; Letter from, to Secretary Popple, 116; Extract from a letter to, relating to Governor Hunter's administration, 118; Referred to, 127, 298—vi, 428, 431.

Docminique (Dominique, Dockminique), Paul, ii, 164, 165, 186–194, 199, 258, 276, 376, 408, 410, 416; Signs surrender of the government, 456–460; Recommends Andrew Hamilton for Governor, 470.—Signs as a Proprietor, iii, 38; Referred to, 49; Memorial from, with others, to the Lords of Trade, relating to New Jersey affairs, 50; Notice of, 51; Signs as a Proprietor, 82, 95, 302; Did not sign Peter Sonmans' commission, 314.—Referred to, iv, 115, 141, 169—v, 432.

Dod (Dodd), David, x, 187.

Dod (Dodd), John, vi, 351—vii, 457—x, 187.

Doequet, Paul, i, 269.

Donaldson, William, ix, 463; Sketch of the reasons why Captain Kennedy's claim to a share of the Bergen Commons was not admitted, 474.— Referred to, x, 137.

Dongan, Thomas, i, 158; Letter from, to Governor Penn, 437; Letter to, from Sir John Werden, 457; Letter to, from East Jersey Proprietors, 463; Letter to, from the Duke of York, 475; Letter to, from Sir John Werden, 476; Letter from, to the Earl of Perth, 483; To Sir John Werden, 485; Referred to, 517, 521; Report of, on the state of the Province of New York, 524; Referred to, 533, 534; Order to, erecting New Perth (Perth Amboy) into a port of entry, 540.—Referred to, ii, 105, 232, 271—vii, 37—viii, Part I, 204, 249, 250, 256—ix. 336.

Donham, Benjamin, iv, 190.

Donnell, ———, i, 310.

Donop, Col., x, 302.

Doremus, John, x, 718.

Dorman, Philip, x, 718.

Dorset, James, ii, 396.

Dotey, Samuel, ii, 397.

Doud, Aaron, Surrogate, ix, 359.

Doughty, Daniel, vi, 202.

Doughty, Jacob, iv, 253, 283, 370—v, 135.

Douglass, William, i, 66, 82, 305, 306, 310.

Douglass, William, Captain, ix, 184, 186.

Dowes, Thomas, iv, 310.

Dowes, William, iv, 310.

Downes, Richard, v, 132, 134, 136, 140.

Downes, Samuel, ii, 541.

Downham, Edmond, ii, 326, 397.

Drake, Andrew, iv, 189.

Drake, Francis, i, 177—ii, 326, 396.

Drake, George, ii, 326, 396.—Petition of, in relation to the supposed Cornbury Fund, iii, 214.

Drake (Dreake), John, ii, 326, 396, 397.

Drake, John, Contributes to a supposed Cornbury Fund, iii, 200; Affidavit in relation thereto, 218; Referred to, 455—iv, 111, 328.

Drayton, William, ix, 621.

Drummon, William, x, 717.

Drummond, Andrew, ix, 445.

Drummond, Gaven, ii, 333, 364, 366.

Drummond, John, An East Jersey Proprietor, i, 383, 412, 433, 434, 439, 441, 446, 451, 454, 457, 460, 463; Interested in goods shipped to East Jersey, 467; Signs as Proprietor, 474; Referred to, 528—ii, 389.

Drummond, Robert, x, 422.

Duake, Anthony, v, 153.

Duane, James, x, 530.

Dudington, William, Captain of the Gaspée schooner, x, 375, 397, 398.

Dudley, John, i, 509.

Dudley, Col. Joseph, ii, 340, 417.

Douglass, John, ii, 339.

Dun, Hugh, ii, 326, 396.

Dun, Samuel, iv, 188.

Dunbar, Col. Thomas, viii, Part II, 17, 92, 140, 143, 172, 202.

Duncan, Alexander, ix, 622.

Duncan, Charles, Recommended for the Council, iv, 133.

Duncan, Thomas, Deposition of, viii, Part I, 42.

Dunch, William, ii, 42–62, 66–74, 76, 79.

Dundasse, James, ii, 35.

Dungan, Thomas, iv, 414, 415.

Dunham, Az, x, 587, 588.

Dunham, Benajah, i, 134—iv, 188.

Dunham, David, iv, 186, 189.

Dunham, Edmond, Contributes to the supposed Cornbury Fund, iii, 200; Affidavit, relative to the same, 217.—Petition, iv, 186, 188.

Dunham, Jonathan, i, 66, 82, 87.

Dunham, Robert, i, 288.

Dunken, John, Affidavit of, against Lewis Morris Ashfield, vii, 619.

Dunn, Hugh, iv, 186, 188.

Dunster, Charles, iii, 314, 315—iv, 141, 241.—Letter from, to one of the Proprietors in England, v, 100; Notice of, 100; Signs certificate, 155.
Dunster, Dan. Donaldson, vi, 139—vii, 128, 129, 416, 426, 427.
Dunzoy, Louis Demarest, x, 717.
Durrell, Commodore Philip, ix, 110.
Dutch Reformed Churches, Charter for in Middlesex, Somerset and Hunterdon counties, considered by the Council, viii, Part I, 108.
Du Trudle, Jacob, ii, 326.
Dyckman, Hugh, i, 128.
Dyer, Eliphalet, x, 529.
Dyre, William, i, 186, 318.

E.

Earl, Edward, ii, 270; Recommended to be one of the Council, 417.—Referred to, ix, 451, 454.
Earsken (Ersken) John, ii, 129, 326.
Easom, Captain John, vi, 380, 382, 383; Examination of, relative to the sloop St. Migel, 390.
East Jersey, Warrant to prepare a patent for, to Sir George Carteret, i, 160; Release of, to the same, 163; Directions, instructions, etc., to the inhabitants of, by Sir George Carteret, 167; A General Court convened in, 176; Lease for, from the Trustees of Sir George Carteret, 366; Appointment of Secretary and Register, also of Receiver-General for, 376; Proposal to hold the government directly from the Duke of York, 380; Release from the Duke of York to the twenty-four Proprietors, 383; Fundamental Constitution of, 395; Letter from the Proprietors of, to the Planters, 411; Gawen Lawrie's commission as Deputy-Governor of, 423; His instructions, 426; Letter to, from Charles II, 438; Additional provisions to the Constitution of, 443; Letter from the Proprietors of, to Governor Lawrie and Council, 446; Agreement, respecting the taking up of lands in, 452; Letter from the Proprietors of, to the Planters, 454; Letter from the same, to Governor Dongan, 463; Account of shipment to, by some of the Proprietors, 464, 466; Instructions, relative to the setting out of land in, 470; Confirmation of former orders respecting, 488 ; Order of Proprietors of, for laying out lands, and censuring Deputy-Governor Lawrie and Thomas Rudyard, 492; Quo warranto against, 501; Order to examine into the affairs of, 502; Letter to the Governor and Council of, from the Proprietors in England, 514; Minutes of New York Council, relative to line between, and West Jersey, 517; Agreement to submit the dividing line between the Provinces to arbitration, 519; Award, respecting the division line, 523; List of Proprietors of in 1687, 528 ; Revocation of all Governor Lawrie's powers in, 531; Petition of the Proprietors to the King, relative to the entering of their vessels at New York, 533; Representations and

proposals of the Proprietors of, respecting their rights to a port, and a government distinct from that of New York, 535; Letter from Governor Barclay and the Proprietors in England, to the Deputy-Governor and Council of, 541.—Commission from the Proprietors of, to Samuel Winder, John Campbell and Miles Forster to confer with the Governor of West Jersey, relative to running the line between the two Provinces, ii, 1; Part of a letter without signature to the Proprietors in England, relative to the division line, 18; Agreement between the Governor of and the Governor of West Jersey, in regard to the partition line, 34; Accounts of the several rates of assessments laid upon the Proprietors of, 37; Instructions from the Proprietors in London, to Governor Andrew Hamilton, 84; Communication of the Proprietors of, to the Board of Trade, 90; Letter from the Proprietors of, to Governor Hamilton, 101; Instructions from the Proprietors of, to Thomas Gordon, 106; Petition of the Elizabethtown people against the Proprietors of, 124; Letter to the Proprietors of, from the Lords of Trade, 134; Opinion of Sir Cresswell Lewinz, on the liability of, to New York for customs, 136; Letter to the Proprietors of, from the King, relating to the Plantation trade, 140; Memorial of the Proprietors of, asking the appointment of Jeremiah Basse as Governor, 149; Petition of the Proprietors of, relative to customs, 163, 165, 169; Order in Council, relative thereto, 169; State of the case of the Proprietors, submitted to the Lords of Trade, 171; Communication from Proprietors in England, to the Governor and Council of, announcing the dismissal of Andrew Hamilton as Governor, and the appointment of Jeremiah Basse in his stead, 176; Opinion of the Attorney General and the Solicitor-General as to the rights of the Province to establish Ports of Entry, 177; Representation from the Lords of Trade, against the rights of the Proprietors of, to establish ports, 180; George Willocks authorized by the Proprietors to receive quit rents, 186; Rip Van Dam likewise so authorized, 194; Disbursements by the Proprietors of, 202, 205; Petition of the Proprietors of, that Andrew Hamilton be approved of as Governor, 249; Order of Council, referring a petition from the Proprietors, to the Lords of Trade, 254; Memorial of the Proprietors of, to the Lords, relative to the seizure of the ship Hester, 259; The same to the same, asking for speedy report upon their petitions, 263; Claims of, to a port in, to be tried in Westminster Hall, 267; Memorial to the Lords of Trade, relative thereto, 268; Memorial of the Proprietors of, to the Lords of Trade, relative to a surrender of their government, 294; Memorial of the Proprietors of, insisting upon establishing Perth Amboy as a Port of Entry, 308; Remonstrance of the inhabitants of, to the King, against the Proprietors in asking for the appointment of a competent Governor, 322; Disturbances in, 329; Answer from the Proprietors of, to the Remonstrance of the inhabitants of, 344; The transmission of the pro-

posed surrender of the government of asked for by the Lords of Trade, 353; Memorial of Jeremiah Basse to the Lords of Trade, asking for a consideration of the remonstrance of the inhabitants of, 357; A retreat for pirates as charged by Edward Randolph, 360; Petition of the Governor and Council of, to the King, asking that the authority of Governor Hamilton might be upheld, 369; Memorial from the Proprietors of, to the Lords Justices, asking for the approval of Andrew Hamilton as Governor of East Jersey, 374; Letter from the Council of East Jersey, to the Proprietors in England, objecting to Andrew Bowne as Governor, 385; Surrender of the government of, by certain Proprietors, 387; Petition of the inhabitants of, to be taken under the government of the King, should the Proprietors not appoint a suitable person as Governor, 394; Memorial of the Proprietors of, relative to the surrender of their government of, 404, 415; Surrender of the government of, to the Crown, 452. Reply of Proprietors of, to the complaints of Mr. Dockwra and Mr. Sonmans against Andrew Hamilton, 475; Letter from the Council of, announcing the death of Governor Andrew Hamilton, 540; Memorial of the Proprietors of, to the Lords of Trade, asking that Peter Sonmans be appointed a member of the Council, iii, 129.—Account of money received and paid by the Treasurer of, v, 142–151.—Quota of assistance to the defence of New York, viii, Part I, 195. See also New Jersey.

Eastell, William, ii, 396.
Eaton, John, vi, 202; Prepares draft of message to the Governor, 246.
Eaton, Michael, i, 186.
Eaton, Robert, v, 139.
Ecclesiastical Jurisdiction in the Plantations; Order in Council, relative to, v, 126; Instruction relating to, 264, 265.
Eckley, John, x, 225.
Eden, Governor, x, 596.
Edmonds, John, ii, 396.
Edridge, John, ii, 50.
Edsall, John, ii, 327.—Affidavit of, against Morris and Willock, iii, 477.
Edsall, Samuel, I, 81, 82, 89, 91, 92, 97; Affairs with the Council of New Netherlands, 125, 131, 146; Interpretor with the Indians, 182.
Edwards, Abiah, ii, 332.
Edwards, Esther, viii, Part I, 89.
Edwards, Herman, i, 49.
Edwards, Rev. Jonathan, viii, Part I, 89.
Edwards, William, x, 717.
Egburtse, Lawrence, Newark rioter, vii, 179.
Egremart, Earl of, Secretary of State, ix, 125; Circular letter from, relative to military affairs, 330; Announces to the Lords of Trade the appointment of William Franklin as Governor of New Jersey, 368; Informs Governor Hardy of his removal, 374; Letters to, 379, 393.
Eires (Eiers), William, iv, 370.—Recommended for the Council, v, 34; Referred to, 61; Money paid to, 146.

Eistell, Thomas, ii, 397.

Eldridge, John, i, 200, 220, 225, 233.

Elections. Instructions respecting, iv, 3; Act regulating, rejected, 55.

Elizabethtown, Application for grant of, i, 14; Indian deed for, 15; Confirmation of the purchase of, 17; Oath of Allegiance of the inhabitants, 49; Special Court held at, 65-80; The Duke of York respecting the grant, 97; Directions of Berkely and Carteret respecting quit rents, 106; Notice to the inhabitants to take out their patents, 120; Relations with Council of New Netherlands, 122, 124, 126-129, 133, 135, 149; Petition of the inhabitants of, to the Council of New Netherlands, 155; Opinions of certain English lawyers on Governor Nicoll's patent for, 272; Visit to, by Governor Andros, 305; Officers at, 321; Court held at, 334, 354; Controversy with Neversink, 477; Affidavits relative to the grant, 504.—Petition of the people of, against the East Jersey Proprietors, ii, 124; Letter from, condemning Governor Basse, 270, 273; Sundry inhabitants of, indicted, 339; Soundings between, and Amboy, 355.—Grant to the people of, iii, 30. —Petition of, relative to the controversy with the Proprietors, vi, 205. —Address of the corporation of, to Governor Belcher, vii, 17.—Petition to have the charter altered, viii, Part I, 104.—Proceedings of the Committee of Observation, x. 536.

Elkinton, Edward, iii, 165.

Elkinton, George, i, 288.

Elleot, William, i, 223, 224.

Ellis, Daniel, x, 15, 17, 202.

Ellis Joseph, viii, Part ii, 151—ix, 184.

Ellis, Simeon, ii, 380.

Elliott, Andrew, ix, 582, 591, 624, 631, 632.

Elliot, John, ix, 622.

Elmore, Daniel, x, 531.

Elsby, John, i, 355.

Else, John, iv, 189.

Elsley, Elisha, i, 50.

Elston (Alston), John; Deposition of, relative to piracies, ii, 223; Referred to, 235, 313.

Elton, Anthony, ii, 384.

Elton, Anthony, viii, Part I, 107—viii, Part II, 151, 152, 232, 233.

Ely, Sarah, x, 512.

Embargo, viii, Part II, 127, 248, 254.

Emet, Mr., iv, 93.

Emley, Peter, ii, 332.

Emley, William, i, 268, 523—ii, 17, 24.

Emly, William, One of the first Commissioners to buy and lay out lands, iii, 221.

Emmons, Nicholas, ix. 251.

Emott, James, Secretary of East Jersey Council, Signature of, 3.

Englie, William, ii, 316.

Ennis, Dr., iii, 75.

Epke, Hendrick, ii, 326.

Epke, Seba, ii, 326.

Erickson, John, i, 236.

Ersken, John, See Earsken, John.

Erwing, Nehemiah, ii, 42-62, 66-74, 79.

Esler, Conrad, x, 718.

Espinosa, Captain Joseph, Letter to Governor Clinton, complaining of his imprisonment, vi, 280; Petition of, 381; Affidavits of, relative to the seizure of the sloop St. Migel, 381, 385.

Essex County, Proceedings of the Court in, relative to Samuel Carter, ii, 313; Minutes of a Court of Sessions held September 10, 1700, 333; Proceedings against sundry persons connected with Newark riots, 336-339.—Taxes, iv, 368, 369.—List of rioters in, vi, 234, 351.—Riots in, vii, 382, 457 (See also Rioters of Essex County and Newark).— Petition of the possessors of lands in, viii, Part I, 54-56; Justices of the Peace for, 105.—Riots in, x, 172, 180, 192, 198; Letter from the committee of the people of, to the inhabitants of Monmouth County, commenting on the events in Boston, and recommending a meeting in New Brunswick, 459; Resolves of the freeholders of, 465.

Essler, John, x, 718.

Estell (Estal, Eistell), Thomas, ii, 326, 332.

Euertson, Admiral, i, 152.

Evans, Colonel, Begins to erect a fort at New Castle, iii, 230, 231, 232.

Evans, Peter, v, 187.

Evens, Thomas, v. 187.

Evens, William, iii, 165.

Everett, Daniel, Sheriff of Orange County, N. Y., ix, 182.

Evers, John M., v, 153.

Everson, Hendrick, i, 269.

Everson, Nicholas, vi, 465, 466.

Evertse, Cornelius, Jr., i, 122.

Every, the pirate; See Avery.

Eves, Thomas, i, 270, 288—iii, 165.

Evillman, William, iv, 310.

Evrington, Jeremiah, ii, 363.

Ewbank, George, iv, 189, 190.

Ewing, Joshua, x, 531.

Ewing, Maskell, Surrogate, ix, 359.

Ewing, Thomas, x, 531.

Exchange, Ship, Account of shipment to East Jersey in August, 1683, by some of the Proprietors, i, 464-469.

F.

Fairchild, Benjamin, x, 717.

Fairchild, Caleb, Sheriff of Morris County. vii, 256.

Fairman's Island, v, 42. 44.

Falconer, David, i, 467, 508, 530.

Falconer, Gilbert, ii, 460.

Falkner, William, Lieutenant, ix, 187.

Fane, Francis, Report of, on the act for enforcing an ordinance made for establishing fees, and regulating the practice of the law, v, 377; Referred to, 406.—Acts submitted to, for opinion, vi, 150.

Farmer, Christopher, i, 195.

Farmer, Capt. Robert, vi, 103, 388, 391.

Farmer, Thomas, iv, 9; Statement of, respecting Peter Sonmans, 15; Removal of, from the Collectorship of Perth Amboy, 49; Referred to, 68; Affidavit of, relative to maladministration in the Courts of Justice in New Jersey, 74; Referred to, 77, 119, 123; Notice of, 123; Referred to, 124; Judge of the Middlesex and Somerset Courts, 129, 132; Letter from, to Governor Hunter, relative to supplies for troops, 135; Letter to, relative to the movement of his troops, 137; Appointed Judge of the Supreme Court, 139; Candidate for High Sheriff, 186; Member of the Council, 253; Salary as Second Judge, 368, 369-371.—Referred to, v, 187, 344, 366, 374, 402, 443, 454, 456, 469, 478—vi, 14. 15, 202, 203.

Farrall, Garrett, x, 718.

Farrand, Ebenezer, vi, 247.—vii, 457.

Farrand, Phineas, x, 718.

Farrand, Samuel, x, 718.

Farrington, John, i, 268.

Farris, William, ix, 622.

Fauconier's Patent, viii, Part I, 275.

Fauconier, Peter, Receiver-General, refused to furnish vouchers, iii. 283; Accounts of, 350-356; Report on papers retained by Lord Cornbury, 357; His accounts and vouchers demanded by the Assembly, 379; Recommends the adjustment of the line between New York and New Jersey, 388.

Fauquier, Francis, Lieutenant-Governor of Virginia, ix, 531.

Fawkener, Everard, Postmaster-General, informs the Lords of Trade of the establishment of packets to the Colonies, viii, Part II, 144.

Fees taken in the different offices of the Province of New Jersey, ix, 593; See also Law.

Fell, John, ix, 446.

Felt Makers' Company, Memorial of, to the Lords of Trade, asking that the inhabitants of the plantations be required to wear hats made in Great Britain, v, 306.

Fenimore, Richard, i. 270—ii, 384—iii, 165.

Fenix, John, vii, 218.

Fenton, Eleazer, i, 269.

Fenwicke, John, i, 118; Note of the arrival of, and family, in West Jersey, in 1675, 185; Before New York Council, 186; Presentment of Samuel Leete against, 186; Special warrant against, from Governor Andros, 187; Proceedings against in New York, 188; Ordered to be arrested by the authorities of New Castle, 191; Letter from New York Council, relating to, 196; Order of the same, relating to the same, 197; Letter to, inclosing said order, 198; Reply from, thereto, 199; Letter to, from the authorities of New Castle, 203; Reference to in Quintipartite deed, 209; Instructions to Commissioners concerning, 220, 228; Minutes of New York Council relative to his granting patents in New Jersey, 235; Proceedings at a Court for the trial of, 236; Proceedings against, under presentment of Samuel Leete, 238; Depositions relating to the conduct of, 274; Proclamation of, to claimants of land, 276; Order of New York Council against, 278; Letter from the same to the Court at New Castle, relative to, 280; Letter to, from authorities at New Castle, 281; Deed from, to William Penn, for half of New Jersey, 370; Referred to, 381, 382; Lands sold by, 413; Agreement between the Executors of, and William Penn, 507; Referred to, ii, 50—iv, 127.

Ferris, Samuel, iii, 165.

Fessenden, Thomas, x, 612.

Field, Jeremiah, iv, 9.

Field (Fell), John, ix, 339.

Field, John, iv, 10, 303.

Filhing, Josiah, iv, 215.

Finch, Samuel, Complains of being wrongfully taken prisoner, viii, Part II, 13.

Fines and Recoveries, Opinions of the Attorney and Solicitor Generals in relation to, v, 291.

Finlay, Hugh, x, 610.

Finns-pointe, Lands at, sold by John Fenwick, i, 413.

Fisher, Hendrick, vii, 336—x, 202, 458, 640.

Fisher, Henry, Inspector of the Press, viii, Part II, 70, 229.

Fisher, Thomas, ii, 122.

Fisher, William, iii, 152, 153, 154—iv, 98.

Fisher, William, x, 718.

Fisher's Island, v, 43, 44, 46.

Fithian, Joel, x, 531.

Fithian, Philip V., v, 532,

Fitzrandolph, Christian, iv, 215.

Fitz Randolph, John, ii, 396—iv, 189.

Fitz Randolph, Joseph, ii, 397; Affidavit against Lord Cornbury, iii, 198; Contributes to supposed Lord Cornbury Fund, 200; Grand Juror, 446.

Fitzrandolph, Nathaniel, Grand Juror on Woodbridge riot, iii, 486, 487. —Referred to, iv, 186, 189.

Fitzrandolph, Peter, iv, 215.

Fitz Randolph, Richard, Affirmation of, relative to riot at Perth Amboy, vi, 466.

Fitz Randolph, Thomas, ii, 395.

Fitzroy, Mr., ix, 15–17, 641.

Flags borne by ships having private commissions, vi, 128.

Fletcher, Governor Benjamin, Letter to, from the Proprietors of West Jersey, ii, 89; Letters to, from Governor Hamilton of East Jersey, 105, 113, 115; William Penn's observations on the proceedings of, 132; Referred to, 265.

Floyd, William, x, 530,

Flypsen, ———, i, 457, 517.

Folsom, Nathaniel, x, 529.

Foort, Roger, v, 187.

Forbenor, Samuel, ii, 396.

Forbis (Forbes), Arthur, an East Jersey Proprietor, i, 460.

Forbes, Brigadier General, ix, 160.

Forbes, John, i, 530.

Ford, Colonel, viii, Part II, 179.

Ford, Jacob, viii, Part II, 229.

Ford, John, iv, 10.

Ford, Robert, ii, 470.

Ford, Samuel, x, 413, 416, 419, 421.

Forman, Alexander, ii, 327, 396—iv, 215.

Foreman, Samuel, ii, 327, 363, 396.

Forman, Thomas, ii, 327.

Forest, Captain James, ix, 227.

Forest, John, i, 269.

Forrester, Major, ix, 228.

Forrester, Mr., viii, Part I, 145—Part II, 245.

Forster, Miles, Commission to, from the East Jersey Proprietors to confer with the Governor of West Jersey relative to the line between the two Provinces, ii, 1; Desires to report, 24; Signs as Proprietor, 376, 408, 411; Surrenders the Government of East Jersey, 387; Recommended to be one of the Council, 417; Signs the surrender of the government, 456, 460; Objected to as a member of Council, 488.— Proposed for the Council, iii, 51, 95; Referred to, 154; Proposed as a member of Lord Lovelace's Council, 299, 302; Notice of, 302; Did not sign Sonmans' Commission, 314; Grand Juror, 446; Recommended for Council of Governor Hunter, 498.—Referred to, iv, 375; Dead, 377.

Forster, William, Inspector of the Press, viii, Part II, 70.

Foster, Ezekiel, x, 531.

Foster, John, i, 15—vi, 207.

Foster, William, ix, 356.

Fowle, Thomassin, iii, 358.

Fowler, John, ii, 397.

Fox, James, ii, 396.

Fox, George, iii, 413.

Fox, Hon. H., Circular letter from, relative to the appointment of the Earl of Loudon as Commander-in-Chief, viii, Part II, 209; Letter to, from Governor Belcher, commenting on the recent proceedings of Government, 220.

Fox, John, iv, 310.

Fox, Thomas, Deposition of, viii, Part I, 48.

Fox, William, iv, 310.

Fox, Mr., Naval officer for Perth Amboy, vii, 381, 650.

Foxcraft, Mr., Postmaster-General, x, 657, 663; 669.

Foye, John, vii, 150, 320—viii, Part I, 22.

Francisco, Peter, x, 718.

Franklin, Benjamin, iii, 116; To Governor Belcher relative to an electrical apparatus, viii, Part I, 7; Letter from, relative to Post routes in New Jersey, ix, 265; Referred to, 369; Commissioner for settling the boundary line, 582, 591, 624, 631, 632; Accounts of, x, 29; Referred to, 48; Appointed agent for New Jersey, 135; Letter from, relative to the appointment of Colonial agents in England, 330; In relation to the attachment of the property of persons who have never resided in the Colony, 337; Referred to, 381, 393, 445; Salary of, 450; Letter from, to Governor Franklin on American affairs, 494; Referred to, 610, 692, 710.

Franklin, Mrs., ix, 640.

Franklin, William, Appointed Governor of New Jersey, ix, 368; Commission of, 368; Notice of, 369; Commission of, as Vice-Admiral, 372; Announces to the Lords of Trade his arrival in New Jersey, and notifies them of vacancies in the Council, 383; Incloses to the same minutes of Council and six acts of the Assembly, 388; Announces to the Lords of Trade, and to the Earl of Egremont that he will appoint a day of thanksgiving; that the Indians had re-commenced hostilities, and measures taken for protection against them, 391, 392; A house to be provided for, 396; Gives an account to the Lords of Trade of his proceedings with the Assembly in respect to the means of repelling the hostilities of the Indians, 398; To the same, relative to an act for raising levies for the defence of the Provinces, 400; To the same, relative to the revenue, and to issuing money in paper bills for erecting public buildings, 402; Announces to the Lords of Trade the death of Chief-Justice Morris, and the appointment of Charles Read to succeed him; also recommends Richard Stockton for the Council, 426; Writes to the Lords of Trade, relative to raising levies; also to some acts passed by the Assembly, and to Mr. Ashfield's claim to precedence in the Council, 428; Letter from, to the Earl of Halifax relative to rais-

ing troops, 431; Informs the Lords of Trade in relation to the friendly aid of the Six Nations of Indians, 433; Is complimented by Lord Halifax for his zeal in protecting the frontier of New Jersey, 439; Conduct of, approved by the Lords of Trade, 444; Named as Commissioner for running the boundaries between New Jersey and New York, 447; Expresses his thanks to the Earl of Halifax, 453; Replies to a letter from the Lords of Trade, relative to certain acts of the Assembly, 458; Writes to the Lords of Trade, transmitting copies of letters and papers relating to the complaint of Capt. Kennedy in the matter of the common-lands of Bergen and enclosures, 459-475, 478; Sends to the Earl of Halifax list of instruments used in the Province, marking such as will bear the highest stamp duty, 479; Writes to the same in relation to illicit trade in New Jersey, 484; To the same relative to measures for improving the correspondence between the Colonies, 485; Has commissioned Frederick Smyth Chief Justice, 486; Transmits petition from owners of islands in the Delaware, to be annexed to the Province of New Jersey, 488; To the Lords of Trade in relation to bounties for raising hemp and silk, 490; Letters from, relative to the Stamp Act, 492, 494, 497, 499; Authorized to call for land and naval forces to quell the disturbances in the Colony, 501; Informs the Lords of Trade of the seditious spirit aroused in New Jersey, 505, 507, 524; Letter from, to Captain James Hawker, 519; To his father, Benj. Franklin, relative to the success of Col. Croghan in his negotiations with the Indians, 521; Congratulations from, on the repeal of the Stamp Act, 555; Transmits votes of the Assembly to the Lords of Trade, 567; Acknowledges receipt of acts of Parliament, 568; Conduct of, approved by the King, 570; Writes to the Earl of Shelburn concerning outrages committed on the Indians, also respecting barracks, 574; Announces to the same the trial and execution of one Seymour for the murder of an Oneida Indian, 578; Gives a statement of the salaries annually granted to the officers of the Government of New Jersey, 579; Information from, relative to annual expenses of the Government and to quit-rents, 586; Fees taken in the different offices, 592; Vice-Admiral, 621; Letter from, to his father, 625; Notified of the King's displeasure with the Assembly for not obeying the act of Parliament, in regard to mutiny and desertion, 636; Acknowledges receipt of new seal for New Jersey, 640; Letter from, to his father in relation to rumors of an attempt to remove the Governor, 640; Writes to Secretary Shelburn relative to inequality of the expense of quartering troops in the Colonies, 642.—Commissions Joseph Reed as Surrogate, x, 8; In relation to the case of John Wilkes, 28; Gives an account of the manufactures, produce and trade of New Jersey, 29; In relation to an act for quartering the troops, 32; In relation to the Massachusetts Assembly circular, 34; Recommends Richard Stockton for the Council, 44; Rebuked for assenting to a law contrary to an act of Parliament, 45; Writes to Secretary

Hillsborough respecting an act for striking £100,000 in bills of credit, 48; To the same, relative to the complaint by the Commissioner of Customs in America to the King, 53 ; Commissions Charles Read, John Smith and Samuel Smith to take charge of the the seals during his absence, 54; Writes to Secretary Hillsborough relative to a treaty with the Indians, 55; Defends his conduct against the censures of the Earl of Hillsborough, 64; In relation to the treaty with the Indians for settling the boundary lines between them and the British Colonies, 95; Letter from, to Cortlandt Skinner, 97; Gives further reasons for issuing £100,000 in bills of credit, 99; Writes to his father respecting his farming operations and other matters, 111; Letters of acknowledgement from, to Earl of Hillsborough, 118, 130; Announces the death of Mr. Ashfield, a member of the Council, 131; Writes to Secretary Pownall relative to the provision for the King's troops, 141; Transmits Chief Justice Smyth's memorial respecting his salary, 144; Writes in relation to the riotous proceedings in Monmouth County, 148; Observations of, on the act for striking £100,000 in bills of credit and on the act relating to the common-lands in the township of Bergen, 150; Speech of, in relation to the riots in Monmouth and Essex Counties, 172; Offers a reward for the discovery of the persons who set fire to the stables, etc., of David Ogden, 183; Writes to the Earl of Hillsborough relative to matters of public interest, 191; Complimented by the Earl of Hillsborough, 198; Informs the Earl of Hillsborough of the displeasure of the Assembly at the disallowance of the Paper Money Act, 200; Announces to the Earl of Hillsborough the action of the Assembly in the matter of supplies for the troops, and the appointment of Barrack Masters, 201; Message from, to the Assembly, relative to supplies for the troops, 203; Answer to the same, 204; Proclamation of, in relation to assault on John Hatton, 205; Writes to Secretary Hillsborough in regard to the war with Spain, and Indian affairs, also announces the death of John Ladd, 221; Letter to Major William Trent, relative to private matters, 227 ; To the Earl of Hillsborough relative to recruiting parties, also to making provisions for the King's troops, 230; Promises assistance in recruiting men, 233; Writes to his father relative to the Ohio affair, also the Assembly's insolvent laws, 236; Announces the refusal of the Assembly to provide for the King's troops, 237; Speech of, to the Assembly and Council, 238; Answer to the same, 242; Message of, to the Assembly, 243; Reply to, 251; Rejoinder. 256; Writes to the Earl of Hillsborough in relation to the complaint of John Hatton, 275; Writes to the Commissioners of Customs at Boston, relative to the Hatton difficulty, 287; Informs the Earl of Hillsborough of the continued refusal of the Assembly to grant supplies for the troops, 297, 304; Complimented by the Earl of Hillsborough for his efficiency in recruiting the King's troops, 301; Disputes with

the Assembly in regard to the resignation of Mr. Ogden as a member
of the House, 306; Writes to the Lords of Trade relative to the proposed repeal of the act authorizing the emission of paper bills, 315;
His position in the matter approved, 318; Informs the Lords of
Trade that an agent for New Jersey had been appointed, 320; Announces that the Assembly had consented to pay arrears due to
the troops, and debt of the Colony incurred during the late war, 321;
Transmits public papers, 333; Writes in relation to the dispute concerning the resignation of Mr. Ogden as a member of the Assembly,
334; In relation to the act concerning the property of non-residents,
337; Transmits the petition of the Presbyterian Clergy of New Jersey, 339; Proclamation of, dissolving the Assembly, 356; Informs
the Earl of Hillsborough that the Assembly had granted money for the
support of the King's troops, 378; Writes to the same in relation to
care and custody of idiots and lunatics, 382; Transmits minutes of
Council and Assembly with observations on the Boundary Act, the
act to enable all subjects to inherit real estate, and the Lottery Act,
385; To the Earl of Dartmouth in regard to papers relative to the
Gaspée schooner, 389; To the same, relative to memorial from Attorney-General Skinner, with observations on the fees of the Governor
and other officers, 389; To the same, relative to the petition of the
Presbyterian Clergy, 400; To the same, relative to the pay of
Government officers, 405; To the same, in relation to the boundary
line, 407; Message of, to the Assembly relative to the resignation of
the Treasurer, Stephen Skinner, 420; Writes to the Earl of Dartmouth on the same subject, and recommends Francis Hopkinson for
the Council in place of Charles Read, 425; Answers from, to inquiries
relative to the condition of the Province of New Jersey, 433, 451;
Salary of, 450; Writes in relation to the Boston Port Act, a Congress
of the several Houses of Assembly, and removal of the seat of Government from Burlington to Perth Amboy, 457; Transmits Acts of the
Assembly to the Earl of Dartmouth, 461; Transmits to the same,
resolutions of the freeholders of Essex County, 464; Writes to the
same, in respect to the first Congress in Philadelphia, and gives
"secret intelligence," 473–478; Sends to the same a pamphlet published by the Continental Congress, 500; Is complimented by the
same, 501; To the same, in relation to the Congress and transmitting
a plan of a proposed union between Great Britain and the Colonies,
503; Speech of the Council and Assembly, 538; Replies to, 541–545;
Letter from, in relation to the seizure of arms and ammunition imported without license, 548; Gives a list of the names of the members of the Council of New Jersey, 560, 561; Gives to the Earl of
Dartmouth secret intelligence, 570; Gives to the same an account of
the proceedings of the King's troops at Concord, 590; Also an account of proceedings, and the effect of the affair at Lexington, 601;
Speech of, to the Assembly. 620; Reply thereto, 633; Rejoinder, 638;

Informs the Earl of Dartmouth as to the movement of troops in New Jersey and Philadelphia, 644; Gives to the same intelligence of the arrest of Major Philip Skeene, 648; His speech to the Assembly approved by the Earl of Dartmouth, 651; Announces that Congress has declared war, 652; Complains that his dispatches are opened at the Post Office, and gives notice that the Congress of New Jersey had assumed command of the militia, 656; Writes that Lord Stirling had accepted a Colonel's commission from the Provincial Congress, and no gentleman would consent to be nominated for the Council, 662; Announces to the Earl of Dartmouth the raising of troops in New Jersey, 669; Transmits to the same his speech to the Assembly, 674; Writes to the same, relative to the sentiments of the people, the proceedings of the Assembly, etc., 676; Gives an account of his arrest, 698, 702; Note on, 710; Message to the Legislature of New Jersey, 719.

Franklin, William Temple, ix, 371.

Frasier, Mr., Collector for the Port of Salem, vii, 381; Returns of, 587, 650.

Frazer, William, vi, 98.

Frazey, Eliphalet, vii, 180.

Frederick, Martin, Sr., x, 718.

Fredricksen (Fredericks), Thomas. i, 49, 125—ii, 326.

Freehold, Letter from the town of, condemning Governor Basse, ii, 273. —Letter from the Committee of Inspection to the inhabitants of Shrewsbury, x, 559.

Freeman, Edward, iv, 189.

Freeman, Gilman, Ensign, ix, 187.

Freeman, Henry, iv, 188—x, 351.

Freeman, John, i, 50—iv, 10.

French, Information concerning the state of the Plantations conveyed through their vessels, iii, 60; Report of an attack by, on New York, 149, 162; Strength of, in Canada, 271.—Hostile attempts of the, on the river Ohio, viii, Part I, 292; The Lords of Trade, in relation to said attempts, 294.—The necessity of driving them from America, viii, Part II, 133; Threatened invasion of, 158, 163, 174.—Defeat of, in Canada, ix, 183.

French, Philip, vi, 368.

French, Thomas, i, 269.

Frettwell, Peter, ii, 148; Recommended to be one of the Council, 417.

Fretwell, Peter, iv, 21, 126; Member of the Council of the West Jersey Proprietors, 152; Referred to, 283; Recommended for the Council, 326, 334; Appointed a Councillor, 331; Notice of, 333; One of the Commissioners to try pirates, 340; Referred to, 373, 374.

Frost, William, iii, 447.

Fullerton, James, vi, 212—vii, 268.

Fullerton, Robert, An East Jersey Proprietor, i, 460, 499, 529—ii, 2.

Fullerton, Thomas, An East Jersey Proprietor, i, 460, 499, 529.
Furch, William, ii, 396.
Furins, Samuel, v, 139.
Furman, Mr., viii, Part I, 154.
Furniss, Samuel, iv, 276–282.

G.

Gadsden (Gadson), Christ., x, 530, 649.
Gage, Thomas, vi, 465, 466.
Gage, General Thomas, ix, 399; Letter from, to Governor Franklin, relative to military operations, 432; Places troops at the command of Governor Franklin, 495.—Referred to, x, 592, 593, 613, 645, 654.
Gales, Samuel, x, 502.
Galloway, Andrew, i, 529.
Galloway, John, x, 717.
Galloway, Joseph, x, 48; Notice of, 111, 197; Referred to, 227, 378, 492, 529, 535, 571; Extracts from letters of, 572, 579.
Gam, Hananiah, ii, 148.
Gannet, Reheboth, ii, 397.
Gardner, Benjamin, Newark rioter, vii, 179.
Gardner, Captain, ix, 122, 123.
Gardner, John, ii, 338—vii, 458.
Gardner, Richard, Complains of Dekey and others of New York, viii, Part I, 220; Intrusted with money to relieve persons distrained, 221, 222; Beaten and robbed by Thomas Dekey, 226; Referred to, 283; Affidavit of, against Dekey and sons, 285.—Complained of, viii, Part II, 13.
Gardner, Thomas, i, 270—ii, 148, 380; Recommended to be one of the Council, 417.—Objected to as a member of the Assembly, iii, 151; Summoned by Lord Cornbury to show his authority for acting as one of the Council of West Jersey, 158; One of the agents of the Proprietors, 221; Referred to, 415; Recommended for Council of Governor Hunter, 498, 499.—Referred to, iv, 13, 119, 120, 128; Notice of, 128, 132, 133, 142; Letter from, to Governor Hunter, respecting Jeremiah Basse, 144; Forbidding surveys, 147; Refuses to take his affirmation instead of oath of office, 148; Referred to, 152, 164; Dead, 175.—Referred to, vi, 245.
Gardner, Thomas, Jr., Newark rioter, vii, 179, 457.
Garner, John, vi, 351.
Garretsen, Garrett, i, 49.
Garretsen, Geart, i, 49.
Garrett, John, iv, 310.
Garrison, John, vii, 606.
Garritse, Henry, x, 467.
Gaspée, Schooner, The plundering and burning of, x, 375, 389, 395.

Gaston, Robert, x, 717.

Gateau, Nicholas, iv, 310, 313.

Gates, Horatio, ix, 427—x, 672.

Gautier, Andrew, x, 365, 366.

Gee, Joshua, v, 6.

Geedes, Jo., iv, 371.

Geere, Elinor, i, 186.

Geere, Ruth, i, 186.

Geere, Zachariah, i, 186.

Gellebrand, Samuel, Deputy Secretary, Letter from, relative to the claim of Lewis Morris for salary, vi, 153.

Gemoenepa, Relations with Bergen, i, 145.

Germain, Lord George, Announces to Governor Franklin the King's concern that New Jersey had submitted to the Continental Congress, x, 675.

Gerrard, William, i, 529.

Gerrdtsden, Hendrick, ii, 326.

Gerrish, Col., x, 671.

Gerritse, Derk, i, 151.

Gerrits (Gerretze), Gerret, i, 125, 320.

Gibbins, Mardia (Mordecai), ii, 326, 366.

Gibbon, Edmund, i, 414.

Gibbon, Grant, x, 471.

Gibbon, John, x, 531.

Gibbon, Nicholas, viii, Part II, 158, 230, 231.

Gibbons, Richard, i, 44.

Gibson, Captain, ii, 223.

Gibson, Bartholomew, i, 468.

Gibson, Elizabeth, An East Jersey Proprietor, i. 490, 500, 507—ii, 32.

Gibson, William, i, 376; An East Jersey Proprietor, 383, 412, 424, 433, 434, 437, 442, 446, 451, 454, 457, 474—ii, 205.

Giljansen, Gillis, i, 194, 276.

Gill, Michael, ix, 622.

Gillmann, Charles, iv, 186.

Gillman, Joseph, iv, 189.

Gilman, Freeman, ix, 187.

Gilman, John, i, 147, 149, 307, 319, 320.

Gilman, William, Affidavit of, relative to the New Jersey rioters, vii, 231.

Ginnins, John, ii, 326.

Glass Manufacturers in New Jersey, vi, 98—viii, Part I, 108, 109—x, 31.

Glen, William, viii, Part I, 27.

Gloucester (Gloster) County, Population of, in 1699, ii, 305.—The magistrates of, commended by Governor Hunter, iv, 158; Taxes, 368, 369 —v, 132, 133.—Money received from collector of, viii, Part I, 66–68; From commissions, 71; Interest money from, 73, 74.

Godbolt, Anne, iv, 81–85.

Godbolt, Francis, iv, 81-85.

Godolphin, Charles, ii, 254.

Godyn, Samuel, Patent to, for the east side of Delaware river, now Cape May County, i, 1.

Goelet, Francis, ix, 334.

Goff, Captain, ii, 97.

Gold, John, ii, 397.

Gold, Lieutenant, x, 607.

Gold and Silver Coins, ix, 135.

Goldsmith, Josias, x, 717.

Gomar, Peter, vi, 166—ix, 179.

Goodman, Charles, Collector at Perth Amboy, letter from, to the Commissioners of Customs, relative to goods seized by him, and rescued by armed men, ii, 291.

Goodson, John, i, 416—ii, 120, 187-193.

Gooldy, Jacob, iv, 147.

Gookin, Charles, Governor of Pennsylvania, letter to him from Governor Hunter, complaining of his proceedings, iv, 160; Going to England as Coxe's ambassador, 255.—Petition for grant of islands in the Delaware, v, 6; Representation of the Lords of Trade, respecting his petition, 18; Order in Council, relative to, 28; Referred to, 447.

Gordon, Andrew, viii, Part I, 42.

Gordon, Augustin, ii, 26.

Gordon, Charles, i, 529.

Gordon, John, i, 529, 530.

Gordon, Peter, Lottery made by, ix, 443, 446, 458; Act to make void, repealed, 487.

Gordon, Sir Robert, One of the East Jersey Proprietors, i, 383, 412, 425, 433, 434, 437, 439, 442, 446, 448, 451, 454, 457, 460, 462; Interested in goods shipped to East Jersey, 467; Signs as Proprietor, 482, 483, 500, 513; Referred to, 528, 529, 530; Disbursements by, on account of East Jersey, ii, 204.

Gordon, Thomas, An East Jersey Proprietor, i, 460, 529—ii, 2, 101.—Instructions to, from the East Jersey Proprietors, 106; Notice of, 106; Referred to, 113; Named as a Proprietor, 187-193, 198; Disbursements by, on account of East Jersey, 204; Signs instructions to Governor Basse, 213; Deputy Secretary, 317, 335; Surrenders the government of East Jersey, 387; Signs the surrender, 456-460; Objected to as a member of Council, 488; Appointed High Sheriff, iii, 15, 16; Complained of, 135; Referred to, 141, 185, 189, 214, 216, 219, 253, 254, 263; Elected Speaker of the Assembly, 292, 359; Signs as such, 298, 372, 378; Complained of by the Council, to Lord Lovelace, 393, 394, 398, 400, 403, 405; Referred to, 414, 415, 431, 433, 448, 453, 479; Indicted, 481; Referred to, 489; Recommended for the Council by the Lords of Trade, 499; Letter from, to the Secretary of State asking for restoration to the office of Chief Justice, 500—iv, 15, 40, 74; The case of, 76; Referred to, 106, 119-121, 128, 129,

133; The opinion of Rev. Jacob Henderson respecting, 157; Further reference to, 164; Letter from, to Rev. Jacob Henderson, inclosing certificates relating to his own and Colonel Anderson's characters, 176, 180, 181; Accounts of, as Receiver-General of New Jersey, 185; Referred to, 200; Attorney-General in place of Mr. Griffith, removed, 209; Certain payments by him sanctioned, 217, 228; Member of Council, 253; Indictment of, 258; Referred to, 266, 267; Signs as member of Council, 310; Referred to, 334; One of the Commissioners to try pirates, 340; Referred to, 363; Account of, as Receiver-General, 368, 369; Referred to, 373, 394.—In Governor Burnet's Council, v, 3; Dead, 33; Money to, 147.

Gorham, Joseph, ix, 590, 591.

Gosling, John, i, 269—iii, 164—iv, 147—v, 36.

Gosnell, John, i, 419.

Gould, Edward T., x, 613.

Gould, James, v, 187.

Gould, John, ii, 327.

Gould, John, x, 717.

Gould, Nathan, Account of the circumstances leading to the capture of New York by the Dutch, i, 121.

Gould, Thomas, Affidavit of, respecting the state of the Province, vii, 375; Affidavit of, relative to the riots, 446.

Goulding (Golding), William, i, 44, 98.

Gouldy, Samuel, iv, 238.

Governors of Colonies, See Colonies and Plantations.

Grachoise, Robert, iv, 9.

Grafton, Duke of, ix, 9, 15, 626, 641.

Graham, Augustus, ii, 461.

Graham, James, i, 299.—In relation to Perth Amboy as a free port, ii, 231.

Grant, James, Jr., ix, 621.

Grant, William, vi, 296.

Granville, Earl of, viii, Part I, 27; Letter to, from Governor Belcher, 97.

Graves, Admiral, x, 645.

Graves, Zackery, i, 50.

Gray, Galfredus, Letter from, on the encroachments of the Indians, v, 107.

Gray, John, i, 50.

Grear, James, Grand Juror on Woodbridge riot, iii, 486.

Gregory, Alexander, Affidavit of, against Lewis Morris Ashfield, vii, 619.

Gregory, Mr., i, 52.

Green, Enoch, x, 345.

Green, Joseph, vii, 604.

Greenaway, Henry, Autograph, v, 510—vii, 326.

Greenaway, Richard, ii, 42-62, 66-74, 79; Signs the surrender of the government, 456-460; Asks that Andrew Hamilton be appointed Governor, 470.—Signs, iii, 95.

Greenland, Henry, i, 299, 319, 320, 364, 478, 523.

Greenville, Bernard, i, 366—ii, 388.

Greenville, Henry, viii, Part I, 27.

Greenwich, Disapproval of the destruction of the tea at, x, 530.

Greenwood, Jonathan, ii, 41-62, 74, 460—vii, 320.

Griffin, Thomas, Indicted, vii, 458—ix, 185, 187.

Griffith, Alexander, Attorney-General, iv, 184; Salary, 185; Removal, 209; Salary, 368, 369.

Griffith, Benjamin, ii, 315-317, 373, 386—iii, 478—iv, 107.

Griffith, John, iv, 186.

Groome, Samuel, i, 227; An East Jersey Proprietor, 366, 373; Commission of, as Receiver-General of East Jersey, 376, 378; Among the twenty-four East Jersey Proprietors, 383; His proprietary right transferred to his son, 432; Instructions to, relative to laying out Perth Amboy, 434; His honesty and fidelity referred to, 447; Notice of, 527, 529.—Referred to, ii, 232.

Gronen, Lafly, ii, 396.

Grorne, Cornelius, v, 153.

Grover, James, i, 44, 88—ii, 396—iii, 212.

Grover, James, Jr., ii, 363.

Grover, Safetie, ii, 363.

Grover, Sefty, Affidavit of in support of the Assembly's remonstrance, iii, 211.

Growden, Lawrence, vii, 130.

Grubb, John, i, 269.

Grub, Thomas, iv, 10.

Grummon, Aaron, Newark rioter, vii, 179.

Guerrish, Joseph, ix, 590, 591.

Gunner, James, ii, 397.

Gunston, John, ii, 42-61, 65-73, 79.

Guy, Bridget, iii, 358.

Guyon, Peter, ii, 41-62, 74—vii, 320.

Guy, Richard, Instructions to, as one of the Commissioners in West Jersey appointed by William Penn and others, i, 219, 228; Name to concessions, etc., to settlers in West Jersey, 268; Resident of Salem, 283; Overseer at, 284; Magistrate, 291, 292; Land sold to, by John Fenwicke, 413, 414.

H.

Habbersfield, Edward, ii, 42-62, 66-74, 79.

Hackett, John, ii, 72.

Hackett, John, Affidavit of, respecting the riots on the estate of Allen and Turner, vii, 377; Referred to, 515—ix, 7.

Hackett, William, Captain of the sloop Indeavor, Proceedings against, i, 64, 67, 71.

Hackshaw, Robert, ii, 42-62, 66-74, 76, 79, 88, 90, 92, 99.

Haddon, John, iii, 313—iv, 94, 95, 98.

Haig, William i, 268.

Haines, John, iii, 165.

Haines, Jonathan, ii, 315, 334.

Haines, Joseph, ii, 315.

Haines, Richard, iii, 164.

Hale, Samuel, ii, 315–317, 373, 386, 488, 541.—Petitions the Assembly in the East Jersey records, iii, 220; Referred to, 479.

Haleday, T., iv, 174; Certificate from, relating to the character of Thomas Gordon, attacked by Jacob Henderson, 180.

Halgard, John, iv, 147.

Halifax, Lord, Letter from, relative to complaints against Governor Belcher, vii, 594.—Letter to, from Governor Belcher, relative to Lewis M. Ashfield, viii, Part I, 8; Referred to, 117.—Letter to, from Governor Belcher, relative to Attorney-General Skinner, viii, Part II, 200; Referred to, 246—ix, 210, 344, 431; Compliments Governor Franklin, for his zeal in protecting the frontiers of New Jersey, 439; Circular letter from, to the Governors in North America, informing them that certain stamp duties would be charged in the Colonies, 448; Writes to Governor Franklin, in relation to Captain Kennedy's complaint, 461.

Halker, John, iv, 190.

Hall, Clem, vi, 139—viii, Part I, 68.

Hall, David, viii, Part I, 74—ix, 625.

Hall, John, i, 51.

Hall, Jutt, ii, 396.

Hall, Reuben, Ensign, ix, 185.

Hall, Thomas, iv, 253, 370—v, 146.

Hall, William, ii, 148, 380.—Proposed for the Council, iii, 95; One of the Council of the Proprietors, 221; Proposed as a member of Lord Lovelace's Council, 299, 302, 309; Appointed as such, 317.—Member of Governor Hunter's Council, iv. 2, 19, 48; His removal from the Council recommended by Governor Hunter, 61; Complaint against from the Assembly, to Governor Hunter, 79, 80: Answer of, to the charges brought against him, 82; Referred to, 115, 124, 125, 130, 141; Removal of, from Council urged by Governor Hunter, 149, 150, 153; Referred to, by Rev. Jacob Henderson, 157; Further reference to, 164, 169, 182; Dead, 216, 293.

Hallis, John, A West Jersey Proprietor, iii, 498.

Halsey, Jeremiah, x, 345.

Hallsey, Joseph, ii, 129, 326, 395.

Halstead, Josiah, x, 533.

Halstead, Timothy, Testimony relating to Elizabeth purchase, i, 504.

Hamans, William, vi, 177.

Hammel, Bryan, ix, 180, 181.

Hammell, John, iv, 98, 310.

Hamilton, Andrew, Instructions to, i, 508; Notice of, 509, 513; Proprietor of East Jersey, 522; Appointed Deputy Governor of East Jersey, 541.—Signs as Proprietor, ii, 2; Named as one, 26; Letter from, to William Dockwra, relative to private affairs, 27; Attest, 84; Instructions to, as Governor, from the East Jersey Proprietors in London, 84; Commissioned to be Governor of West Jersey, 87; Referred to, 92, 93; Letter to, from William Dockwra, 101; Letters from, to Governor Fletcher of New York, 105, 113, 115; Referred to, 107; Signs as Proprietor, 113; Referred to, 122; Signs agreement, 146; Signs address to the King, 147; Communication from the Proprietors in England, announcing his dismissal as Governor, 176; Disbursements by, on account of East Jersey, 205; Petition of East Jersey Proprietors that he be approved of as Governor, 249; Opinion of the Attorney-General asked and given as to his eligibility to the office of Governor, 250; Proprietors of West Jersey ask his appointment as Governor, 257; Letter from, to Secretary Popple, relative to his appointment as Governor of New Jersey, 258; Note on, 259; Order of Council referring the approval of his appointment as Governor of West Jersey to the Lords of Trade, 275; Commission to, as Agent of the West Jersey Society, 299; Referred to, 303, 318; Letter from, to the Secretary of State, 321; Referred to, 324, 328, 329, 330, 349-351, 356; Presides at the Monmouth County Court, 362, 366; Referred to, 368; Petition to the King, from the Council, asking that his authority might be upheld, 369; The Proprietors of East and West Jersey ask the Lords Justices to approve of his appointment as Governor, 374; A petition to the same effect to the King from the Council and Representatives of West Jersey, 377; Referred to, 382, 385, 394, 400-402, 413-428; Recommended by the Proprietors of West Jersey for Governor, 429; Objections to his appointment, by William Dockwra, 432; Letter from, to the Proprietors in England, 437; Reply to these objections by Lewis Morris, 442; Referred to, 463, 464; Complained of to the Queen, by William Dockwra and Peter Sonmans, 466; Petition of the Proprietors to the Queen, that he be appointed Governor, 469; Objections to him as Governor, from William Dockwra and Peter Sonmans, to the Lords of Trade, 470; Reply of the Proprietors of New Jersey to the complaint aforesaid, 475; Opposed by Colonel Quarry, 479; Referred to, 482, 484, 536; Death of announced, 540.— Favors the Quakers, iii, 13, 15; Referred to, 187, 223, 275, 276, 489— iv, 414, 434—viii, Part I, 239, 249, 288.

Hamilton, Andrew (of Philadelphia), v, 101, 102.

Hamilton, Gustavus, ii, 120, 122.

Hamilton, John, Affidavit against Lord Cornbury, iii, 154; Proposed for the Council, 299, 302, 498.—Recommended for the Council, iv, 62, 153, 154, 169, 170, 182; Notice of, 183; Member of Council, 253, 310, 334, 340, 363; Payments to, 370, 372; Referred to, 373, 394.—One of Governor Burnet's Council, v, 3; Money paid to, 146; Commis-

sioner to try pirates, 197; Signs memorial, 301, 443; As President of the Council of New Jersey, announces to the Lords of Trade the death of President Anderson, and his own assumption of the government, 445; Letter to, from Secretary Popple, relative to vacancies in the Council, 454; Referred to, 455, 456, 459–462; Letter from, to the Duke of Newcastle, relative to the claims of Lewis Morris to the administration of the government, 467; Proclamation of, against Lewis Morris, 469; Complaints of, against Lewis Morris, to the Lords of Trade, 478; Referred to, 479, 480; Reasons why he is rightfully entitled to the government of New Jersey, 482; Observations of Lewis Morris, on his reasons above mentioned, 492—vi, 14, 15, 59; Complains to the Lords of Trade of certain proceedings of Governor Morris, 69; Rank in the Council, 109; Autograph, 145; Letter from, to the Lords of Trade, on the claim of Lewis Morris for salary while striving to obtain the Presidency of New Jersey, 151; Reply to said letter, 153; Instructions from, to John Lawrence, for running the partition line between East and West Jersey, 154; Referred to, 352; Assumes the Presidency, on the death of Governor Morris, 367–378; Letter from, to the Council of New York, relative to the destruction of the beacon on the Highlands of Neversink, 379; Referred to. 414; In Council, 424; Letter to, from David Ogden, transmitting affidavits respecting the riots, 426; Message of, to the House of Assembly, 435; Letter to the Lords of Trade, written at the request of, 446; Letter from, to Colonel Peter Schuyler, commander of New Jersey troops, 447; Death of announced, 462; Referred to, 473—vii, 5, 6, 116. 139, 169, 174, 175, 213, 214, 217, 394, 396, 477—viii, Part I, 76, 79—ix. 7, 242.

Hamilton, Robert, ii, 396.

Hammond, Peter, vii, 326.

Hammond, William, ii, 194, 199, 258; Signs the surrender of the government, 456–460.—Referred to, vii, 326.

Hampton, Andrew, ii, 129—iii, 479.

Hampton, Elizabeth, vii, 179; Affidavit of, relative to the riots at Newark and Perth Amboy, 181; Referred to, 224.

Hampton, James, vi, 430, 431—vii, 219, 421.

Hampton, Jonathan, vii, 439—viii. Part II, 230—x, 362, 363, 367, 369, 588.

Hanbury, Mr., viii, Part II, 123.

Hancock, Francis, ii, 187–193, 198; Signs the surrender of the government, 456–460; Asks that Andrew Hamilton be appointed Governor, 470.—Proprietor, iii, 314.

Hancock, Godfrey, i, 269.

Hancock, John, i, 437, 448, 529—iv, 98.

Hancock, Richard, i, 187, 284, 292, 414.

Hancock, William, i, 414—vi, 202, 246, 251—vii, 99—viii, Part II, 150, 155, 233.

Hand, Elijah, x, 531.

Hand, John, ii, 380—iii, 351, 352.

Hand, Shamgar, ii, 384.

Hankins, Jonathan, Deposition of, viii, Part I, 41.

Hankison (Hanackson), Thomas, Presented by Monmouth County Grand Jury, ii, 332; Signs petition, 396.

Hankson, Richard, ii, 396.

Hanlock, Edward. See Hunloke.

Hannington, Samuel, ii, 461.

Hanoe, John, i, 128.

Hanton, John, i, 464, 465, 467, 468, 510, 511-513—ii, 32, 33.

Haracis, John, i, 268.

Harburt, Thomas, ii, 326.

Harcourt, Earl of, viii, Part I, 23.

Hardenbergh's, Patent, viii, Part I, 278.

Hardenbrook, Adolph, i, 49.

Harding, Thomas, i, 269, 288.

Hardinge, N., Letter from, to the Lords of Trade, relative to division of appropriation of Parliament, viii, Part II, 205.

Hardwick, Lord, Letter to, from Governor Belcher, viii, Part I, 95—viii, Part II, 188.

Hardy, Sir Charles, Governor of New York, Letter to, from the Lords of Trade, recommending the appointment of a Commissioner to arrange the boundary difficulties, viii, Part II, 129; Complimentary letter to, from Governor Belcher, 141; From the same, relative to the boundary line, 142, 183, 207.

Hardy, Josiah, ix, 235; Appointment of, as Governor of New Jersey, approved, 259; Commission of, approved in the Privy Council, 262; Commission of, 270; Instructions, 274; Commission of, as Vice-Admiral, 280; Named as a Commissioner for trying pirates, 283; Instructions for, approved by Privy Council, 285; Informs the Lords of Trade of his arrival in New Jersey, and asks to have the suspension of Edward Antill confirmed, 316; Notice of, 316; Referred to, 343; Re-appoints Mr. Morris Chief-Justice, and Messrs. Nevill and Saltar, second and third Justices, 345; Letter from, relative to the duty on imported negroes, 347; Memorandum relative to the validity of his appointment of Judges during good behavior, 349; His removal asked for, 360; Letter from, relative to the declaration of war against Spain, 363; Informs Secretary Pownall that the Commissions during good behavior had been relinquished by the Judges; also recommends R. H. Morris for Chief-Justice, and announces the death of Andrew Johnston, 364; Recommends Stephen Skinner to be appointed Treasurer of New Jersey, 366; Informed of his removal from the Governorship, 374; Announces to the Lords of Trade the appointment of Anthony White, as Judge of the Admiralty, in room of Lewis Morris, deceased, 377; Acknowledges the letter announcing his removal, 379; Opinion of the Attorney-General as to his appointments, 380; In-

closes acts and papers to the Lords of Trade, 382; Referred to, 387, 459.

Harford, Lord, ix, 9, 15.

Hargue, William, i, 394.

Hariott, David, iv, 98, 99.

Harkent, Daniel, ii, 326, 327.

Harker, Captain Samuel, ix, 184.

Harmenson, Downs, i, 49.

Harmer, James P., ix, 18.

Harper, Alexander, iv, 185, 368.

Harriman, John, x, 718.

Harriman, John, Jr., ii, 129, 327, 395.

Harriman, Joseph, x, 717.

Harriman, Richard, x, 717.

Harrington, Henry, ii, 43–61, 65–73, 79.

Harris, Daniel, i, 50.

Harris, Elizabeth, ii, 46.

Harris, Ephraim, x, 531.

Harris, Samuel, x, 717.

Harris, Stephen, iv, 310.

Harrison, Amos, vi, 351—vii, 458.

Harrison, Benjamin, x, 530.

Harrison, Daniel, ii, 336—vi, 149, 402—viii, Part I, 214, 215.

Harrison, Edmund, ii, 41–61, 65–73, 76, 78, 87, 88, 90, 91, 95, 99.

Harrison, Edward, iv, 9.

Harrison, Francis, Member of the New York Council, v, 2; Letter from, relative to carrying copper ore from New Jersey to Holland, 7; Commissioner to try pirates, 197; Referred to, 350, 396, 397, 409.

Harrison, Jake, x, 718.

Harrison, James, Deputed by Governor Penn to go to East Jersey, i, 395; Appointed a Commissioner to treat with West Jersey, 415, 419.

Harrison, John, Proposed for the Council, iii, 95; Referred to, 154; Proposed as a member of Lord Lovelace's Council, 299, 302, 309; Peter Sonman's memorial against, 306; Superseded by Lewis Morris in Lord Lovelace's Council, 329; Moneys paid by, to the Receiver-General, 351; Referred to, 429, 430, 448, 458, 459, 460—iv, 10, 98, 102, 253; Referred to by Rev. Jacob Henderson, 157; Payments to, 371; Referred to, 375, 377; Instructions to, relative to the boundary line, 391; Witness, 399; Referred to, 417, 436—v, 146—vi, 147, 350, 352 —vii, 457.

Harrison, John, Deputy Surveyor, viii, Part I, 207; Sent to examine what branches might be between the Delaware and Susquehanna, 241, 252, 253.

Harrison, Joseph, ii, 336.

Harrison, Richard, Signs the Surrender of the Government, ii, 456, 460; Asks that Andrew Hamilton be appointed Governor, 470.

Harrison, Sarah, iv, 109.

Harrison, Samuel, ii, 336, 339—iv, 108, 109—vi, 346, 350, 361, 365—vii, 64, 74, 436.

Harrison, William, iv, 9—x, 226.

Harsh, Henry, ii, 396.

Hart, Edward, Raises troops for the expedition to Canada, vi, 371-376 —x, 269.

Hart, John, of Hunterdon County, x, 269.

Hart, Moses, x, 273.

Hart, Thomas, An East Jersey Proprietor, i, 366, 373, 383, 412, 424, 433, 434, 437, 442, 446, 451, 454, 457, 460, 462, 474, 482, 483, 490, 499, 500, 504, 528—ii, 26, 149, 164, 165, 171, 177, 186-193, 198, 213, 257, 263, 270, 376, 408, 410, 437, 470—iii, 314, 315, 488—x, 131.

Hartshorne, Hugh, An East Jersey Proprietor, i, 366, 374, 383, 412, 528 —viii, Part II, 39, 230, 232.

Hartshorne, Richard, i, 88, 143; Instructions to, as one of the Commissioners in West Jersey, appointed by William Penn and others, 219; Letter to, from the Proprietors of West Jersey, 227; Referred to, 292; Elected Deputy for Assembly, 307.—Referred to, ii, 101; Disorders in New Jersey, 327; Note on, 329; Signs petition, 396; Nominated for Council, 487.—Contributes to Cornbury Fund, iii, 212; Referred to, 479, 482, 483—iv, 111, 285, 318.

Hartshorne, Robert, In charge of beacon on Navesink Highlands, vi, 374.—Affirmation respecting John Coxe, vii, 541.

Hartshorne, Thomas, ii, 326.

Hartshorne, William, Contributes to the supposed Cornbury Fund, iii, 213.

Harvard College, vii, 118.

Hasell (Haswell), Richard, Signs the surrender of the Government, ii, 456-460; Asks the appointment of Andrew Hamilton for Governor, 470.

Haselwood, George, i, 269.

Hasenclever, Peter, Petition of, to be allowed to purchase lands, ix, 583; Notice of, 583.

Haskoll (Haskell), John, Salary as Doorkeeper of the Council, iv, 369—v, 55, 56, 135, 137, 141, 145.

Hatfield (Hettfield), Abraham, ii, 129, 334, 339—iii, 496.

Hatfield, Abner, x, 463, 512, 551, 552, 558.

Hatfield (Hetfield), Cornelius, ii, 129, 325, 334.

Hatfield (Hetfield), Isaac, ii, 326, 334, 339—iii, 496.

Hatfield (Heathfield), Matthias, i, 50, 65—vii, 223, 651.

Hathaway, Silas, x, 718.

Hats. See Felt Makers' Company.

Hatter, Benjamin, ii, 129.

Hatton, John, Collector of Salem, x, 53, 205; Arrest of, 207; Complains to Governor Franklin of the action of the Justices of Cape May, 209,

215; Opinion of the Attorney-General thereupon, 216, 217; Complaints of, to the Commissioners of Customs at Boston, 218; Complaint of, with papers, sent to the Earl of Hillsborough, 275, 276, 304, 305; Referred to, 314.

Hanse, John, i, 88, 307.

Havens, John, i, 51.

Hawk, Sir Edward, viii, Part II, 131.

Hawke, Admiral, ix, 210.

Hawker, Captain James, ix, 511; Letter from, to Governor Franklin, respecting stamps for New Jersey, 513; Answer thereto, 514; Referred to, 515.

Hawles, Sir John, Solicitor-General, ii, 138; Consulted as to East Jersey ports, 174; His reply, 177.

Hayes, Thomas, ii, 336, 339.

Hayes, William, Affidavit of, in relation to the taking of New York by the Dutch, i, 152.

Hayle, Samuel, i, 66, 71, 82.

Haynes, John, i, 50.

Haynes, Joseph, vii, 321, 322, 326.

Hayward, Daniel, x, 718.

Hayward, Nicholas, ii, 41-61, 65-73, 76, 78.

Hazard, Mr., viii, Part I, 95.

Hazen, Colonel, ix, 339.

Headley, Levand, i, 50.

Heard, John, iii, 446.

Heard, Captain John, vii, 231, 232, 282, 283.

Heard, Nathaniel, x, 719, 720.

Hearn, Nathaniel, x, 588.

Heathcote, Caleb, iii, 64; Recommended as Governor of New Jersey, 284.—Referred to, iv, 340.

Heathcote, George, i, 316, 318—ii, 80.

Heathcote, Sir Gilbert, iii, 284.

Heathfield, Hethfield, Hetfield. See Hatfield.

Heaton, Gideon, x, 531.

Hedden, Aaron, x, 718.

Hedge (Hedges), Samuel, Surveyor-General of West Jersey, i, 193, 269, 275, 284, 373, 413, 414, 508—ii, 146, 380.

Hegeman, Adrian, His son breaks the goal at Perth Amboy, viii, Part I, 50, 51.

Hegemen, Dollings, vi, 455, 465—vii, 64, 206, 456—viii, Part 1, 50, 51.

Helme, Israel, i, 182.

Helmighsen, Roelof, ii, 326.

Helmsby, Joseph, i, 239, 241, 271, 291—iii, 221.

Hemingway, Robert, Grand Juror on Woodbridge riot, iii, 486, 487.

Hemp, The production of, iv, 286.—Bounties upon, ix, 405, 490.

Henderson, Jacob, Representation by, of the state of the Church, iv, 155;

Governor Hunter's account of him in a letter to John Chamberlayne, 158; Remarks on his representations, 161; Letter to, from the Clergy of New York and New Jersey, disapproving of his course toward the Council of New Jersey, 173; Referred to, 174.

Henderson, Michael, Ensign, ix, 187.

Hendricks, Abraham, vii, 421–424.

Hendricks, Isaac, vii, 422.

Hendricks, William, ii, 363.

Hendrickse, Daniel, iii, 356.

Hendrickse, Jacob, ii, 326.

Hendrickson, Daniel, ii, 326, 366—x, 600.

Hendrixson, Jacob, iv, 113.

Hendrickson, John, i, 114—vii, 377.

Hendrickson, Kend., ii, 396.

Hendrickson, Peter, i, 114.

Henley, Robert, Commissioner of Customs, ii, 168, 179.

Hennion, Henry, x, 718.

Henry, Patrick, x, 530.

Herber, Thomas, x, 352.

Herbert, Walter, ii, 326.

Heritage, Richard, ii, 148.

Herman, Augustine, i, 17, 204.

Herman, Casp., i, 268.

Herman, Ephraim, i, 276, 281, 283.

Herne, John, ii, 397.

Heron, Joseph, ii, 239, 240.

Herring, John, viii, Part I, 220, 227, 228; Affidavit of, against Thomas Dekey and sons, 282.

Herresons, Peter, i, 288.

Hertford, Countess of, viii, Part I, 85.

Hester, Case of the ship, ii, 245, 255, 259, 303, 311, 341, 367, 398—iii, 478.

Hetfield, and Hethfield. See Hatfield.

Heulings, William, i, 268—iii, 164.

Hewes, Joseph, x, 530.

Hewes, William, i, 414.

Hewght, Abner, ii, 363.

Hewett, David, iv, 10.

Hewitt, Thomas, ii, 332.

Hewlings, Abraham, iv, 147—x, 15, 17, 139, 358.

Hewling, Jacob, iv, 147; Expelled from the Assembly, 292; Signs, 309.

Hewlings, William, x, 15, 17.

Hews, Richard, i, 177.

Heyndrotch, ii, 327.

Heysen, Peter, i, 1.

Heywood, John, An East Jersey Proprietor, i, 366, 374, 383, 412, 529.

Heywood, Thomas, i, 332.

Hickey, Israel, vii, 427.

Hicks, Isaac, One of the Commissioners to run partition line, iv, 383, 394, 429, 435—viii, Part I, 239, 264.

Hicks, Jasper, ii, 417.

Hieckens, Roger, i, 414.

Hieston, Obadiah, Salary as Sergeant-at-Arms, iv, 369, 371.

Higgins, Jediah, ii, 326—iv, 9, 15, 98.

Higgins, Jedediah, ii, 396—iii, 458, 459, 484.

Higgins, John, x, 711.

Higgins (Higgens), Thomas, ii, 316, 326, 396—iii, 486, 487.

Hiler, Jacob, x, 718.

Hiler, John, x, 718.

Hiler, Nicholas, x, 718.

Hiler, Peter, Jr., x, 718.

Hiler, Philip, x, 718.

Hill, Abraham, ii, 129.

Hill, Richard, Member of the Pennsylvania Council, iv, 393—vii, 543.

Hill, Secretary Thomas, Letter from, to Mr. Fane, relative to two acts of the New Jersey Assembly, vi, 150.

Hill, Thomas, v, 132, 134, 136.

Hill, William, ii, 327.

Hillsborough, Earl of, Secretary of State for the Southern Department, ix, 342—x, 10; Writes to Governor Franklin, relative to providing quarters for the King's troops, 12; Letter from, relative to the Massachusetts Assembly circular, 14, 45; Instructs the Governors of America how to transmit duplicates, 35; Cautions the Governors in America in regard to letters received from the King's Secretaries of State, 57; In relation to the Massachusetts Assembly circular, 58; In relation to the bill for issuing £100,000, and the unwarrantable proceedings of the Assembly in connection therewith, 60; Governor Franklin defends himself against the censures of, 72; Writes to Governor Franklin, relative to the bill for issuing £100,000, 103; Informs the Colonial Governors that the King has no design to tax America for purposes of revenue, 109; Announces the appointment of Cortlandt (Stephen) Skinner as a member of Council, 139; Corrects his error in regard to the Christian name of Mr. Skinner, 147; Compliments Governor Franklin and the Council of New Jersey, 198; Transmits to Governor Franklin two orders of the Council, 213; To the same, in regard to providing for the King's troops, 219; To the same, relative to the dispute with Spain, the Indian trade, etc., 274; Letter from Governor Franklin, in relation to the complaint of John Hatton, 275; Approves the conduct of Governor Franklin in the matter of recruiting the King's forces, 301; Writes to Governor Franklin, relative to Mr. Hatton's complaint, and the obstinacy of the Assembly in refusing to provide for the King's troops, 304; Ap-

proves Governor Franklin's position in regard to the resignation of a member of the Assembly, 318; Writes to Governor Franklin, relative to arrears due to the troops, 323; To the same, in relation to the dispute with the Assembly, and the salary of the Chief-Justice, 361; To the same, in relation to a writ for the election of a new member of Assembly for Essex County, 374.

Hinchman, James, vii, 99.

Hinchman, John, x, 15, 17, 458, 697.

Hinckman, John, v, 211.

Hind, John, ii, 46, 62.

Hindes, James, x, 718.

Hindes, John, ii, 327, 397.

Hindse, Joseph, ii, 396.

Hinney, John, iii, 306.

Hite, John, vii, 612, 614, 619–622.—Deposition of, viii, Part I, 40.

Hodgson, General, ix, 277.

Hoff, Charles, x, 717.

Hoff, Garrett, x, 717.

Hoff, John, x, 717.

Hoff, Joseph, x, 717.

Hoffman, Christian, x, 717.

Hoge, William, ii, 332.

Hogelandt, Henry, vi, 456, 465, 469.

Hogg Island, v, 42, 44.

Hogg, John, Recommended for Council of Governor Hunter, iii, 498.

Hoghtelin, Johannes, vi, 167.

Hoits, Obadiah, i, 128.

Holburn, Admiral, viii, Part II, 249; To command the fleet in American waters, 251.

Holdernesse, Earl of, viii, Part I, 23; Letter from, to the Lords of Trade, 32; Referred to, 92; Removes the embargo upon corn, Part II, 248.

Holks, Thomas, Jr., Sheriff of Burlington County, iv, 142.

Holland, Captain, v, 54.

Holland, Ferdinando, Signs the surrender of the Government, ii, 456–460.

Holland, Samuel, ix, 582, 591, 624, 631, 632—x, 518, 599, 660.

Holland, Mr., viii, Part I, 94.

Hollander's Creek Island, v, 42, 44, 45.

Hollenkous, Philip, x, 718.

Holles, Joseph, Opinion of, on Elizabethtown Patent, i, 271.

Hollingshead, John, ii, 148.

Hollingshead, Joseph, viii, Part II, 40, 154, 229, 230.

Hollingshead, Mr., ix, 338.

Hollingsworth, John, iv, 113.

Hollis, John, ii, 470.

Holme, John, ii, 146, 384, 486, 488.

Holme, Thomas, i, 373.

Holmes, Abijah, x, 531.

Holmes, James, Member of the Assembly, viii, Part II, 94; Warrants to, 152, 153, 234.

Holmes, Jonathan, i, 307.

Holmes, Joseph, x, 717.

Holmes, Josiah, x, 600, 667.

Holmes, Obadiah, i, 44, 88—ii, 363, 384, 396, 486.

Holmes, Thomas, i, 394 ; Appointed a Commissioner to go to East Jersey, by Governor Penn, 395 ; Commissioner to treat with West Jersey, 415, 419.

Holt, Joseph, Opinion of, On Elizabethtown Patent, i, 271.

Homan, Benjamin, i, 50.

Home, Archibald, Recommended for the Council, vi, 109 ; Appointed as such, 127; Deceased, 237.

Honan and Handen's Patent, viii, Part I, 275.

Honblon, Peter, ii, 470.

Hood, Clawson, vi, 417.

Hooghteline, Johannes, viii, Part I, 212.

Hooglandt, D., iv, 190.

Hooglandt, Hendrick, vii, 449, 451 ; Indicted, 458 ; Referred to, 575, 577.

Hoolmann (Holman), Robert, 327, 396.

Hooper, Capt. James, v, 102.

Hooper, Robert Lettice, Nominated for Chief-Justice, v, 97 ; Money received of on account of Bills of Credit, 134 ; Money paid to, 147, 148, 150 ; Appointed Chief-Justice of New Jersey, 182; Referred to, 344, 374, 401, 402 ; Recommended for Council of New Jersey, 410, 454, 469.—Member of Council, vi, 14, 15; Died, 109, 127.—Affidavit of, relative to the riots, vii, 447.—Referred to, ix, 215, 231, 339—x, 303,

Hooper, Robert, Recommended for the Council, ix, 127.

Hooper, William, x, 530.

Hoost, William, iv, 10.

Hooton, Thomas, i, 268.

Hopemyre, Samuel, ii, 332.

Hoper, Robert, vii, 638.

Hopkins, Ebenezer, vii, 99—viii, Part I, 74; Part II, 229, 235.

Hopkins, Governor, Letter to from Governor Belcher relative to a Convention of the Commissioners for the several Colonies, viii, Part II, 167.

Hopkins, Mr., Magistrate in Rhode Island, vii, 69.

Hopkins, Samuel, i, 66, 121; Appointment by the Council of New Netherlands as a civil officer and his acts as such, 129, 130, 139, 149, 152, 153; Note on, 152; Referred to, 300.

Hopkins, Stephen, x, 529.

Hopkinson, Francis, x, 270; Recommended for the Council, 426; Notice of, 426, 455.

Hopkinson, Thomas, vii, 130—ix, 622—x, 426.

Hoppe, Jost, Indicted, vii, 458.

Hopper, George, vi, 456, 465—vii, 458.

Hopper, John, vi, 465—vii, 458.

Hoppon, Jacob, x, 718.

Hornblower, Josiah, ix, 321.

Horner, John, Grand Juror on Woodbridge riot, iii, 486, 487.—Referred to, vii, 620, 621.

Horseneck, Controversy concerning the lands at, vi, 354.—Riots at, vii, 364, 368, 370.

Horsley, Charles, i, 17.

Horsemanden, Daniel, v, 323—ix, 178, 283—x, 375; Notice of, 377.

Horton, John, iii, 165.

Horton. William, iii, 165.

Hoshell, Michael, x, 531.

Hoskins, Robert, i, 289.

Hossett, Gillis, i, 1.

Houdon (Howdon, Hardon), Michael, Surrenders the Government of East Jersey, ii, 387; Signs the surrender, 456-460; Objected to as a member of Council, 488.

Houghton, Joab, x, 273.

Houlings (Hewlings), Abraham, Signer of bills of credit, viii, Part II. 40, 154, 155, 229.

House of Representatives. See New Jersey.

Houston, Alexander, ix, 625.

Houthout, Fabius, i, 51.

How, John, vii, 533.

Howard, Charles, ix, 621.

Howard, Hannah, ii, 470.

Howard, Hiram, x, 718.

Howard, William, x, 718.

Howett, Randle, i, 17.

Hoyle, John, Opinion of, on Elizabethtown Patent, i, 271.

Hubbell, Nathaniel, Lieutenant, ix, 185.

Hubbert, James, i, 150.

Huchings, Roger, iv, 113.

Hudd, James, Jr., Surrogate, ix, 360.

Hud (Hude, Hudd), Adam, iii, 424, 447; High Sheriff of Middlesex and Somerset, affidavit of, respecting the proceedings of Peter Sonmans, 457.—Referred to, iv, 10, 88, 89, 186, 303, 334, 375, 377.

Hude, James, v, 443.—Recommended for the Council, vi, 233; Notice of, 233; Recommended by the Lords of Trade, 237; Member of Council, 367-378—vii, 5; Member of Governor Belcher's Council, 6, 11, 98, 102; Referred to, 127; Autograph, 184; Unites in a communication

from the Council to Governor Belcher, 188; Also in an address to the King, 191; Signs, 237, 455; In Council, 335, 541; Referred to, 504, 618—viii, Part I, 43, 103, 107—ix, 5, 22; Member of Council, 274; Named as one of the Commissioners for trying pirates, 283: Death of, 386; Referred to, 394.

Hude, Robert, vi, 465, 466.

Huddy, Charles, iv, 344, 345.

Huddy (Hoddy), Hugh, Proposed for the Council, iii, 95, 299, 302, 340; Appointed a member of Council, 317; Referred to, 357; Signs, 473. —Member of Governor Hunter's Council, iv, 2, 19; Referred to, 41, 42, 48, 61, 75, 99; Obtains a patent for carriages, 129; Referred to, 130, 132, 141, 153; By Jacob Henderson, 157; Further reference to, 164, 296; Dead, 326, 331, 363; Money paid to, 369, 372; Referred to, 374.

Hudson, Peter, ii, 470.

Hugg, John, ii, 148; Appointed a member of the Council by Governor Hunter, iv, 363, 373, 375.—Member of Governor Burnett's Council, v, 3; Money paid to, 137, 141; Commissioned to try pirates, 197; Dead, 293; Notice of, 293.

Hugg, John, Jr., ii, 148.

Hughes, Humphrey, v, 133, 137, 141.

Hughes, John, ix, 516, 518.

Hughes, William, i, 369.

Hughes, ——, x, 206, 210, 212, 277, 279.

Huit, Joseph, i, 51.

Hulet, George, contributes to the supposed Cornbury Fund, iii, 213, 214.

Hull, Benia, ii, 326.

Hull, Benjamin, ii, 326, 395.—Meetings at his house, iii, 198; Contributions to the supposed Cornbury Fund, 200; Petition of against said Fund, 205; Referred to, 209, 218—iv, 189.

Hull, Hopewell, iv, 188.

Hull, Joseph, x, 718.

Hull, Robert, x, 502.

Hull, Samuel, ii, 397.

Hullett, George, i, 51.

Hulmes, Jonathan, i, 134.

Humbly, Peter, iv, 344, 345.

Hume, Lord, viii, Part I, 93.

Humphreys, Charles, x, 529.

Humphreys (Humphries), Joshua, ii, 148—iii, 165—iv, 152, 278.

Hungerford, Ducie, Deposition of, relative to the seizure of a vessel at Perth Amboy, ii, 238, 243 ; Referred to, 245, 247, 255.

Hunloke (Hunlock), Edward, ii, 41, 146, 147, 380 ; Recommended to be one of the Council, 417, 429, 486, 488 ; Referred to, 481 ; Remarks concerning, 502 ; Appointed member of the Council, 507.—Dead, iii, 1, 47, 78.

Hunloke, Thomas, v, 132, 134, 136, 138, 187.

Hunt, Abraham, x, 202, 471, 588.

Hunt, Enoch, Ensign, ix, 187.

Hunt, Mansfield, vii, 433, 442.

Hunt, Ralph, ii, 384.

Hunt, Samuel, Major, ix, 184, 186.

Hunt, Wilson, viii, Part II, 229, 235.

Hunt, ———, iv, 299.

Hunter, Andrew, x, 345.

Hunter, Dam'd, iv, 263.

Hunter, Robert, i, 19—iii, 497.—Governor of New Jersey, Instructions to, iv, 1, 2; His arrival in New York, 6; Letter from, to Lord Dartmouth relative to Lady Lovelace, 10; Notice of, 11; Letter from, to the Lords of Trade, respecting an intended meeting of the New Jersey Assembly, 11; To the same, respecting the place of meeting of the Assembly, 16; Address of the Council to, 17; Representation of the Assembly to, relative to the administration of Lord Cornbury, 24; Letter from to the Commissioners of Customs relative to the removal of the Collector at Perth Amboy, 49; Communication from, to the Lords of Trade, with documents, referring to affairs in East Jersey, 51; Recommends John Kiel for Surveyor-General of New Jersey, 78; Complaint of the Assembly of New Jersey to, against William Hall, 79; Memorial of the same to, relative to the perversions of justice in the courts of law, 87; Address to, from inhabitants of Salem relative to taxes, 111; Letter to, from the Lords of Trade in reply to his communication of May 7, 1711, 113; Letter from to Captain Coy, relative to dispatching troops to Albany, 135; Letter to, from Colonel Farmer, relative to supplies for troops, 135; Letter from, to Colonel Cox relative to discharging volunteers, 136; Letter from, to Secretary St. John, relative to New Jersey affairs, 137; Letter from, to Jeremiah Basse, relative to Supreme Court Judges, 139; From, to the same, relative to swearing officers, 141; Letter to, from J. Basse, relative to survey, 142; Letter to, from Thomas Gardner, complaining of Jeremiah Basse, 144; Letter to, from Basse concerning Thomas Gardner, 148; Letter from, to the Lords of Trade, relative to changes in New Jersey Council, 149; Asks the action of the Lords of Trade in relation to the New Jersey Council, 151; Remarks upon his conduct by Rev. Jacob Henderson, 155, 156; Letter from, to Magistrates of Gloucester County commending them, 158; His account of the Rev. Jacob Henderson, 158; Letter from, to J. Basse respecting the seizure of a shallop at Gloucester, 159; Letter from, to Colonel Gookin, Governor of Pennsylvania, complaining of his proceedings, 160; Referred to, 163; Letters from, to the Lords of Trade, relative to New Jersey affairs, 171, 174; Letter to, from the Lords of Trade, relative to the Council of New Jersey, 182; Letter from, to Attorney-General Griffith, relative to delinquent taxpayers, 184; Salary, 185;

Letters from, to the Lords of Trade, relative to New Jersey affairs, 195, 206, 210, 213; New commission issued to, 202; Letter to Secretary Popple relative to support of the Government of New Jersey, 211; Acknowledges the receipt of his commission, 215; Letter from, to Secretary Popple relating to certain appointments by the Bishop of London, 218; Letter from, respecting certain proceedings of Rev. Mr. Vesey, 219; Letter from, to the Lords of Trade, relative to certain acts of the New Jersey Assembly, 221; Letter from to Secretary Popple relating to Rev. Mr. Talbot and Rev. Mr. Vesey, 223; Letters to, from the Lords of Trade relative to New Jersey matters, 227; Letter from, to the Lords of Trade, relative to the same, 230; Letter from, to Secretary Popple, enclosing two Quaker speeches relating to Mr. Coxe, 242; Speech of, to the Assembly of New Jersey, 249; Address to, from the Assembly, relating to the expelling of their Governor, 250; Letter from, to the agent for New York in London, 254; Letter from, to the Lords of Trade, relating to New Jersey affairs, 255; Letter from, to Secretary Popple, relating to Mr. Coxe and others, 258; Letter from, to the Lords of Trade, relative to proceedings of Mr. Coxe, 260; Letter from Samuel Bustall, against, 262; Letter from, to the Lords of Trade, relative to dissolving the Assembly, 264; Speech of, to the Assembly, 267; Address of the Assembly to, 268; Letter from, to the Lords of Trade, 273; Referred to, 282; Letters to, from George Willocks and Rev. John Talbot, 290, 291; Letter from, to the Lords of Trade, with acts of the New Jersey Assembly, 291; Letters from, to Secretary Popple, 294, 295, 297; Address of the House of Representatives of New Jersey to, 303; Answer to the same, 304; Letter from, to Secretary Popple, enclosing a minute of the Council, 305; Complaint against, 306; Letter from, to the Lords of Trade, 311; Letter from, to Mr. Phillips, in answer to the charges against him, 312; Letter from, to Secretary Popple, recommending these Councillors to fill vacancies, 326; The King satisfied with his conduct, 327; Warrant to use a new seal for New Jersey, 332; Letter from, to Secretary Popple, relative to vacancies in the Council, 333; Letter to, from the Lords of Trade, concerning his various communications, 335; Named as one of the Commissioners for trying pirates, 339; Letter from, to the Lords of Trade, relating to New Jersey affairs, 363; Message and Speech to the New Jersey Assembly, 364, 365; Salary, 368, 369, 371; Letter from, to the Lords of Trade, relating to the old seal, 373; Letter to, from the Lords of Trade, relative to the members of the Council, 374; Letter to Secretary Popple, relative to the same, 376; Letter from, to the Lords of Trade, transmitting papers, 386; Letter from, to Secretary Popple, announcing his intention to return to England, 387; Proceedings of the Pennsylvania Council, relative to his departure, 393; Answer of to queries relating to New Jersey, 449.—Referred to, v, 1, 10, 12, 14, 53, 54; Letter to, from James Alexander,

55; Referred to, 113; Letters from, to James Alexander, 179, 187, 261; Referred to, 198, 338, 344, 350; Letter to, from James Alexander, relative to Governor Cosby, 359; Referred to, 374, 477, 495—vi, 71.—On the boundaries between New York and New Jersey, viii, Part I, 132, 133, 137, 142, 148, 149, 167, 233.—Referred to, x, 225.

Hunter, Samuel, iii, 358.

Hunter, Thomas Orby, vi, 77.

Hunterdon County, iv, 368, 369—v, 12, 13, 61, 73, 83, 84, 132, 133.—Riot in, vii, 382.—Money received from Collector, viii, Part I, 66–68; From Commissioners, 71, 74.—Assemblymen of, instructed to oppose the quartering of troops in the provinces, x, 269.

Huntington, Lady, viii, Part I, 85; Letter to, from Governor Belcher, 87.

Huntingdon, Samuel, ii, 336.

Hutchings, Sarah, i, 186.

Hutchinson, George, i, 242, 270, 522, 523.

Hutchinson, Thomas, i, 241.

Hutchinson, Thomas, ix, 390.

Hyde, John, ii, 47.

Hyde, Lord, i, 353.

Hyler, Peter, x, 718.

I.

Idiots, Governors of Colonies authorized to issue commissions for the care and custody of, x, 370; Governor Franklin in relation to, 382.

Ike, Philip, vi, 455—vii. 458.

Ilnes, Abner, ii, 397.

Ilslee, John, iii, 446.

Ilslee, Jonathan, iii, 446.

Ilsley, William, iv, 186, 188.

Indians, Deed from for Elizabethtown Grant, i, 15 ; Murders by at Matiniconck Island, 72, 76 ; Governor Lovelace to Mr. Tom, relative to, 74 ; The same, to Capt. Carr, relative to, 79 ; Conference between, and the Council of New Netherlands, 131 ; Letter to Capt. Cantwell, relative to, 179, 181; Conference with, 182; Proceedings of Council, relative to, 458.—Attempt to defraud them of their land, iv, 276, 285.—Friendly to the inhabitants, v, 22; Method of protection against, 107, 112.—Act regulating the purchase of lands from, vi, 142; Grants from, referred to, 339, 341; Expedition against, 369 ; Opinions respecting purchases from, 420.—Deeds from, referred to, vii, 31, 37, 40, 83; Proposed conferences with, 135, 596 ; Number of in New Jersey, 245; The Six Nations of, 582; Missionary to be sent among, 597.—Proposed interview with the Six Nations, viii, Part, I, 156; Number of in New Jersey, 158, 163, 174; Imprisonment of in Pennsylvania, 191.—Conflict with on the Delaware, ix, 117; Plan for protection against, proposed by the Quakers, 118; Invasion of, 120 ; Message from Governor Bernard to the Minisinks, 125 ; Deputation of to Governor Bernard, 128; Conferences held with at Easton, 139 ;

Peace concluded with, 160, 164 ; Trade with them recommended, 165; Co-operation of, 172: Town laid out for in Burlington County, 174; Settlements on the borders likely to interfere with, 321 ; John Brainard appointed Superintendent of, at Brotherton, 355 ; Recommence hostilities in the back country, 391, 392; Proceedings with respect to repelling the hostilities of, 398; The Six Nations of, likely to render aid that will end the war for the summer, 433; Col. Croghan. negotiations with, 521 ; Complaints concerning the murdering of, 569; Outrages committed upon, 575 ; Murder of an Oneida Indian, 578.—Treaty with relative to boundary line between them and the Northern Colonies, x, 55, 95; Commerce with, 222 ; Complaints of, 241; Trade with, 275 ; Number of in New Jersey, 447.

Indian, Peter, vi, 407.

Ineth, John, iv, 310.

Ingersoll, Jared, ix, 582, 591, 625, 631, 632.

Inians, John, ii, 18.

Inglis, Charles, x, 313.

Ingoldsby, Richard, iii, 64; Letter from, to Lord Cornbury, 67; Reply to the same reprimanding him, 68; Letter from, to the Lords of Trade, complaining of Lord Cornbury's treatment of him, 109; Commission as Lieutenant-Governor of New York revoked, and appointed one of the Council of New Jersey, 145, 146, 340; Affidavit of, relating to the arbitrary proceedings of Lord Cornbury, 150; Referred to, 160, 181, 231; Notice of, 290; Proposed as a member of Lord Lovelace's Council, 299; Signs addresses, 367, 373, 415; Resentment of the Assembly to him, 371; Defence of, 372, 401; Orders, as Lieutenant-Governor, Peter Sonmans' answer to the Assembly to be printed, 460; Letters'from, to the Lords of Trade, relativeto New Jersey affairs, 460, 467; The validity of his commission of Lieutenant-Governor referred to the Queen, 469; Representation from, to the Queen, relative to the Quakers, 470; His commission revoked, 474.—Referred to, iv, 10, 5 6, 57, 66, 129, 130, 230, 234.

Innes, Alexander, iv, 174; Certificates from, sustaining the character of Thomas Gordon, 177; And of Colonel John Anderson, 178.

Inness, Robert, Presented by Monmouth Grand Jury, ii, 332.

Insolvent Laws, x, 236.

Ipan Kickan, Indian Chief, i. 182.

Iron, Memorial relative to the production of, iv, 286.—Encouraging th e making of, vi, 140.—The importation of, vii, 554, 557-570.—Accou nt of the quantity imported into England from the Colonies, between Christmas, 1749, to Christmas. 1752, viii, Part I, 118, 119; In Morr is and Sussex Counties, Part II, 79.—Peter Hansenclever & Co.'s work s for the manufacture of, ix, 583.—Number of furnaces, etc., in Ne w Jersey, x, 31.

Irwin, John, ii, 76, 79 (See Jurin).

Islands in the Delaware, See Delaware.

J.

Jaborowsky, Alberdt, ii, 327.

Jackson, Daniel, x, 718.

Jackson, Edward, x, 717.

Jackson, J., x, 717.

Jackson, Richard, Report of, on certain acts of the New Jersey Legislature, x, 233, 365, 369, 508, 701.

Jackson, Stephen, x, 717.

Jacobs, Henry, x, 516.

Jacobs, Thomas, iv, 85.

Jacobse (Jacobs), Hendrick, i, 286; Petition in favor of, as tenant in possession of Matiniconck Island, 287.

Jacobse, Lymar, i, 151.

Jacobson, Gruna, i, 270.

Jacobus, Abraham, x, 718.

Jacobus, James, x, 718.

Jacobus, Brant, x, 718.

Jacobus, Cornelius A., x, 717, 718.

Jacobus, Hendrick, vi, 245—vii, 457.

Jacquet, Jean Paul, Repossessed of lands taken from him, i, 117, 189; Justice of New Castle, 190, 195, 201, 203; His complaint against John Fenwicke, 235, 236; Letter from, to Fenwicke, 281.

James, Duke of York, Patent to, for New Jersey, i, 3; Lease from, to John, Lord Berkeley and Sir George Carteret, for New Jersey, 8; Release for the same to the same, 10; Letter from, to Governor Lovelace, confirming his grant to Berkeley and Carteret, 97; Lease from, to Sir George Carteret for the northern half of New Jersey, 161; Release from, to the same, for New Jersey, 163; Grant to William Penn and his associates for West Jersey, 324; Release from, to Sir George Carteret (grandson and heir of the original Proprietor) for East Jersey, 337; Release from, to the twenty-four Proprietors, 383; Letter from, to Governor Dongan, 475.

James, Richard, ii, 326, 396—iii, 213.

Jamison, David, ii, 114; Notice of, 114, 115.—Appointed Chief Justice, iv, 70, 131, 140; Recommended for the Council, 217, 227; Indictment of, 236; Referred to, 266; Salary, 185, 368, 369, 371.—Referred to, v, 77, 135, 139, 143, 344, 374.

Jan, Gerrard, ii, 326.

Janqueno, i, 1.

Jansen, Aert, i, 268.

Jansen, Pieter, i, 49.

Jaques, Henry, Jr., i, 50.

Jarbowsky, Jackor, ii, 327.

Jarratt, Allane, One of the Commissioners to run the partition line, iv, 383, 390, 394; Petition of, respecting the line between New York

and New Jersey, 403; Report of New York Council on his petition, 406, 409; Letter from Peter Schuyler relating to, 431.—Referred to. vi, 146-148, 170.—New York Surveyor, viii, Part I, 172; Petition of to a Committee of the Colony of New York, 173; Petition to President Schuyler, 233; Report on the same, 235; Referred to. 240. 247, 253, 254, 258, 265, 277.

Jauncey, James, ix, 18.

Janson, Claas, i, 269.

Javis, Jabus, vii, 377.

Jaxon, John, i, 285.

Jay, John, x, 530, 691.

Jeans, Henry, i, iii.

Jeffers, Edward, vii, 213, 415, 417.

Jeffers, John, vi, 455, 465—vii, 458.

Jeffery, Richard, ix, 18.

Jeffreys, Sir George, i, 324, 345.

Jeffries (Jefferies), Edward, vi, 415.

Jeoffry, Andrew, i, 529.

Jegon, Peter, x, 515-517.

Jegon, Peter, i, 51, 111, 286, 288.

Jenings, John, ii, 397: Recommended for Council. 429.

Jenings, Henry, i, 269.

Jenkins, Griffin, A brief vindication of the purchasers against the Proprietors, in a Christian manner, vi, 266 ; Notice of, 288; Referred to, 311, 320, 322, 323.

Jenkins, Nathaniel, v, 133, 135, 141.

Jennings, James, x, 718.

Jennings, Samuel, i, 268 ; Governor of West Jersey, 421 ; Memorial to from the people of Salem. 421; A Proprietor of West Jersey, 522, 523—ii. 64, 65, 380 ; Recommended to be one of the Council, 417 ; Objected to. 488 ; Remarks concerning, 502; Appointed member of the Council, 507.—One of Lord Cornbury's Council, iii, 2, 65. 155 : Summoned by Lord Cornbury to show his authority to act as one of the Council of West Jersey, 158 : Notice of, 158; Referred to, 160, 192, 194; One of the Council of Proprietors, 221; Complained against by Lord Cornbury, 224, 226; Resolves to leave the Queen's Council, 235; Colonel Quarry's remarks concerning, 237; Referred to, 268, 269; Comments upon, by Colonel Quarry, 273; The Council's opinion of him, 288, 365,[398, 406, 407, 409, 412-415.—Referred to. iv, 33-35, 77, 78, 131.

Jesop, Jeremiah, ii, 339—iii, 496.

Jewell, George, ii, 315, 335.

Jewell, John, ii. 209, 384, 486, 502.

Johnson, Abraham, ix, 251.

Johnson, Cornelius, vi, 455, 465—vii, 458.

Johnson, Eliphalet, vii, 439; Affidavit of, relative to the riots, 44 .

7

Johnson, Everett, ii, 121.

Johnson, Ezekiel, vii, 434.

Johnson, Fopp, i, 118.

Johnson (Johnstown), James, An East Jersey Proprietor, i, 460, 499, 529.

Johnson, John, Affidavit of, relative to the riots in Essex County, vii, 432; Referred to, 628.

Johnson, Jonathan, x, 717.

Johnson, Joseph, ii, 336, 339.

Johnston, Andrew, v, 61, 155; Letter from, relative to Governor Montgomerie, 183; Recommended for the Council, 317; Signs petition, 443.—Speaker of the Assembly, vi, 142; Instructions from, to John Lawrence, for running the partition line between East and West Jersey, 154; Recommended for the Council, 233; Notice of, 233; Recommended by the Lords of Trade, 237; Pall-bearer of Governor Morris, 368; Mayor of Perth Amboy, 467.—Member of Governor Belcher's Council, vii, 5, 6, 11; Autograph of, 14, 184; In Council, 86, 88, 102; Referred to, 108, 109; Unites with other members of the Council in a communication to Governor Belcher, 188; Also in an address to the King, 191; Referred to, 218; Signs, 237; Referred to, 281; In Council, 335, 343; On the state of the paper currency, 357; Signs, 455; Referred to, 504, 644—viii, Part I, 16 ; Letter to, from Governor Belcher, relative to the imprisonment of Simon (Cornelius) Wyckoff, 37; Referred to, 38, 44, 46; Accounts of, as Treasurer, 65, 76; In Council, 102; Salary, 106; Referred to, 191; Bond of indemnity, 200; Referred to, 221, 232.—Ordered to muster his troops, viii, Part II, 157; Account of, as Treasurer, 171; Directions to, from Governor Belcher, 178, 182; Account of, as Treasurer for East Jersey, 223.—Referred to, ix, 274; Named as one of the Commissioners for trying pirates, 283; Commissioner to purchase lands of the Indians, 356; Death of, 364, 366, 386, 394.—Referred to, x, 422.

Johnston, David, iv, 41.

Johnston, Captain Heathcote, x, 711.

Johnston, John, viii, Part I, 239.—Signer of bills of credit, viii, Part II, 39; Member of Assembly, 94.

Johnston, Colonel John, ix, 184–187.

Johnston, Lewis, Commissioned to run the line between East and West Jersey, vi, 352.—Agent for West Jersey Society, vii, 320.—Referred to, viii, Part I, 200—Part II, 228, 270.—Recommended for Council, ix, 127; Letter to, from George Otter, 337.

Johnston, Major-General William, Commander of the Colonial troops for New England, New York and New Jersey, viii, Part II, 141, 143, 164.

Johnston, William, vii, 421, 424.

Johnstone (Johnston, Johnson), Dr. John, ii, 336, 337; In relation to the outrage committed in the Monmouth County Court House, 366;

Surrenders the Government of East Jersey, 387; Recommended for
Council, 417; Signs the surrender of the Government, 456, 460;
Objected to as a member of Council, 488.—Proposed for the Council,
iii. 51; Referred to, 154; Affidavit of in support of the Assembly's
remonstrance, 207; Referred to, 262, 277; Complained of by Lord
Cornbury, 335; Referred to, 392, 403—iv, 12; Speaker of the
Assembly, 19, 20; Referred to, 39, 68, 106, 119; Notice of, 119, 121,
125, 127; Appointed Judge, 129; Referred to, 130, 131, 132, 377,
388, 390; One of the Commissioners for running the partition line,
394; Referred to, 406, 416, 435—v, 35, 56-61; Chosen Speaker of
the Assembly, 62; Superseded as one of the New York Council, 70;
Money paid to, 150; Referred to, 179, 263, 288—ix, 185.

Johnstone (Johnston, Johnson), John, Jr., iv, 15; Appointed member of
Governor Hunter's Council, 363, 373.—One of Governor Burnet's
Council, v, 2, 3, 34; Money paid to, 146; Commissioner to try
pirates, 197; Signs memorial, 301.

Johnson, Lamb, ii, 396.

Johnson, Major, vi, 402.

Johnson, Nathaniel, vii, 48, 49.

Johnson, Oukie, vii, 424.

Johnson, Peter, x, 717.

Johnson, Richard, ii, 63—iv, 370.

Johnson, Samuel, vii, 377, 606.

Johnson, Thomas, i, 142, 177, 306, 310, 320, 355—ii, 333, 334, 339,
362, 396.

Johnson, Thomas, Jr., x, 530.

Johnson, Thomas, Ensign, ix, 185.

Johnson, William, i, 50, 268, 413.

Johnson, William Gill, i, 118, 268, 414.

Johnson, Sir William, ix, 172, 178; Named as one of the Commissioners
for trying pirates, 283; Referred to, 522—x, 57, 112, 495.

Johnson, Wm. Samuel, Opinion of, in relation to the common lands in
Secaucus, ix, 454.

Jolly, John, vii, 130.

Jones, Abraham, x, 331.

Jones, Benjamin, iv, 113.

Jones, Cadwallader, ii, 119.

Jones, Ebenezer, Signs the Surrender of the Government, ii, 456-460;
Recommends Andrew Hamilton for Governor, 470.—Complaint
against Lord Cornbury, iii, 95.

Jones, Jeffrey, i, 50, 82, 84—ii, 111, 127—iii, 403—vi, 212—vii, 268.

Jones, John, iii, 165.

Jones, Nathaniel, Recommended by the Lords of Trade to be made Chief-
Justice of New Jersey, ix, 173; Referred to, 177, 210, 211; Proceed-
ings of the Supreme Court in relation to his appointment, 214-218 ;
Dispute between him and R. H. Morris for the office of Chief-Justice,

230, 235, 248; Memorial of, relative to his difficulties in New Jersey, 342; Remonstrance in favor of, 344.

Jones, R., ii, 30.

Jones, Robert, ix, 622.

Jones, Timothy, x, 345.

Jones, Sir William, Opinion of, in regard to duties demanded from the inhabitants of West Jersey, i, 323; Referred to, 354.

Jones, Wm., i, 51, 65—ii, 326, 396.

Jonken, Lonbert, ii, 326.

Joomerijo, ii, 327.

Joyce, Henry, iv, 328.

Judges, Granting of commissions to during good behaviour, ix, 308, 321; Order in Privy Council relative to commissions to, 324, 329; Memorandum relative to the validity of Governor Hardy's appointment of, during good behaviour, 349 ; Appointments during good behaviour relinquished by the Judges, 364; Opinion of the Attorney-General as to the validity of their apppointments, 380.

Jurin, John, ii, 41-61, 65-73, 88, 92, 95; Signs the surrender of the government, 456-460; Asked that Hamilton be appointed Governor, 470. —Signs as a Proprietor, iii, 38.

K

Kay, John, ii, 380—iii, 2, 21.—Speaker of the Assembly, iv, 134, 278 ; Affirmation of, 283; Payments to, 370, 371—v, 137.

Kean, Thomas M., x, 529.

Kearney, Michael, Treasurer of East Jersey, receipts and payments of, v, 142-151; Signs certificate, 155.—Recommended for Council, x, 132; Referred to, 303.

Kearney, Philip, vi. 368—vii, 108, 109, 150—ix, 16, 449; Letter to, from David Ogden, relative to the resumption of business by the lawyers under the Stamp Act, 531; Referred to, 303, 412, 414, 415, 711.

Keasbey, Edward, viii, Part II, 229, 235.

Kebble, John, Proposes to set up a manufacturer of pot-ashes in New Jersey, iii, 304; Report of the Commissioners of Customs on his pro position, 329; Notice of, 329; Petition of, 342, 343; Report on, 343; Proposal of, for the manufacture of pot-ashes in New Jersey, 344, 346.

Keith, George, i, 480; Notice of, 517; Locating the 41st degree of north latitude on Hudson's River, 520.—Reference to map of, ii, 10, 15, 16, 23, 33, 417—iv 412, 414, 424—vi, 155, 156—viii, Part I, 247—x, 426.

Keith, Sir William, Threatened by the Indians, v, 114: Letter from, to the Lords of Trade, relative to certain manufactures in the Plantations, 203; Discourse on the state of the Plantations, 214; Letter to, from Thomas Lowndes, respecting the manufacture of pot and pearl ashes in the Plantations, 245; Answer from, to the same, 246;

Urged by Rev. William Skinner to apply for the Government of New Jersey, 435; Applies for the same, 446; Notice of, 447; Memorial of, relative to the necessity of separating the Government of New Jersey from that of New York, 450.

Kelly, Andrew, Affidavit of, relative to the riot at Perth Amboy, vi, 468.

Kelly, Isaac, x, 718.

Kelly, William, Recommended for the Council of New Jersey, x, 132.

Kemble, Peter, viii, Part I, 43, 103, 107, 188.—Member of Council, ix, 274; Named as one of the Commissioners for trying pirates, 283; Referred to, 511—x, 561.

Kemble, Robert, i, 268.

Kendall, Thomas, i, 288.

Kennedy, Archibald, v, 197.—Named as one of the commissioners to try pirates, ix, 283; Complaint of, relative to the common lands of Bergen, 459; Notice of, 460; Letter from Governor Franklin, relative to his complaint, 461; State of facts concerning the same, 463; Letter from William Bayard, relative thereto, 467, 471; Letter from John Berrien, relative thereto, 470; Deposition of William Bayard, in the same matter, 472; Reasons why his claim was not admitted, 474; Writes to Governor Franklin, relative to the Stamp Act, 512; Referred to, 641.

Kensey, John, i, 291.

Kent, Ely, vi, 351—vii, 457.

Kent, Helmer, x, 718.

Kent, Stephen, i, 128.

Kent, Thomas, i, 269.

Kent, William, i, 268.

Keppell, Commodore, ix, 277.

Kerpright, Mr., vii, 323, 324.

Ketchel, Samuel, vii, 32.

Keyse, John, ii, 317.

Kidd, Captain Robert, ii, 115, 284, 287, 362, 366, 401.

Kiel, John, Recommended for Surveyor-General of New Jersey, iv, 78; Referred to, 139.

Kill von Kull, i, 14, 151.

Killingworth, Thomas, ii, 384—iii, 215, 216.

Kimbol (Kemble), Peter, Recommended for the Council, vi, 233, 238; Pall-bearer of Governor Morris, 368.—Referred to, vii, 5; Member of Governor Belcher's Council, 6, 11, 86, 88, 98, 183, 188, 191, 237, 335, 343, 455, 503, 541.

King, John, vii, 182—x, 413, 717.

Kinney, Thomas, Sheriff, x, 413, 419.

Kingsland, Captain, Proposed for the Council, iii, 340.

Kingsland, Edmund, x, 718.

Kingsland, William, Plantation and effects ordered to be sold by the Dutch Governor Colve, i, 138.

Kinowl, Lord, viii, Part I, 93.

Kinsey, Chief-Justice, of Pennsylvania, vii, 59.

Kinsey, James, x, 370, 414, 458, 546, 575, 576, 680, 730.

Kinsey, John, Speaker of the Assembly, iv, 253; Fees to, 370, 371—v, 146, 150.

Kinsey, John (2d), Member of Assembly from Middlesex County, v, 262; Chosen Speaker, 270; Referred to, 288; Signs petition to the King for a separate government for New Jersey, 443.

Kirby, Benjamin, iv, 310.

Kirby, Richard, iv, 309.

Kirby, William, iv, 310.

Kirk, Gabriel, i, 51.

Kirkbride, James (Joseph), iv, 390; One of the commissioners for running partition line, 394, 453.

Kirkbride, Joseph, ix, 395.

Kirkbridge, Joseph, iii, 165.

Kit Marius, Indian Chief, i, 182.

Kitchell, Samuel, i, 134.

Kite (Kight), Robert, Mayor of London, x, 4, 7.

Klasen, Hendrick, ii, 327.

Knapp, Henry, iv, 10.

Knapp, Thomas, Autograph, v, 510.—Vice-President of West New Jersey Society, vii, 327.

Knott, David, x, 600.

Knowles, Governor, vii, 68.

Knowles, William, x, 113.

Kollock, Shepherd, ix, 627, 628.

Krigiers, Captain, i, 179.

Kuyf, Captain, i, 130, 133, 143.

Kuyper, Justice, ix, 470.

L.

Lackerouse, Michael, i, 269.

Lacy, Edward, ii, 226.

Ladd, John, viii, Part II, 151, 232, 233.—Recommended for the Council, ix, 127, 387, 388; Appointed Surrogate, 359; Member of Council, 394; Notice of, 395; In Council, 509.—Dead, x, 224; Notice of, 224.

Ladds, William, vii, 326, 327.

Laing, William, ii, 275.

Laken, John, Grand Juror for Essex County, iii, 496.

Lamb, John, ii, 42-61, 65-73, 79, 129.

Lamb, Matthew, Letter to, from the Lords of Trade, relative to an act of New Jersey, obliging Sheriffs to give security, vii, 296; Reply to the same, 329.—Official letter to, ix, 351, 443.

Lambert, Colonel, ix, 277.

Lambert, John, i, 268—ii, 325.

Lambert, Roger, ii, 129, 325.

Lambert, Thomas, i, 268, 523—ii, 148—iv, 452—v. 133, 139, 141, 211, 316.

Lamson, Eleazar, vi, 245—vii, 444, 457.

Lamson, Eley, ii, 339.

Lamson, Thomas, vi, 351—vii, 457.

Landevinter, Peter, ii, 396.

Lands, and titles to, See Colonies, etc.

Lane, Cornelius, x, 600, 667.

Lane, Henry, v, 323—vii, 145, 320.

Lane, Sir Thomas, ii, 41-61, 65-73, 76, 78, 79, 87, 91, 92, 95, 99, 149, 164, 165, 171, 186-194, 199, 258, 270, 299, 300, 302, 321, 376, 408, 410; Letter to, from, Secretary Popple, 428; Referred to, 448; Signs surrender of the Government, 456-460; Recommends Andrew Hamilton for Governor, 470; Letter to, from Secretary Popple, 473.—Notice of, iii, 38; Signs as Proprietor, 82, 95, 302; Refuses to sign, 314.—Referred to, vi, 314—vii, 320, 326.

Langstaffe (Longstaff), John, ii, 316, 326, 396.—Contributes to a supposed Cornbury Fund, iii, 200; Petition of the House of Representatives against said Fund, 206.

Langdon, Harry, i, 345.

Laning, John, x, 531.

Lannoy, Peter de, ii, 470.

Lantin, Captain L., i, 517.

La Prairie (Lapriere), See Vanquellin.

Larta, Nicholas, ii, 396.

Laswall, William, i, 270.

Laten, John, vii, 426.

Laten, William, ii, 396.

Lattouch, Mr., vii, 322, 323, 326.

Laurence, See Lawrence.

Laurence, Andries, iii, 351.

Laurence, Thomas, ii, 326.

Law, Report on an act for enforcing an ordinance made for establishing fees and regulating the practice of, v, 377-395; Petition against said act, 403.—Act relative to the practice of, ix, 490.

Laws, Revision of, viii, Part I, 27, 103.

Lawrence, Benjamin, ii, 396—iv, 310.

Lawrence, Elisha, ii, 365, 397—iii, 212—iv, 37, 310, 370—v, 147—ix, 343 —x, 302.

Lawrence, Elisha (2d), x, 459.

Lawrence, James, ii, 326, 396.

Lawrence, John, i, 148, 150, 156—ii, 106, 237, 396—iii, 213—iv, 111, 310.

Lawrence, John (2d), Instructions to, relative to boundary line between East and West Jersey, vi, 154.

Lawrence, John (3d), Recommended for Council, x, 226, 232, 275; Notice of, 302; Referred to, 307, 313; In Council, 351.
Lawrence, Joseph, ii, 397—iv, 310—vi, 245—vii, 457.
Lawrence, Richard, iv, 310—x, 459.
Lawrence, Robert, iv, 310—vi, 202, 203—vii, 29—viii, Part II, 16, 72—ix, 13.
Lawrence, William, ii, 327, 396, 487—iii, 216—iv, 126, 253, 370—v, 60, 142, 144, 146, 149.
Lawrence, William, Jr., 270, 396, 486.
Lawrie (Lowry, Lawry), Gawen, Quintipartite deed to, from Sir George Carteret, i, 205; Instructions from, and others, to their Commissioners in West Jersey, 219; Names to Concessions, etc.. to West Jersey, 268; Grant to him and others from the Duke of York, 324; Referred to, 377; Among the twenty-four East Jersey Proprietors, 383; Commission of, as Deputy Governor of East Jersey, 423; Instructions to, 426, 434; Referred to, etc., as a Proprietor, 442, 448; Notice of, 455; Instructions to, from Robert Barclay and other Proprietors, 459; Interested in goods shipped to East Jersey, 467, 469; Instructions to, 476; Letter to, from William Dockwra, 486; Censured by the Proprietors of East Jersey, 492; Order to inspect the accounts of, 503; Referred to, 517, 521, 528; Revocation of all his powers in East Jersey, 531.—Signs as a Proprietor, ii, 2; Referred to, 62; Disbursements by, on account of East Jersey, 202, 203.—Referred to, iv, 415, 388—viii, Part I, 204.
Lawyers of New Jersey, Agree not to act under the Stamp Act, ix, 506; Meeting of, called in relation to resuming business under the Stamp Act, 531; Attitude of, toward the Stamp Act, 536, 540; Determine to resume their practice regardless of the Stamp Act, 546; Address to, by the Sons of Liberty, 547; Fees of, 605.—Complaints against, x, 148, 192; Agreement among, to prevent unnecessary litigation on account of the disturbed state of the Colonies, 589.
Lawtone, William, ii, 332.
Layden (Ployden?), Sir Edward, i, 272.
Layng, Will., iv, 9.
League Island, v, 42, 44.
Leake, John, ix, 18.
Leaming, Aaron, vi, 202, 203—vii, 336, 502—viii, Part I, 74; Part II, 150, 155, 233—ix, 129.
Leaming, Jeremiah, viii, Part II, 153, 229, 235.
Leaming (Learning), Thomas, x, 207-212, 282.
Leasy Point, x, 515.
Lechmere, Thomas, Surveyor-General of Customs, vii, 6.
Leck, William, Opinion of, on Elizabethtown Patent, i, 272.
Lecroa (Lacroa), Michael, i, 116.
Lee, Sir George, viii, Part I, 23.

Lee, John, x, 717.

Lee, Richard Henry, x, 530.

Lee, Samuel, x, 364, 365, 367.

Lee, William Phillips, ix, 226.

Leeds, Daniel, i, 270—ii, 305; Recommended to be one of the Council, 417, 429, 486; Objected to, 488; Appointed member of the Council, 507—iii, 2, 83, 340; Objects to certain representatives in the Assembly, 88, 112, 137, 150; Referred to, 160, 178, 279, 463; Signs, 290, 367; Again objected as a member of Council, 301; Letter from, William Penn, respecting, 303; Removal asked for, 309—iv, 41; Recommended for Council, 133; Referred to, 143, 145; Protest of, with others, against the Proceedings of the Council of Proprietors of West Jersey, 146; Referred to, 149; Signs, 309; Referred to, 313.

Leeds, Japhet, iv. 147.

Leeds, Philo, iv, 147.

Leeds, Tilan, v, 68.

Leek, Samuel, x, 531.

Leete, Samuel, Presentment of, against John Fenwicke, i. 186, 238.

Le Fetra, Edmund, i, 51.

Lefevre, Hypolite, i, 227, 269, 414.

Legislature of New Jersey, See New Jersey and Assembly.

Leigh, Egerton, ix, 621.

Leisler, Jacob, ix, 337.

Leister, Mr., vi, 386.

Le Montes, John, v, 153.

Lenex, John, viii, Part I, 137.

Lennox, Lord, ix, 15.

Lentin, Josiah, Testimony relating to Elizabethtown Purchase, i, 504.

Leonard, Elijah, x, 717.

Leonard, Henry, ii, 333—iv, 142.—Recommended for the Council, v, 318.—Captain, vi, 425.

Leonard, John, ii, 332.

Leonard, John (2d), x, 207–212, 282.

Leonard, Joseph, Captain, ix, 184.

Leonard, Nathaniel. In charge of Beacon on Neversink Highlands, vi, 374.

Leonard, Samuel, ii, 328-332.—Letter to, from William Penn, ii, 318; Note on, 318; Sits with Governor Hamilton in Monmouth County Court, 362; President of Monmouth County Court, 364; Signs, 386; Recommended for Council, 417, 429, 431; Objected to, 488; Remarks concerning, 502; Appointed member of the Council, 507.—Dead, iii, 1, 40, 78.

Leonard, Samuel (2d), iv, 10—v, 62, 146, 150—vi, 139, 202, 203—viii, Part I, 200; Part II, 228—ix, 360.

Leonard, Thomas, iv, 9, 377—v, 147, 151.—Recommended for Council, vi, 233, 238; Pall-bearer of Governor Morris, 368.—Member of Council,

vii, 5, 6, 86, 88, 98; Referred to, 128; Autograph, 184; Signs, 237; In Council, 343, 347, 455, 503, 618, 644—viii, Part I, 16.—Warrant to, Part II, 152.—Resigns his seat in Council, ix, 127; Notice, 152.

Leonards, Thomas, i, 50.

Lesenby, Henry, i, 50.

Leslie, George, ii, 186.

Letts, William, i, 84, 85.

Leveridge, Mr., ii, 239.

Levy, Benjamin, Signs the surrender of the Government, ii, 456-460.

Levy, Moses, iv, 344, 345.

Lewis, Thomas, Signs the surrender of the Government, ii, 456–460—iii, 95.

Lewinz, Sir Cresswell, Opinion of, on the liability of East Jersey to New York for customs, ii, 134.

Lexington and Concord, How the news of the affair at, were carried through New Jersey, x, 587; Effect of the affair at, in New Jersey, 603; Affidavits relating to, 612, 615.

Ligge, Coll, i, 353.

Light Money, i, 151—x, 264.

Ligonier, Sir John, viii, Part I, 23.

Linch, Dennis, iv, 45.

Lindsley, Ebenezer, vi, 351.

Lindsley, John, ii, 336.

Lindsley, Josiah, vi, 351—vii, 435, 457.

Lindsley, Samuel, x, 717.

Lindsley, Captain, x, 375.

Ling, Mathew, iii, 64—vii, 166.

Link, Henry, x, 717.

Lippet, Moses, ii, 366, 397—iii, 212.

Lipincot, John, Contributes to the supposed Cornbury Fund, iii, 212.

Lipincot, Richard, Contributes to the supposed Cornbury Fund, iii, 213.

Lipincott, Samuel, Jr., iii, 164.

Lippincott, Frederick J., ii, 148.

Lippincott, James, v, 187.

Lippincott, Jerome, v, 187.

Lippincott, Joseph, ii, 397.

Lippincott, Remembrance, ii, 397.

Lippincott, Restore, ii, 380.

Lippincott, Richard, i, 413.

Lispenard, Leonard, ix, 18.

Little, Daniel, vii, 421, 422.

Little (Littell), John, ii, 129, 326—vi, 373—x, 600, 667.

Little, Peter, x, 717.

Little, Robert, ii, 334, 339—iii, 496.

Little, Samuel, ii, 334, 339—iii, 496.

Livingston, James, viii, Part I, 123; Part II, 14.

Livingston, Philip, v, 197.—Speaker of the Council of New York, vii, 142—x, 530.

Livingston, Robert, ii, 369.

Livingston, William, x, 345, 467, 530, 546, 575.

Livingstons, The, viii, Part I, 93.

Loade, John, ii, 327.

Locke, John, One of the Lords of Trade, ii, 185, 304.

Lochart, Alexander, iv, 309.

Lockhart, Gawen, iv, 186.

Lockhart, George, i, 430.

Lockhart, John, vii, 166.

Lodge, Abraham, v, 404.

Lodwick, Charles, iv, 344, 345.

Loften (Lofting, Loftnings), John, ii, 270; Petition of, relating to the Ship Hester, 311; Referred to, 342.

Logan, James, Letter from, to George Willocks, relative to the division line between the Provinces, iv, 377; Notice of, 381; Letter from, to Daniel Coxe, on the division line, 388; Member of the Pennsylvania Council, 393; Referred to, 452.

Logan, James, Letter to, from Governor Belcher, relative to a charter for the new college, vii, 124.—Referred to, x, 231.

Logan, William, vii, 130.

Logan, or Tah-gah-juti, x, 495.

Long, Peter, iii, 356.

Longfield, Cornelius, Recommended for the Council, iii, 340—iv, 133.

Longfield, Thomas, Lieutenant, ix, 187.

Longstaff, John, i, 134.

Longstreet, Garret, x, 600.

Longstreet, Samuel, x, 600.

Looker (Luke, Luker), John, ii, 129, 315, 334, 339, 397.

Looker (Luke, Luker), William, ii, 129, 327, 334, 395.

Loper, Arthur, ii, 339.

Lore, Jonathan, x, 531.

Lords of the Admiralty, Letter to, from the Earl of Bellomont, relative to taking two supposed pirates out of the custody of Governor Basse, ii, 236.

Lords Justices, Order of, referring the petition of the Proprietors of East Jersey to the Lords of Trade, ii, 169; Petition to, from the Proprietors of East Jersey, 169; Representation to, from the Lords of Trade, against the right of the Proprietors of East Jersey to establish ports, 180; Communication to, from the Lords of Trade, relative to the surrender of the Government of New Jersey by the Proprietors, 420.

Lords Proprietors, See Berkeley and Carteret.

Lords of the Treasury, Petition to, in relation to the payment of customs, ii, 163, 165; Letter to, from the Earl of Bellomont, enclosing his

proclamation, relative to ports in New Jersey, 221; Letter to, from
the Earl of Bellomont, relative to the Ship Hester, 341.
Lords of Trade, Letter to, from Governor Andros, ii, 37; Communication to, from the Proprietors of East Jersey, 90; Memorial to, from
Edward Randolph, 131; Extract from minutes of, 132; Memorial to,
from the Proprietors of the several Provinces in America, relating to
Courts of Admiralty there, 133; Letter from, to the Proprietors of
East and West Jersey, 134; Letter from, to Jeremiah Basse, requiring him to give security before being appointed Deputy Governor, 150; Letter to, from Secretary Lownds, transmitting documents referring to the payment of customs in New York, by the
people in East and West Jersey, 163; Petition of the Proprietors of
East Jersey, relating to ports, referred to them, 169; Memorial of
the state of the case submitted to, 171; Answer to their inquiries on
the subject from the Attorney-General and the Solicitor-General,
177; Representation from, to the Lords Justices, against the rights
of East Jersey to establish ports, 180; Customs to be paid in New
York by all vessels trading in Hudson's River, 200; Letter from, to
the Earl of Bellomont, relative to ports in New Jersey, 201; Letters
to, from the Earl of Bellomont, relative to the same, 216, 222, 234,
241; Petition of the Proprietors of East Jersey referred to, 254, 255;
Memorial to, from the Proprietors of West Jersey, asking the appointment of Andrew Hamilton as Governor, 257; Memorial to,
relative to the ship Hester, 259; Further memorial, 263; Representation from, to the King, informing him of their determination to
have the claim to a port in New Jersey tried in Westminster Hall,
267; Memorial to, from the Proprietors of East Jersey, relative
thereto, 268; Letter to, from the Earl of Bellomont, 271; Order
referring to them, the approval of Andrew Hamilton as Governor of
West Jersey, 275; Letter to, from Robert Quary, concerning pirates,
277; Memorial to, from the Proprietors of East Jersey, relative to a
surrender of their Government, 294; Letter from, to the Earl of
Bellomont, relative to New Jersey matters, 302; Memorial to, from
East Jersey Proprietors, relative to establishing Perth Amboy as a
Port of Entry, 308; Letter to, from Governor Basse, with an account of his administration, 310; Letter to, from the same, transmitting papers, 340; Letter to, from the same, 343, 352; Answer of
the Proprietors of East Jersey to the remonstrance of the inhabitants, referred to them, 344; Ask for the transmission of the proposed surrender of the government of East Jersey, 353; Edward
Randolph recommends them to annex East Jersey to New York, and
West Jersey to Pennsylvania, 356; Memorial to, from Jeremiah
Basse, asking for a consideration of the remonstrance of the inhabitants of East Jersey, 357; Letter from, to the Earl of Bellomont,
relative to the boundaries between New York and New Jersey, 367;
Memorial to, from Mr. Basse, relative to the surrender of the Gov-

ernment, 418; Communication from, to the Lords Justices, relative
to the surrender of the government of East and West Jersey by the
Proprietors, 420; Letter to, from Chief-Justice Atwood, 428; Letter
to, from Lewis Morris, relative to Mr. Dockwra's objections to the
appointment of Andrew Hamilton as Governor of New Jersey, 442;
Representation to the King, transmitting draft of commission, etc.,
for the Governor to be appointed over New Jersey, 448; Commission
to Lord Cornbury to proclaim Queen Anne in New Jersey, 450; The
petition of William Dockwra and Peter Sonmans against Andrew
Hamilton, referred to, 465; Petition of the Proprietors that Hamilton by appointed Governor, referred to, 468; Memorial to, from
William Dockwra and Peter Sonmans, objecting to Hamilton's appointment as Governor, 470; Draft of a letter conferring temporary
authority upon Lewis Morris, submitted by them for the signature of
the Queen, 474; Letter to, from Colonel Quary, opposing Andrew
Hamilton, 479; A similar letter to, from Surveyor-General Randolph,
481; Letter to, from Lord Cornbury, relative to proclaiming the
Queen in New Jersey, 482; Communication from, to the Queen.
recommending that some person not connected with affairs in New
Jersey be appointed Governor, 484; Letter to, from the Earl of
Nottingham, recommending a Council for New Jersey, 486; Com-
mission for Lord Cornbury as Governor of New Jersey, submitted
by, 488; Letter from, to the Earl of Nottingham, relative to the
Council of New Jersey, 502; Letter to, from Lewis Morris, 504;
Letter to, from Lord Cornbury, 536; Circular letter from, 539; Letter to Lord Cornbury, relative to the defence of New York, 541;
Letter to, from Robert Quary, relative to the trouble in New Jersey,
544.—Letter to, from Colonel Robert Quary, iii, 7; Letter to, from
Governor Cornbury, 12; Communication to, by Robert Quary, relative to New Jersey affairs, 13; Letter to, from Lord Cornbury, relative to the same, 28; Memorial to, from the Proprietors, adverse to
the appointment of Peter Sonmans and Daniel Coxe as members of
the Council, 35; Answers to the same, 39, 42, 48; Letter to, from
Robert Quary, 52; Letters to, from Lord Cornbury, 54, 64; Circular
letter from, to the Governors of Plantations, 60; Petition relative to
the title to Staten Island referred to, 61; Letter to, from Lord Cornbury, relative to New Jersey affairs, 68; Petition to, from the West
Jersey Proprietors, relative to the proceedings of Lord Cornbury, 81;
Memorial to, from Daniel Coxe and others, relative to New Jersey
affairs, 82; Complaints to, from West Jersey Proprietors, with
request that Lewis Morris be restored to the Council, 85; Letter
from, to Lord Cornbury, 99; Memorial to, proposing Peter Sonmans
for the Council, 101; Letter to, from Lord Cornbury relative to New
Jersey affairs, 103; Complaints to, from Lieutenant-Governor
Ingoldsby, concerning Lord Cornbury, 109; Gentlemen for the
Council of New Jersey proposed by, 115; Observations of, on the

memorial of the West Jersey Proprietors against Lord Cornbury, 117; Letter to, from Lord Cornbury relative to his new instructions, 119; Circular letter from, relative to the appointment of John Bridger as Surveyor of Her Majesty's woods, 122; Letter from, to Lord Cornbury, relative to New Jersey affairs, and to the complaints made against him, 124; Asked to appoint Peter Sonmans a member of Council, 126; Letters from, to Lord Cornbury, 148, 154, 159, 224; Circular letter from, with an instruction relative to the attendance of the members of the several Councils, 241; Letter to, from Lord Cornbury, on New Jersey affairs, 267; Letter to, from Colonel Quary, relative to the same, 271; Letter to, from Lord Cornbury, with an address of the Council to the Queen, objecting to the proceedings of the Assembly, 285; Submit to the Secretary of State a draft of a commission to Lord Lovelace to be Governor of New Jersey, 298; Representation of, on Lord Lovelace's instructions, 309; Communication from, to Lord Lovelace, 323; Letter to, from the Earl of Sunderland relative to Lewis Morris, 328; Reply to the same, 328; Letter to, from Lord Lovelace, 359; Letter to, from Lieutenant-Governor Ingoldsby relative to New Jersey affairs, 460; Letter to, from Colonel Nicholson and Colonel Vetch relative to the Quakers, 464; Letter to, from Lieutenant-Governor Ingoldsby relative to the proceedings of the Assembly, 467; Representation of, to the Queen, relative to the commission of Lieutenant-Governor Ingoldsby, 469; Representation of, to the Queen, relative to an act regulating Negro, Indian and Mulatto slaves, etc., in New Jersey, 473; Memorial to, with documents, relative to Lewis Morris and others, 476; Memorial to, from Proprietors of New Jersey, asking for a change in the Council, 497; Ask for the restoration of Lewis Morris to the Council of New Jersey, 499.—Letter to Governor Hunter, iv, 2; Letter to, from the same, respecting an intended meeting of the New Jersey Assembly, 11; From the same, respecting the place of meeting of said Assembly, 16; Letter to, from Governor Hunter, with documents, referring to affairs in East Jersey, 51; Reply from, to said letter, 113; Memorial to, from the New Jersey Proprietors, relative to the disputes between the Council and the Assembly, 140; Letter to, from Governor Hunter, relative to changes in the New Jersey Council, 149; Action of, in relation to the New Jersey Council, asked by Governor Hunter, 151; Communication from, to the Queen, relative to the changes in the New Jersey Council, 169; Letters to, from Governor Hunter, relative to New Jersey affairs, 171, 174; Letter from, to Governor Hunter, relative to the Council of New Jersey, 182; Letter to, from Governor Hunter, relative to New Jersey affairs, 195; Letter to, from Lord Cornbury, relative to certain acts of the New Jersey Assembly, 199; Prepare new commission for Governor Hunter, 202; Letter of, to the Bishop of London, relative to the character of missionaries, 212; Letter to,

from Governor Hunter, relative to certain acts of the New Jersey Assembly, 221; Letter from, to Governor Hunter, relative to New Jersey affairs, 227; Letters to, from Governor Hunter, relative to New Jersey affairs, 230, 255, 260, 264, 273; Memorial to, from Thomas Coram, relative to hemp and iron, 286 ; Letter to, from Governor Hunter, 311; Letter from, to the King, recommending the approval of the act allowing Quakers to affirm, 334; Letter from, to Governor Hunter, relative to his various communications, 335; Representation from, to the King, naming commissioners for trying pirates, 339; Scheme, or treatise, relating to Plantations, referred to, 345; Letter to, from Governor Hunter, relating to New Jersey affairs, 363; Representation of, to the King, relative to the petition against the Quakers, 366; Letter to, from Governor Hunter, transmitting papers, 386; Letter to, from Peter Schuyler, relating to Surveyor Jarratt, 431, 438; Letter to, from Lewis Morris, relative to the boundary line, etc., 439; Letter from, to Secretary Craggs, transmitting the commission of William Burnet as Governor of New York and New Jersey, 447.—Communication to the King, with draft of instructions to Governor Burnet, v. 1; Letter from, to Governor Burnet, relative to Secretary Smith's fees, 4; Letter to, relative to exportation of copper ore from New Jersey, 7; Letter to, from Governor Burnet, relative to the New Jersey Assembly, 8; Letter from, to the Lords of the Treasury, referring to the matter of exportation of copper ore from New Jersey, 9; Letter to, from Governor Burnet, relating to the proceedings of the Assembly and the Council of New Jersey, 10; Representation of, respecting the Islands in Delaware River, 18; Letter to, from Governor Burnet. relative to New Jersey affairs, 32; Letter from, to Governor Burnet, relative to vacancies in the New Jersey Council, 51; Memorial to, relative to improvements in the production of naval stores in the Colonies, 68; Letter from, to Governor Burnet, 70; Report to, on the proposed alterations in the Constitution of New Jersey, 72; Letter to, from Governor Burnet, relative to paper money, 75; Representation of, to the King, respecting the manner of electing representatives to the Assembly, 83; Letter to, from Governor Burnet, relative to New Jersey affairs, 104; Letter to, from Galfridus Gray, relative to encroachments of the Indians, 107, 112; Letters to, from Governor Burnet, 117; Letter from, to Governor Burnet, relative to gold and silver mines in New Jersey, 120; Letter from, to Governor Burnet, relative to paper money, 156; From the same, relative to interest money, 165; Representation from, to the King, with commissions of John Montgomerie as Governor of New York and New Jersey, 167; Letter to, from Governor Montgomerie, 167; Letter to, from Governor Burnet, transmitting documents, 181; Letter to, from Governor Montgomerie, announcing his arrival in New York, 184; Letter from, to Governor Montgomerie, relative to

interest money and paper bills, 200; Letter to, from Sir William
Keith, relative to certain manufactures, 203; Letter to, from Governor Montgomerie, relative to New Jersey affairs, 206; Representation of, to the Privy Council, relative to certain manufactures in
the Plantations, 207; Representation from, to the King, relative to
the partition line between East and West Jersey, 213; Letter
to, from Governor Montgomerie, relative to New Jersey affairs, 224;
Letter from, relative to certain acts passed by the New Jersey Assembly, 247; Letter to, from Governor Montgomerie, relative to the payment of interest money for incidental expenses, 249; Answer to the
same, 266; Informed of the death of Governor Montgomerie, 294,
295; Letter from, to Governor Montgomerie, 302; Memorial to,
from the Felt Makers' Company, 306; Letter to, from Lewis Morris,
relative to the proceedings of Governor Cosby, 349; Letter to, from
Governor Cosby, respecting certain acts of the New Jersey Assembly,
364; Address of, to the Queen, relative to the complaints against
James Alexander, Lewis Morris and Rip Van Dam, 408; Petition of
Richard Partridge for a separate Governor for New Jersey referred
to, 448; Letter to, from Lewis Morris, asserting his claims to the
Presidency of the Council of New Jersey, 472; Complaints of President Hamilton against Lewis Morris, 478; Letter from, to the Duke
of Newcastle, relative to the difficulties in New Jersey, 479; Announces the appointment of Lord Dela-Warr, as Governor of New
York and New Jersey, 490.—Representation to the King, with a
draft of commission for Lewis Morris, as Governor of New Jersey,
vi, 1; Report of, on the currency in America, 78; Report of, with
additional instructions to the Governors in America, 94–98; Report
of, relative to bills of credit, 122; Communication from, relative to
ensigns borne by ships having private commissions, 128; Letter to,
from Governor Morris, relative to New Jersey affairs, 130; Memorial
to, relative to the purchasing of lands from the Indians, 142; Petition
of the inhabitants of Elizabethtown referred to, 205; Recommendations of, for the Council, 237; Representation of, proposing the repeal of the act regulating fees, 238; Letter to, from James Alexander
and Robert Hunter Morris, giving an account of the Provinces, 419;
Representation of, respecting the petition of Mr. Partridge for liberty to issue bills of credit in New Jersey, 433; Letter to, written at
the request of President Hamilton, 446; Petition of Jonathan
Belcher referred to, 449; Report of, on said petition, 453; Death of
President Hamilton, announced to, 462.—Letter to, from the Duke
of Newcastle, relative to the instructions for Governor Belcher, vii,
1; Reply of, with a draft of commission for Governor Belcher, 2;
Informed of the arrival of Governor Belcher in his government, 29;
Letter of congratulation from, to Governor Belcher, 96; Letter to,
from Governor Belcher, relative to certain acts of the Legislature,
140; Letter to, from Governor Clinton, relative to the New York and

New Jersey division line, 159; Letter to, from Governor Belcher, 170; Petition to, from the executors of Lewis Morris to pay his salary, 171; Extracts from letters of, to Lewis Morris, relative to paper currency, 172; Reply of, to the petition of the executors of Lewis Morris, 173; Petition of, relative to the division line between New York and New Jersey, 226; Letter to, from the Council of New Jersey relative to the riots, 236; Certain queries made by, answered by Governor Belcher, 243; Letter to, from Governor Belcher, relative to the riots, 249, 293; Letter from, to Matthew Lamb, relative to an act of New Jersey, obliging Sheriffs to give security, 296; Proposals from, with regard to the disturbances in New Jersey, 311-316; Letter to, from Governor Belcher, respecting the proceedings of the Assembly, 361; Representation of the Assembly to, relative to arrears of salary due to the late Governor Morris, 359; Representation of, on the state of the Province of New Jersey, 466; Notified of the suspension from Council of John Coxe, 540; Letter from, to Governor Belcher, relative to the behavior of the Assembly, 551; Propose David Ogden as a member of the Council in place of John Coxe, 578; Propose Lewis M. Ashfield to supply a vacancy in the Council by the death of Richard Smith, 585; Object to Samuel Smith and William Morris as members of the Council, 585; Answer to the objections, from Governor Belcher, 607; Governor Belcher to, in relation to Lewis Morris Ashfield, 623.—Letter to, from Governor Belcher, relative to the Council of New Jersey, viii, Part I, 13; Memorial to, relative to the same, 18; Report of, relative to the improper publication in New Jersey of one of their orders, 28; Letter to, from Governor Belcher, relative to the proceedings of the New Jersey Council, 60; Circular letter from, to the Governors of the Colonies, 63; Accounts of various officers transmitted to, 65; Refusal of a seat in the Council to Lewis M. Ashfield, referred to, 111; Governor Belcher's course toward Mr. Ashfield, disapproved by, 124; Opinion of, on the boundaries between New York and New Jersey, 128; Governor Belcher desired by them to give aid to the missionaries for propagating the Gospel in New Jersey, 140; Circular letter from, relative to a proposed interview with the Six Nations of Indians, 156; Draft of instructions to Governors, relative to appeals in cases of error, 188; Recommend the King to allow the Governor of New Jersey to assent to the bill for the issue of £60,000 in bills of credit, 196; Proceedings of the New Jersey Council and Assembly transmitted, 287; Comments of, upon the action of the New Jersey Legislature in regard to the common defence against the French, 294; Letter from, to Lieutenant-Governor De Lancey, relative to the boundary line, 297.—Letter from, to Sir Thomas Robinson, with a plan of general defence for the Colonies, viii, Part II, 1; Memorial of Richard Partridge to, relative to emitting £70,000 in bills of credit, 95; Representation from, to the King, upon the petition of the

House of Representatives of New Jersey, relative to bills of credit,
100; Recommend Thomas Pownall as Lieutenant-Governor of New
Jersey, 102; Communication from, to the Lords Justices, relative to
the boundary between New York and New Jersey, 108; Reply of, to
letters of Governor Belcher, 124; Recommend the appointment of a
commission to arrange the boundary difficulties, 129; Recommend
the establishment of packet-boats between England and the Colonies,
138; Circular letter from, relative to the establishment of packet-
boats, 146; Queries from, to Governor Belcher, and answers from,
185; Commend the services of New Jersey in defending the country,
206; Letter from, to Governor Hardy, relative to commissions for
settling the boundary controversies, 212; Informed of the death of
James Alexander, 214; Direct Governor Belcher, if unable to attend
meetings of the Governors, to depute Lieutenaut-Governor Pownall,
215; Representation of, to the King, on the state of the different
Colonies, 216; Prepare warrant appointing William Aynsley Chief-
Justice, 247.—Letter to, from Thomas Pownall, ix, 1; Propose
Francis Bernard as Governor, 21; Report of, on a bill for issuing
£60,000 in bills of credit, 34; Report draft of instructious for Governor Bernard, 38; Refer certain questions to the Solicitor-General,
112; Report of, on a bill for emitting £89,000 in bills of credit, 113;
Representation from, to the King. relative to a law for issuing bills
of credit without a suspending clause, 147; Answer of, to several
communications from Governor Bernard, 152; Report to the Privy
Council. draft of instructions to, relative to passing bills authorizing
the emission of bills of credit, 156; Letters to, from Governor
Bernard. relative to the raising of troops and money bills, 168, 170;
Propose Nathaniel Jones to be Chief-Justice of New Jersey, 172;
Inform Governor Bernard that he has been appointed Governor of
Massachusetts, 188; Letter from, on the pretentions of R. H. Morris
to resume the office of Chief-Justice, 191; Representation from, to
the King. respecting the dispute between R. H. Morris and N. Jones
for the office of Chief-Justice, 230; Prepare a draft of a proclamation
for the Colonies. of George III as King, 241; Circular letter from, to
the Governors in North America, relative to the old seals, 243;
Instructions from, to the same, relative to alterations in the prayers
for the Royal family, 244; Give directions relative to seals for the
Colonies, 247; Informed by Governor Boone of the amicable proceedings of the last Assembly, 248; Directed to prepare warrants for continuing Christopher Coates and Joseph Worrell as Secretary and Attorney-General of New Jersey, 257; Proposition of, that Josiah Hardy be
appointed Governor of New Jersey, approved, 259; Informed by Governor Boone in regard to raising additional troops, and other matters, 260; Representation of, relative to the dispute for the office of
Chief-Justice of New Jersey, 264; Present instructions for Governor
Hardy, 272; Present to the King the names of persons to be commis-

sioners for trying pirates, 282; Draft instructions to the Governor relative to the alterations in the prayers for the Royal family, 302; Prepare
draft of instructions to the Governors relative to interferences with
the Indians, and the tenure of commissions to judges and other
officers, 321; Recommend the disapproval of two acts passed in
New Jersey in April, 1761, 331; Ask for the removal of Governor
Hardy, 360; Informed by Governor Hardy of the death of Andrew
Johnson and recommended to appoint Stephen Skinner as his successor as Treasurer, 366; Present draft of alterations in the prayers
for the Royal family, 375; Do not object to issuing certain sums of
paper money for providing a house for the Governor, 396; Representation of, relative to hemp, paper money, duties upon beaver skins
and whale fins, 405; Report draft of instructions in regard to fees
taken in the several offices of Government in the American Colonies,
440; Propose Frederick Smyth and James Parker for the Council of
New Jersey, 442; Propose the repeal of an act for rendering void the
lottery made by Peter Gordon, 443; Approve the conduct of Governor Franklin, and do not object to a duty on the importation of
negroes, 444; To Governor Franklin respecting marriage licenses,
520; Transmit to the Duke of Grafton copies of papers relating to
the riots growing out of the Stamp Act, 527; Report the annual expense of the Colonies, and their indebtedness at the end of the late
war, 533; Require from the several Governors an account of the
manufactures in their respective governments, 563; Propose commissioners for settling boundary line between New York and New
Jersey, 623; Announce to Governor Franklin the King's displeasure
with the Assembly for not obeying the Act of Parliament in regard
to mutiny and desertion, 636.—Recommend the repeal of the act
relative to commissioners for supplying barracks, x, 26; Recommend the disallowance of the act for issuing £100,000 in bills of
credit, 106; Also the act relative to the common lands in the township of Bergen, 188; Representation of, in relation to an act regulating the practice of the law in New Jersey, 199; To Governor
Franklin, relative to acts of the Assembly concerning creditors,
and concerning aliens, 300; Present to the King a draft of instructions to Governors relative to the naturalization of aliens, divorces
and title to lands, 410, 411; Recommend Francis Hopkins for the
Council of New Jersey, 455.
Lost, Francis, iv, 188.
Lot, Benthal, i, 49.
Lotteries, Peter Gordon's, ix, 443, 446, 458, 487.—Governors of the Colonies instructed in regard to raising of money by, x, 104, 108; Obser-
vations of Governor Franklin upon the act relative to, 387; Considered by the King, 416; Report of Richard Jackson upon, 508.
Loudoun (Lowden, Loudon), Earl of, viii, Part I, 93—viii, Part II, 206;
Appointed commander-in-chief of all the forces in America, 209;

Referred to, 220, 222, 241; Notified that no further embargo is to be laid on corn or other grain, 248; Informed of the death of Governor Belcher, 259, and objections of John Reading to assume the chief authority, 259; Referred to, 267—ix, 17.

Loughenner, Abraham, x, 718.

Love, John, ii, 42–61, 65–73, 79.

Lovelace, Governor Francis, i, 72, 76; Letter from, to Captain Carr, reproving him for neglecting his duty in regard to the Indian murders at Matiniconk Island, 79; Letter to, from the Duke of York, confirming the grant to Berkeley and Carteret, 97, 108; Referred to, 121.

Lovelace, Lord John, Appointed Governor of New Jersey, iii, 298, 309; Instructions to, as Governor of New Jersey, 316; Communication to, from the Lords of Trade, 323; Letter from, to the Lords of Trade, 359; Notice of, 359; Speech of, to the Assembly, 361; Address of the Assembly to, 362; Address to, from the Assembly, condemning Peter Sonmans, 374; Address to, from the same, relative to Peter Fauconnier, 379; From the same, to the same, expressing their want of confidence in the Council, 379; Address of congratulation to, from Lewis Morris, 380; Verses ridiculing said address, 381–385; Address of the Lieutenant-Governor and Council of New Jersey to, relative to the proceedings of the Assembly, 390; Referred to, 457, 461, 464; Notice of, 466; Referred to, 469, 497, 500—iv, 24, 47, 77, 298— x, 225.

Lovelace, Lady, iv, 10, 46, 131, 371.

Lovelace, Thomas, i, 76.

Loveridge, John, iii, 448, 453.

Lovett, Jonathan, iv, 310.

Lovet, Samuel, i, 269, 288.

Low, Isaac, x, 530, 561, 587.

Low, John, vi, 294, 316, 317, 356, 408—vii, 18, 48, 64, 123, 127, 198, 474 —viii, Part II, 158, 174, 177, 182.

Lowe, Joseph, iv, 344, 345.

Lowerus, Henry, x, 718.

Lowndes, Thomas, Letter from, to Sir William Keith, respecting the manufacture of pot and pearl ashes in the Plantations, v, 245; Answer to the same, 246.

Lownds, William, Secretary to the Lords Commissioners of the Treasury, ii, 163, 165; Letters to, from Secretary Popple, 168, 244.—Referred to, iii, 329; Letter from, relative to the petition of John Keble, 341, 347.

Lloyd, David, ii, 122.

Lloyd, John, iv, 113.

Lloyd, Jo., iv, 344, 345.

Lowrensi, Laurence, ii, 326.

Lubertse, John, ii, 326.

Lucar, William, Affidavit of, in support of the remonstrance of the Assembly against Governor Cornbury, iii, 199; Referred to, 201, 211.

Lucas, John, i, 289.

Lucas, Nicholas, Quintipartite deed to, from Sir George Carteret, i, 205; Instructions from, and others, to their Commissioners in West Jersey, 219; Name to concessions, etc., to West Jersey, 268; Grant to him and others from the Duke of York, 324, 386.—Referred to, ii, 62, 388.

Lucas, Robert, i, 289.

Ludington, Thomas, ii, 336.

Ludwell, Colonel, ii, 120.

Luke, John, ii, 315.

Luke, William, ii, 315.

Lunatics, Governors of Colonies authorized to issue commissions for the care and custody of, x, 370, 371; Governor Franklin in relation to, 382.

Lurting, Robert, v, 153, 154.

Luse, Zepheniah, Captain, ix, 185, 186.

Lydall, Thomas, vii, 427.

Lyell, David, ii, 171, 177, 186-193, 198, 213, 263; Surrenders the Government of East Jersey, 387; Signs the surrender of the Government, 456-460; Objected to as a member of Council, 488.—West Jersey Proprietor, iii, 314.—Recommended for the Council, iv, 63; Notice of, 63; Recommended for the Council, 217, 227; Member of Council, 253, 299; Referred to, 313, 334; One of the Commissioners to try pirates, 340; Payments to, 370, 371; Referred to, 373, 394.—Member of Council, v, 3, 34; Money paid to, 135, 143, 146, 148, 151.—Dead, vi, 352.

Lyell, Fenwick, v, 155.—Member of Governor Morris' Council, vi, 14, 15, 109; Deceased, 237.

Lyman, Major-General Phineas, second in command to Major-General Johnston, viii, Part II, 164.

Lynch, Thomas, x, 530.

Lyndsley, Ebenezer, vii, 458.

Lyndsley, Elisha, v, 351—vii, 458.

Lyon, Benjamin, ii, 129, 326, 334, 339—iii, 199, 496.

Lyon, Ebenezer, ii, 129, 334, 397—iii, 486—v, 155.

Lyon, Eliphalet, x, 717.

Lyon (Lyen), Henry, i, 306, 320—ii, 129, 327.

Lyon, Isaac, vi, 402.

Lyon, Jacob, x, 718.

Lyon, Joseph, ii, 123, 327, 334, 339, 396—iii, 199, 211, 496.

M.

McConnel, John, x, 718.
McConnell, Thomas, Affidavit of, respecting the Newark riots, vi, 430.
McCook, ———, x, 520.
McDonald, William, Captain, ix, 186.
McEleson, Joamis, ii, 327.
McEvers, John, vi, 169-171—ix, 179.
Machielson, Elias, iii, 483; Justice of the Peace for Essex County, 495.
McKay, James, vii, 423.
Mackdowalle, Alexander, v, 155.
McKean, Rev. Robert, ix, 338, 340.
McKean, Thomas, x, 728.
McKeilson, Elias, ii, 313, 333.
Mackelson, Enoch, Member of the Assembly, iii, 295.
McKenzie, Æneas, iv, 174; Certificate of, in behalf of Thomas Gordon,
     attacked by Jacob Henderson, 181.
McKenzie, Sir George, ix, 337.
Mackhackamack, viii, Part I, 207; Riots near to, 208, 209.
Mackinsey, Thomas, iv, 310.
McKnight, Charles, x, 345.
McPherson, Gillis, x, 717.
McRanke, Edward, x, 717.
McUrdy, James, x, 717.
McWhertor, Alexander, x, 345.
Macy, George, i, 369.
Maddocks, John, i, 269, 414.
Madge, Charles, ii, 47.
Madge, Humphrey, ii, 47.
Magie, John, x, 717.
Magriger, Patrick, An East Jersey Proprietor, i, 460.
Mahurin, Seth, x, 718.
Mair, Arthur, ix, 365.
Major, Mr., His Majesty's Chief Engraver of seals, ix, 247.
Maker, Joseph, Jr., ii, 396.
Mall, Jorat, ii, 396.
Malows, Henry, iii, 355.
Malster, William, i, 227, 283, 284, 414.
Manamowaone, i, 16, 18.
Maneten, Lands at, sold by John Fenwick, i, 413.
Manickty, Indian Chief, i, 182.
Manning (Mannen), Benjamin, ii, 316, 326, 397—iii, 486, 487.
Manning, James, ii, 326, 396.
Manning, John, ii, 327, 397.
Manning (Mannen), Joseph, ii, 316, 326, 396—iii, 486.
Manufactures, Letter relative to, from Sir William Keith, v, 203; Letter

respecting the same, from another source, 204; Representation by the Lords of Trade, relative to, 207; Memorial, asking that hats worn in the Colonies be all made in Great Britain, 306; Memorial against laws prejudicial to manufactures in Great Britain, 308.—Promotion of, viii, Part 1, 108, 109; Quality and sorts of New Jersey, Part II, 82.—Suppressing those prejudicial to commerce, ix, 273; Disadvantages to, in England, 420; Circular letter, relative to, 563; Of pig and bar iron, 583.—In New Jersey, x, 29, 442.

Marcelissen, Peter, i, 125.

March, George, i, 50.

March, Hugh, i, 50.

Marinus, John, x, 718.

Markham, William, ii, 120.

Marlow, Gregory, i, 239.

Marriages, births and burials, x, 452.

Marriage licences, ix, 504, 520.

Marriott, Abraham, v, 187.

Marriot, Isaac, i, 269.

Mars, Joseph, ii, 326.

Marsh, John, i, 465—ii, 326.

Marsh, Robert, ii, 129.

Marsh, Samuel, i, 50, 82.

Marshall, John, iv, 310.

Martin, David, Letter from. to Governor Belcher, relative to the riots in Hunterdon County, vii, 86.

Martin, Hugh, vii, 606.

Martin, Josiah, ix, 283.

Martin, Richard, i, 480.

Martin, Samuel, x, 717.

Martin, Sarah, Affidavit of, relative to the riot at Perth Amboy, vi. 469 —vii, 449.

Martyn, John, i, 82.

Maryland. Quota of troops from, for the defence of New York, ii, 134; Illegal trading in, 360.—Contribution from, for the fortification on the northern frontier, viii, Part I, 194, 196.

Maskell, Daniel, x, 531.

Maskell, Thomas, iv, 215—x, 531.

Mason, John, v, 133, 137, 141.

Mason, Thomas, v, 133, 137, 141.

Massacher, John, vii, 372, 373, 444.

Massachusetts, Illegal trade with, ii, 123, 361; Quota of troops for the defence of New York, 134—viii, Part I, 195; Raising troops, Part II, 128; Controversies between it and New York and New Jersey, 212.— Letter of the Speaker of the House of Representatives, denounced by the King, x, 14; Governor Franklin, relative to the same, 34, 36; Secretary Hillsborough, relative to the same, 45, 58.

Master, Frances, i, 51.
Master, William, i, 269.
Mathamek, i, 1.
Mather, Increase, vii, 618.
Mathews, Richard, i, 268.
Mathews, Thomas, Charges against, i, 416, 420; Proclamation of Governor Penn against, 422.
Mathews, Vincent, vi, 166.
Mathie, John, iv, 10.
Matiniconck Island, Indian murders at, i, 72, 74; Lease of, to Robert Stacy, 286; Petition in favor of Henry Jacobs, tenant in possession of, 287; Referred to, 417—x, 515.
Matlock, William, i, 288—v, 187.
Matson, Peter, ii, 146.
Mattano, i, 16, 18.
Matthews, Captain Peter, ii, 113, 255, 399.
Mattiven, James, x, 273.
Mattowacks (Matawacks), or Long Island, i, 3, 157—x, 120.
Mattulx, Luis, i, 51.
Mavericke, Samuel, Letter from, to Lord Arlington, relative to the grants to Berkeley and Carteret, i, 57.
Maxwell, William, Ensign, ix, 185, 187.
Mayo, Richard, ii, 42–62, 66–74, 79.
Meaker (Meeker), Benjamin, ii, 129, 326, 334, 397—iii, 199, 211.
Meaker (Meeker), John, ii, 129, 334, 339, 396—iii, 201, 486, 496.
Meaker (Meeker), Joseph, i, 82, 84—ii, 129, 326, 334, 397—iii, 202, 210.
Meaker (Meeker), William, i, 50, 65; Indicted for riotous conduct, i, 82, 84; Letter relative to his conduct, from Lords Berkeley and Carteret, to the Governor and Council of New Jersey, 104; Complaint against Samuel Moore, 149; Petition from, 320; Case of, against William Pardon, 334; Note on, 334; Referred to, 336, 337—ii, 339—iii, 496.
Meckenzie (McKinzie), Sir George, An East Jersey Proprietor, i, 441, 457, 460, 463.
Meckenzie, Keneth, i, 530.
Medcalfe, Matthew, ii, 148.
Meech, Thomas, ii, 481.
Meekat, John, ii, 326.
Meeker (Miaker), Timothy, vi, 351—vii, 458.
Meeker, See also Meaker.
Megie, John, ii, 129, 326, 397.
Mehelm, John, x, 458, 479, 697.
Mehemickwon, Indian King, iv, 277.
Mekowetick, i, 1.
Melfort, Earl of, An East Jersey Proprietor, i, 490, 499, 500, 508, 513, 528—ii, 10, 26, 32, 202.
Mellechap, i, 369.

Mellin, Robert, Difficulties with Peter Sonmans, iii, 376, 423-429, 447, 452.
Melven, James, ii, 332.
Melyn (Moleyn), Jacob, i, 122, 128, 133.
Menville (Mienville, Monviele), Gabriel, ii, 106, 237.
Mercell, William, ii, 396.
Merret, Isaac, Recommended for Council of Governor Hunter, iii, 498.
Merrett, William, i, 521—ii, 326.
Merrick, William, ii, 226, 313.
Merry, Mr., iv, 152.
Meservie, Captain, i, 317, 318.
Mew, Richard, i, 268; An East Jersey Proprietor, 366, 383, 424, 433,
    434, 437, 442, 446, 448, 451, 454, 462, 474, 482, 483, 529—ii, 205.
Meyer, E., i, 269.
Mice, Pier, ii, 397.
Michell, Archibald, ii, 148.
Michel (Mitchell), Charles, ii, 42-61, 65-73, 79, 99; Signs the surrender
    of the government, 456-460; Asks the appointment of Andrew Ham-
    ilton as Governor, 470.—Signs Memorial, iv, 396.
Michel, Charles, Jr., A West Jersey Proprietor, iii, 95, 498.
Michel (Mitchell), Francis, ii, 42-62, 66-74, 79; Signs the surrender of
    the government, 456-460; Asks the appointment of Andrew Hamil-
    ton as Governor, 470.—Signs, iii, 38, 82, 95, 302, 498—iv, 141.
Michell, Richard, i, 83, 84.
Michel, Robert, ii, 42-61, 65-73, 76, 79, 88, 92, 95, 99, 186-194, 258, 276,
    300, 302; Signs the surrender of the government, 456-460; Asks the
    appointment of Andrew Hamilton as Governor, 470.—Signs as a
    Proprietor, iii, 38, 51, 82, 95, 302; Refuses to sign Sonmans' Com-
    mission, 314, 498.—Referred to, iv, 141.
Michelses, Hartman, ii, 326.
Mickle, John, v, 133, 139, 141, 211—vi, 202.
Mickle, William, viii, Part II, 151.
Micklethwart, Joseph, Signs the surrender of the government, ii, 456-
    460.—Memorial of, iii, 95.
Mico, Joseph, Autograph, v, 510.—Referred to, vii, 326.
Middlesex County, Minutes of the Court of, ii, 315.—Petition of, to the
    Assembly, against Peter Sonmans, iii, 445; Report on said petition,
    447.—Further petition of, iv, 8; Freeholders' books altered, 97-99;
    Petition of, against the election of Thomas Farmer, 186; Taxes, 368.
    —Petition of, for a separate Governor, v, 444.—List of rioters in, vi,
    455; Charge to the Grand Jury of, 456.—The jail of broken open,
    viii, Part I, 43; Petition of land owners in, 54-56.
Middleton, Henry, x, 529.
Middleton, Hugh, iv, 36, 125.
Middleton, Nathan, v, 187.
Middleton, Thomas, v, 187.
Middletown, Oath of allegiance taken by the inhabitants, i, 51; Proclam-

ation of the Governor and Council relative to the inhabitants of, 58; Warrant from Governor Carteret for the seizure of a paper against the laws, signed by the inhabitants of, 61; Confirmation to, of certain privileges, 83; Relations with the Council of New Netherlands, 123, 125, 127, 129, 130, 134, 135, 142, 143, 333.—Courts at, ii. 362, 364.

Mifflin, John, Jr., i, 289.

Mifflin, John, Sr , i, 289.

Mifflin, Thomas, x, 529, 574.

Miggle, Archibald, ii, 380.

Miles (Myles), John, ii. 129, 326, 334, 330, 395—iii, 496.

Military Affairs, The immediate dispatch of troops to Albany urged by Governor Hunter, iv, 135; Supplies for troops, 135; Discharging volunteers, 136; Troops at Amboy, 137; Troops and money raised by Governor Hunter for the Canadian expedition, 138.—Condition of militia in New Jersey, v, 319.—Number of fighting men, including regular forces, in the Colonies. vi, 89, 90; Troops raised in New Jersey, 99, 102; Abstract of a bill for settling and better regulating the militia of New Jersey, 191; Action of the Assembly on said bill, 247-249; Troops raised for the expedition to Canada, 371, 378; Number of men in the several companies under command of Colonel Peter Schuyler, 424; Mutiny of the troops under command of Colonel Schuyler, 447; Payment of the troops sent against Canada, 451.— The New Jersey Assembly vote £15,000 for the support of Colonel Schuyler's regiment, viii, Part II, 11; Four new regiments to be raised, 17; Order settling the rank of officers serving with the Provincial forces in North America, 29; Number of militia in New Jersey, 84; The King intends to augment the regiments in America. 92; A regiment raised by the Assembly, 106; Governor Shirley in relation to, 111; Reported defeat of General Braddock, 117-120; Letter from Governor Belcher to Governor Dinwiddie, relative to, 122; Message from Governor Belcher relative to, 128; Condition of the forces on the frontier, 131; Governor Belcher relative to raising additional troops, 135; Supplies for the troops, 140; Movements of the same, 143; Letter from Governor Belcher relative to, 148; Invasion of the Province, 156; Colonels of militia ordered to muster their regiments, 157; Threatened invasion of the French and Indians, 158; Movement of troops, 160; Condition of, 161. 162, 168; Colonels of regiments directed to move to the Delaware River, 174; Defence of the frontier, 179; Letter from Governor Belcher relative to, 180; Augmentation of the forces in New Jersey asked for, 201; Earl of Loudoun appointed Commander-in-Chief of all the forces in America. 209; Additional troops called for, 241.—Warrant settling the rank of Provincial officers, ix, 10; Invasion of Canada, 111; Money required for continuing the war, 137; Estimate for raising, paying and clothing 1,000 men, 143; Preparations urged for the invasion of Canada,

149; Act for raising 1,000 men passed, 166, 168; Amount of money raised for purposes of the war, 167; The New Jersey regiment arrives at Albany, 174; Defeat of the French army in Canada, 183; Officers of the New Jersey regiments in the French war, 184-187; Comments of Governor Bernard on the bill for raising troops in the Province, 224; David Price ordered to impress vessels to transport troops to New Jersey, 246; Act passed for raising additional troops in New Jersey, 260, 261; Part of the New Jersey regiments continued, 299; Circular letter to the Governors relative to recruiting the regular regiments in America, 330; Condition of the militia in New Jersey, 367; Forces raised for marching against the Indians, 398, 400, 428, 431; Letter from General Gage relative to, 432; Inequality of the expense of quartering the troops in the Colonies, 642.—Law for providing quarters for the King's troops, x, 12; Commissioners for supplying barracks, 26; Act of Legislature for quartering the troops, 32; Act relative to supplying barracks repealed by the King, 41; Governor Franklin in relation to barracks, 84; The same, in relation to provision for the King's troops, 141, 201, 203; Secretary Hillsborough in relation to the same, 219; Recruiting parties, 230; Assembly refuse to provide for the King's troops, 237; Assemblymen of Hunterdon County instructed to oppose the quartering of troops in the Province, 269; Supplies for the troops still refused by the Assembly, 297, 304; The Assembly consents to pay the arrears due to the troops, and the debt incurred during the late war, 321; Secretary Hillsborough in relation to arrears due to the troops, 323; Money granted for the support of the King's troops, 378; Number of men in New Jersey capable of bearing arms in 1772, 446; Proceedings of the King's troops at Concord, 590; Movement of troops in New Jersey and Philadelphia, 644; Congress of New Jersey assumes command of the militia of that State, 659; Troops and money raised in New Jersey, 669.

Militia, See Military Affairs.
Millard, Charles, iv, 310.
Miller, Charles, iv, 98.
Miller, Eben, viii, Part II, 151–153, 233, 234.
Miller, Elizabeth, Signs the surrender of the Government, ii, 456–460.
Miller, Ephraim, Lieutenant, ix, 185.
Miller, Henry, i, 510.
Miller, Isaac, x, 717.
Miller, John, x, 718.
Miller, John, Jr., of Jrs., x, 718.
Miller, Richard, ii, 334.
Miller, Samuel, ii, 339.
Miller, Thomas, ii, 470.—Affidavit of, respecting the Newark riots, vi, 430; Referred, to, 431.
Miller, William, ii, 129, 397.

Mills, Daniel, ii, 148.

Mills, James, ii, 417.

Mills, Jedediah, x, 207–212, 279.

Mills, William, ix, 4.

Milner, Samuel, Grand Juror, Essex County, iii, 496.

Mines, Memorial of John Gosling respecting, v, 36; Letter from Governor Burnet, relative to gold and silver mines in, 74; Opinion of the Attorney and Solicitor Generals as to the ownership of, 64; Letters from the Lords of Trade, relative to, 120, 156.—Articles of association to work in New Jersey and elsewhere, ix, 318.—In New Jersey, x, 445.

Mingaghqué, Relations with Bergen, i, 145, 151.

Minisink, Indians of, i, 458; Lands, 459—ii, 48; Journal of a visit to, by Arent Schuyler, 103.—Island of, vi, 163, 165, 166, 170.—Patent, viii, Part I, 135, 174, 208, 210, 211, 223, 232, 266, 274–276, 281, 290, 291. —Memorial of the Proprietors of, viii, Part II, 20; Highways laid out through, 23; Referred to, 28, 180; Claimed by New York, 33, 75; A town burnt in, 181, 184, 185.

Minnevarre, Laird of, ix, 337, 338.

Minniell, G., Mayor of New York, Letter from, to Sir John Werden, i, 491.

Minshall, Edward, iii, 314.

Minshall, Francis, ii, 194, 199, 276, 416, 470; Signs the surrender of the Government, 456–460; Asks for Andrew Hamilton as Governor, 470.

Minshull, Francis, Autograph, v, 510—vii, 326.

Minuit, Peter, i, 2.

Mitchell, Jacob, ii, 129, 326.

Mitchell, James, x, 717.

Mitchell, William, ii, 395.

Mitchell, See Michel.

Mitchelsen (Michaelse, Michaelye), Elias, i, 49, 125, 320.

Mohawk River, Patents for lands upon, ix, 308.

Moll, John, i, 190, 195, 201, 203, 282.

Molleson, Gilbert, ii, 187–193, 198, 257, 263, 376, 408, 416; Signs the surrender of the Government, 456–460; Recommends Andrew Hamilton for Governor, 470.

Molleson, John, iii, 446—iv, 9.

Mompeson, Roger, Recommended for the Council, iii, 78, 115; Appointed Chief-Justice, 79, 125; Notice of, 116; Appointed a member of the Council, 125; Referred to, 130, 155; In council, 290; Proposed as a member of Lord Lovelace's Council, 299; Appointed as such, 317; His position as Chief-Justice sought for by others, 360; Signs, 367; His removal as Chief-Justice asked for by the Assembly of New Jersey, 371; Defence of, 373; Signs addresses, 415, 473; The Proprietors ask that he may be left out of Governor Hunter's Council, 497; Referred to, 501.—Member of Governor Hunter's

Council, iv, 2; Referred to, 31, 41, 48, 61; Resigns the office of Chief-Justice, 70; Presides, 101; Referred to, 130, 131; Salary, 185, 368; Dead, 208, 214, 216; Referred to, 324.—Referred to, v, 344, 374.

Monckton, Robert. Named as a commissioner for trying pirates, ix, 283; Referred to, 390, 400.

Monk, James, ix, 621.

Monmouth County, Disturbances in, ii, 328, 330; Indictment of sundry persons in, 332; Proceedings of the Court of Sessions of, 362, 364, 371.—Taxes, iv, 368, 369.—Watches stationed on the coast of, vi, 373; Beacons destroyed, 378.—Riotous proceedings in, x, 148; Speech of Governor Franklin in relation to the riots in, 172; Address of the Assembly in relation to the same, 180; The same referred to, 198; Letter to, from Essex County Committee relative to events in Boston, 459; Letter to, from Committee of Correspondence at Boston, 498.

Monmouth Patent, From Governor Nicolls, i, 43, 97.

Morrow, John, x, 15, 17.

Montague, Lord Charles, ix, 621.

Montague, Edward, x, 25.

Montgomerie, John, Drafts of commissions of, as Governor of New York and New Jersey submitted to the King, v, 167; Letter from, to the Lords of Trade, 167; Instruction to, 169–178; Referred to, 179, 181, 183; Letter from, to the Lords of Trade, 184; Notice of, 185; Letter from, to the Lords of Trade, inclosing Governor Burnet's remarks on acts of the New Jersey Assembly, 189, 190; Letter to, from the Lords of Trade, relative to interest money and paper bills, 200; Letter from, to the Lords of Trade, respecting New Jersey affairs, 206, 234; Letter to, from the Lords of Trade, relative to certain acts of the New Jersey Assembly, 247; Letter from, to the Lords of Trade, respecting the payment of interest money for incidental expenses, 249; Answer to the same, 266; Letter from, to the Duke of Newcastle, relative to New Jersey copper ore, 267; Letter from, to the Lords of Trade, relative to New Jersey affairs, 268; Memorial to, from James Alexander, relative to the West Jersey surveyorship, 273; Letter from, to Lords of Trade, relative to several acts passed by the New Jersey Assembly, 285; Letter from, to Secretary Popple, 291; Letter from, to the Duke of New Castle, relative to vacancies in the New Jersey Council, 293; Death of, announced, 294, 295; Letter to, from the Lords of Trade, relative to acts of the New Jersey Assembly, 302; Referred to, 314, 315, 319, 371, 399, 457, 484, 492—vi, 71.

Montgomery, Michael, x, 718.

Montgomerie, William, vii, 542.

Moody, Daniel, ii, 113.

Moore, Alexander, viii, Part II, 228,

Moore, Benjamin, iii, 165.

Moore, Cornelius, Indicted, vii, 458.

Moore, Francis, ii, 327.

Moore, George, i, 192.

Moore, Sir Harry, Governor of New York, ix, 511; Proclamation of, relative to the robbing of the Treasury of East Jersey, 564; Vice-Admiral, 621; Referred to, 626.—Proclamation of, relative to the robbery of the East Jersey Treasury, x, 39.

Moore, John, i, 195, 201.

Moore, John, iv, 98, 186—v, 398, 402, 409, 410.

Moore (Moor), Sir John, ii, 164, 165, 194, 199, 258, 276, 299, 300, 302—vi, 314.

Moore, J., Letter from, to the Governor of Maryland, relative to irregularities in New Jersey, ii, 464.

Moore, Joshua, x, 717.

Moore, Matthew, ii, 113, 292—iii, 482—iv, 9, 15.

Moore, Samuel, i, 50, 83: Commissioned to represent the New Jersey Council in England, 93; Grant to, from Lords Berkeley and Carteret, 104; Complaints against, 141, 142, 150; Appointed Provost Marshall, 178, 319; Warrant for the arrest of, 321; Disposition of, by the New York Council, 322.—Grand Juror, iii, 486, 487.

Moore, Rev. Mr., iii, 270.

Moravians, viii, Part II, 160, 165.

Moore, Enoch, iv, 215.

More, John, ii, 397.

More, Matthew, iii, 446.

More, Thomas, i, 50.

More, ———, x, 113.

Morford, John, ii, 396.

Morford, Thomas, x, 600.

Morgan, Joseph, Improvements in modes of navigation, iv, 190, 194.

Morgann, Maurice, Commissioned Secretary of the Colony of New Jersey, x, 1; Note on, 3; Deputes Joseph Reed, Jr., to be Deputy Secretary, 5, 8, 133.

Morgan, Simeon, iv, 80-85.

Morice, Thomas, ii, 470.

Morrey, Ferry, iv, 129.

Morris, Benjamin, vii, 603, 606.

Morris, Charles, ix, 582, 591, 621, 624, 631, 632.

Morris, Col., i, 299, 300.

Morris County, Letter from the Lieutenant Governor of New York, relative to the erection of, viii, Part I, 266; Iron in, Part II, 79; Proclamation of Governor Belcher relative to the defence of, 182.—When set off, x, 298; Association of the inhabitants of Pequanock in, to sustain the action of the Continental and Provincial Congress, 716.

Morris, Dennis, ii, 325.

Morris (Moores), John, Deputy Sheriff of Essex County, ii, 336.—Grand Juror, iii, 486, 487.

Morris. Lewis, i, 134; Certificate relative to the boundary line between New York and New Jersey, 521.—Notice of, ii, 217; Commitment of, for contempt of court, 217; Appointed one of Governor Hamilton's Council, 328-331; President of Monmouth County Court, 332; Present at the same, 362; Note on, 390; Letter from, to the Lords of Trade, relative to the disorder in New Jersey, 398; Letter from, to Secretary Popple, relative to the surrender of the Government of East and West Jersey by the Proprietors, 412; Signs for Proprietors, 416; Recommended for Council, 417, 429, 451, 486; Letter from, to the Lords of Trade, relative to Dockwra's objections to the appointment of Andrew Hamilton as Governor of New Jersey, 442; Witness, 460; Recommends Andrew Hamilton for Governor, 470; Referred to, 472; Temporary authority conferred upon him by the Queen, 474; Referred to, 478; Objected to as a member of Council, 488; Letter from, to the Lords of Trade, relative to the difficulties in New Jersey, 504; Appointed member of the Council, 507; Announces the death of Governor Andrew Hamilton, 541.—One of Governor Cornbury's Council, iii, 2; Influence over the Scotch settlers, 14; Referred to, 47; Commissioner for New Jersey, 64; Criticism upon his conduct by Lord Cornbury, and his suspension from Council announced to the Lords of Trade, 73-77; His restoration to the Council asked for by the Proprietors of West Jersey, 85; His suspension recommended to be taken off by the Lords of Trade, 118, 124; Referred to, 132, 136, 138, 140, 143, 154, 188, 192-196, 223, 225; Colonel Quary's remarks concerning, 236, 237; Referred to, 260, 268; Letter from, to the Secretary of State, transmitting documents explanatory of the difficulties in New Jersey. 274; Opinion of the Council concerning him, 288, 365; Proposed as a member of Governor Lovelace's Council, 299; Appointed as such, 317, 328, 329; Referred to, 335; Order of the Privy Council, restoring him to the Council of New Jersey, 349; Congratulatory address from, to Governor Lovelace, 380; Verses ridiculing said address, 381-385; Referred to, 392-415; Suspended from the Council by Lieutenant-Governor Ingoldsby, 464; Documents relative to, 476-496; Before the Court of Common Rights, in 1698, 479-486; Questions the right of the Proprietors to govern, 488; Letter to the Assembly, 491; His restoration to the Council asked for by the Lords of Trade, 499.—A member of Governor Hunter's Council, iv, 2, 19; Referred to, 12, 33-35, 118, 119, 127-133; Remarks upon, by Rev. Jacob Henderson, 156, 162, 163; Appointed a member of the Council, 182; Referred to, 200; Appointed Chief-Justice, in place of Mr. Monpesson deceased, 208, 214; Indictment of, by the Grand Jury of Burlington County, 239; Signs as member of the Council, 253, 310;

Referred to, 316, 334; One of the commissioners to try pirates, 340; Referred to, 363; Fees to, 372; Referred to, 373; Proclamation of, as President, in regard to the neglect of the assessors of some Counties in New Jersey, 400; Memorial of the Proprietors to, relative to the survey of the boundaries between New Jersey and New York, 408; Letter from, to the Lords of Trade, relating to said boundary, 439; Notice of, 444; Letters from, to Peter Schuyler, relating to the boundaries between New York and New Jersey, 446, 448.—One of Governor Burnet's Council, v, 3, 34; Referred to, 59, 60, 103; Money paid to, 147, 151; Commissioner to try pirates, 197; Announces to the Lords of Trade the death of Governor Montgomerie, 295; Address and memorial of the Council to, 296; Letter from, to the Duke of Newcastle, in relation to the separate government for New Jersey, 314; Referred to, 328; Complained of, by Governor Cosby, 329-345; Letter from, to the Lords of Trade, relative to the proceedings of Governor Cosby, 349; Governor Cosby's reasons for removing him from the Chief-Justiceship, 366; Letter from Governor Cosby to the Lords of Trade, relating to, 395-401; Referred to, 402; Goes to England, 403; Complaints against, laid before the Queen, 408; Referred to, 431, 432; Petition of, to the King, relative to his dismission from the Council, 433; The King and Council declare the reasons for his removal from the Chief-Justiceship insufficient, 437; Referred to, 439, 449, 454; Letter from, to the Duke of Newcastle, in support of his claim to the Presidency of the Council, 455; Demands the administration of the Government, 463; Proclamation issued by, as President of the Council, 464-467; His claims submitted to the Duke of Newcastle by President Hamilton, 469; Letter from, to the Lords of Trade, relative to his claims to the Presidency of the Council of New Jersey, 472; Report of four of the Council on his claim to the Presidency thereof, 474; Complaint made against him by President Hamilton to the Lords of Trade, 478, 481; Proclamation by, 489; Letter from, to the Lords of Trade, transmitting his observations on Mr. Hamilton's reasons, 491; Made Governor of New Jersey, 511.—Commission for, as Governor of New Jersey, vi, 1, 2; Instructions to, 13; Acknowledges the receipt of his commission, 57; Letter from, to Sir Charles Water, relating to affairs of New Jersey and New York, 60; Complained of, to the Lords of Trade by John Hamilton, 69; Referred to, 73; Letter from, to the Duke of Newcastle, relative to the raising of troops in New Jersey, 99; Letter from, to the Duke of Newcastle, on New Jersey affairs, 100; Proclamation of, relating to the currency of foreign coins, 117; Letter from, to the Lords of Trade, relative to New Jersey affairs, 130; Memorial to, from the Proprietors of East and West Jersey, relative to the line between New York and New Jersey, 138; Representation to, relative to the making of iron, 140; Address to, relative to the partition line between New York and New Jersey, 144; His claim for

salary while striving to obtain the Presidency of the Council, 151; Letter from Deputy Secretary Gellibrand relative thereto, 153; Letter from, to Governor George Clinton, relative to the boundary line between New York and New Jersey, 162; Speeches of, to the Assembly and answers thereto, 178-190; Dissolves the Assembly, 190; Memorial to, respecting the boundary line between New York and New Jersey, 216; Representation to, from the Council, giving reasons for rejecting several acts of the Assembly, 219; Recommendation of, for the Council, 232; Certificate of, concerning the Proprietors' surrender of the Government, 234; Illness of, 246; Message of, to the Assembly, 251; Decease of, 363, 367; Names of his pall-bearers, 368; Referred to, 423, 434, 444.—Succeeded as Governor by Jonathan Belcher, vii, 1, 2; Referred to, 77, 116; Executors of, petition the Lords of Trade to pay his salary, 171; Letters to, from the Lords of Trade, relative to paper currency, 172; Reply of the Lords of Trade to the petition of the executors, 173; Referred to, 213; Proceedings of Council relative to arrears due to the family of, 335; Referred to, 353; Representation of the Assembly relative to said arrears, 459; Comments of the Lords of Trade upon the action of the Assembly, 551—viii, Part I, 76-78, 209; Memorial to, from the New Jersey Proprietors, relative to the boundary line between that Province and New York, 244.—Referred to, ix, 216, 231, 339.

Morris, Lewis, Jr., Suspended from the Council, v, 270.—Referred to, vi, 169—vii, 57; In relation to the division line between New York and New Jersey, 163.—Death of, ix, 377; Notice of, 378.—Referred to, x, 114.

Morris, Richard, ix, 321, 621.

Morris, Robert Hunter, Letter from, to James Alexander, commenting on the proceedings of Governor Cosby, v, 431.—Member of Governor Morris' Council, vi, 14, 15, 109; Report of, concerning the northern boundary, 168; Referred to, 294, 314, 315, 316, 317, 329; Commission to, to run the line between East and West Jersey, 352; Referred to, 355, 359, 360, 367-378, 395; Letter from, to the Lords of Trade, giving an account of the Province, 419: In Council, 435; Message of President Hamilton, relative to, 436; Letter from, to the Lords of Trade, at the request of President Hamilton, 446; Informed of the riot at Perth Amboy, 463; Letter from, to James Alexander, respecting New Jersey affairs, 471—vii, 5; Member of Governor Belcher's Council, 6; Letter from, to James Alexander, 17; Autograph of, 18; In Council, 86, 88; Commends sundry officers, 102; Letter from, to James Alexander, relative to the appointment of Samuel Nevill as Judge, 108; Referred to, 124; Address of, to the Speaker of the Council of New York, 141; Attempts, with other members of the Council, to advise Governor Belcher, 183; Communication from, to the same, 185; Address of, with other members of the Council, to the King, relative to the riots, 189; Letter from, to F. J. Paris,

relative to the same, 197; Referred to, 204; Answer of, to the rioters, 233; Signs as member of Council, 237; Referred to, 259; Letter from, to J. F. Paris, 262; Referred to, 280, 284, 285, 287, 288; Empowered to act for the Proprietors of East Jersey, in matters relating to the riots, 318; Letter from, relating to the riots in Newark, 328; Letter from, in relation to reuniting New Jersey to New York, 331; In Council, 335; Referred to, 347, 353-354; Petition of, relative to the disorders in the Province, 379; Complains of the injustice of the Assembly in refusing to pay arrears of salary due the late Governor, his father, 401; Referred to, 403; Deposition of, relative to the riots, 408; Opinion of, against passing an act of general pardon in favor of the rioters, 409; Signs letters to Governor Belcher, 452-456; Referred to, 463, 467, 472, 474, 477, 479, 501, 503, 507, 508, 511, 521, 525; Letter to, from Cadwallader Colden, 552; Referred to, 574, 603; Letters to, from J. Alexander, 626, 644, 651.—Letter from, to the Lords of Trade, relative to the Constitution of the Council of New Jersey, viii. Part I, 13; Papers relative to the state of affairs in the Province, 28; Letter to, from Governor Clinton, 92; Referred to, 102; Letter to, from the Secretary of Governor Clinton, relative to Provincial affairs, 116, 120; Referred to, 135; Letter to, from Mr. Paris, relative to the boundary line between New York and New Jersey, 152; Reply to the same, 157; Letter to, from Charles Read, 186; Bond of indemnity, 200; Referred to, 213; Memorandum concerning line between New York and New Jersey, 267; Referred to, 269.—Appointed Governor of Pennsylvania, viii, Part II, 91; Letter to, from Governor Belcher, relative to Indian affairs, 116; Referred to, 117, 120; Letter to, from Governor Belcher, relative to the threatened invasion of the French and Indians, 158; From the same, relative to the condition of military affairs, 161, 165; Referred to, 173; Letter to, from Governor Belcher, relative to military movements, 180; Petition of, as a Proprietor, 228; Informs the Earl of Loudon, of the death of Governor Belcher, and objections of John Reading to assume chief authority, 259; Referred to, 266-270—ix, 7; Pretension of, to the office of Chief-Justice of New Jersey, 176; Letter from the Lords of Trade on said pretension of, 191; Shows Governor Bernard why he ought to be permitted to resume the office of Chief-Justice, and incloses to him a copy of his patent, 206, 207; His claims presented to the Lords of Trade, 209; Proceedings of the Supreme Court in relation to the claims of, 212, 214-218; Dispute between him and Nathaniel Jones, respecting the office of Chief-Justice, 220; Informs Governor Boone of said dispute, 235; Referred to, 248, 264; Member of Governor Hardy's Council, 274; Named as one of the Commissioners for trying pirates, 283; Referred to, 324, 342, 343; Re-appointed Chief-Justice, 345, 351; Referred to, 355, 361, 362; Recommended for Chief-Justice, 364; Death of, 426, 427; Referred to, 430, 442, 445—x, 131.

Morris, Stephen, vii, 436.

Morris, William, Recommended for the Council, iv, 63, 153; Referred to, by Rev. Jacob Henderson, 157; Recommended for the Council, 169, 170; Dead, 171, 376.

Morris, William, Nominated for the Council, vii, 575, 577; Referred to, 593–595, 600; Memorial of Richard Partridge, respecting him, 602; Certificates in defence of his character, 603–606; Letter from Governor Belcher, to the Lords of Trade, relative to him, 607; From the same, to Lord Hardwicke, respecting him, 611; Referred to, 628, 629; Deposition of Samuel Tucker, as to the character of, 636; Affirmation of, relative to the conduct of Lewis M. Ashfield, 642; Referred to, 651—viii, Part I, 111.

Morrison, Archibald, vii, 282.

Morse, Robert, ii, 327.

Morton, George, i. 413.

Morton, John, x, 529.

Morton, Thomas, ii, 291.

Mosse, Peter, i, 50.

Mosse, Robert, i, 50, 85.

Mott, Gersham, ii, 363.—Contributes to the supposed Cornbury Fund, iii, 212.—Referred to, iv, 37; Expelled from the Assembly, 126.—Referred to, vi, 154.

Mott, William, vi, 202—viii, Part II, 151.

Moullains, Jacob, i, 50.

Mount, Humphry, Deposition of, viii, Part I, 41.

Mount, William, i, 523.

Mourison, Henry, x, 718.

Mourison, Mouris, x, 718.

Mudie (Mudy), David, An East Jersey Proprietor, i, 460, 499, 528, 530.

Mudie, Janet, ii, 107.

Muilman, Henry, vii, 326.

Muirhead, John, iv, 377.

Mulford, Benjamin, x, 531.

Mulford, Samuel, iv, 293, 294, 296, 344, 345.

Munday, Nicholas, iv, 186, 189.

Munson, John, x, 717.

Murch, John, x, 285.

Murder within the limits of the Admiral's jurisdiction, Bill for the punishment of, ix, 352.

Murray, James, ix, 622.

Murray, John, x, 562.

Murray, Joseph, v, 404—vi, 393, 396.—Letter to, from James Alexander, vii, 77; Papers sent by, 80, 81.—Memorandum, relative to New York and New Jersey boundary line, submitted to, viii, Part I, 267; Referred to, 269–274.

Murray, Robert, x, 562.

Murray, W., Solicitor-General, Report of, upon certain acts passed in
    New Jersey, vii, 305.
Musise, Cornelius, ii, 326.
Mutineers and enemies to the Government, Peace and welfare of the
    Province, i, 90, 176.

N.

Nahihan, John, ii, 396.
Nane, W. P., iii, 306.
Nassau Hall, Erection of, viii, Part II, 146.
Nassau, John, Lieutenant-Governor of New York, ii, 237.
Naturalization, Acts relating to, x, 411.
Naval Stores, Memorial relative to improvements in the production of,
    v, 68.
Navell, James, i, 268, 284.
Navesink, Oath of allegiance taken by the inhabitants of, 1667–68, i, 51;
    To produce the laws and publish them, 59; Notice to the inhabitants
    to take out their patents, 120; Controversy with Elizabethtown, 477.
Neal, Henry, v, 155.
Ned, A slave of Hatton, x, 207, 208, 279.
Negroes imported into New Jersey, v, 152.—Number of, in the Colonies,
    vi, 90.—Bill for laying a duty on the importation of, ix, 344, 347,
    383, 444, 458.
Neilson, James, x, 471, 587, 588.
Nelson, Benjamin, Signs the surrender of the government, ii, 456–460;
    Asks the appointment of Andrew Hamilton as Governor, 470.
Nelson, James, vii, 108.
N——s, Lord, Political creed with respect to America, x, 492.
Net, Rene, v, 153.
Netheway, Jonathan, ii, 42–62, 66–74, 79.
Nethorp, Edward, i, 268.
Neuman, Wm., i, 51, 134.
Neversink, Beacon on the Highlands of, vi, 378, 379.
Nevill, James, i, 118; Appointed Secretary of West Jersey, 275; Magis-
    trate, 292; Letter from to Governor Penn, 381, 413; Signs, 508.
Nevill, Samuel, vi, 139; Vote on the Militia Act, 202, 203; Referred to,
    255; Speech in the Assembly, in answer to the rioters' petition, 323;
    Notice of, 323; Referred to, 409, 410, 417, 418; Charge of, to the
    Grand Jury of Middlesex County, 456; Referred to, 468, 470.—An-
    swer of the rioters to his speech, vii, 30; Appointed Second Judge,
    97; Comments upon his appointment, by Robert H. Morris, 107; Re-
    ferred to, 114, 212, 215, 254, 258, 283: Speaker of the Assembly,
    351, 353; Referred to, 364, 450, 475, 478, 544, 546.—Letter to, from
    Governor Belcher, relative to the riot at Perth Amboy, viii, Part I,
    38; Letter from, to Governor Belcher, relative to the trial of Lewis

M. Ashfield, 40; To the same, relative to the riot at Amboy, 46; Salary, 105; Bond of indemnity, 200; Memorandum concerning line between New York and New Jersey, 267; Referred to, 269.—To agree with printer for printing bills of credit, viii, Part II, 71; Warrants to, 151-153; Jurat, 224; Petition of, as a Proprietor, 228; Warrants 232, 234.—Referred to, ix, 21, 214, 217, 224; Re-appointed, 345, 427.

Nevill, Thomas, vi, 465, 466.

Newark, Letter from Governor Carteret, to the Indian Sachem Oraton, relative to, i, 55; Directions as to the arrears of quit-rents of, 106; Notice to the inhabitants of, to take out their patents, 119; Relation with the Council of New Netherlands, 122, 124, 126, 128-130, 134, 137, 138, 142; Petition of the inhabitants of, to the Council of New Netherlands, 155; Officers at, 320.—Letter from the town of, to the other towns in East New Jersey, in reference to a certain act of the Legislature, and reflecting upon the conduct of Governor Basse, ii, 270; Letter from, condemning Governor Basse, 273.—Riots at, vi, 250, 292; Publication of the East Jersey Proprietors, relative to, 297; Referred to, 321, 336; State of facts, concerning, 397; Remarks of James Alexander, and Robert Hunter Morris, upon said riots, 420; Letter from David Ogden, with affidavits respecting, 426-432; Observations upon, by President Hamilton, 436; Increase of, 446.—Indian deed of sale to, vii, 31; Treatment of the settlers referred to, 43; Riots at, 210, 219; Affidavits respecting them, 178-182.

Newbold, Barzillai, viii, Part II, 151-153, 233, 234.

Newbold, John, i, 269.

Newbound, Michael, iv, 310.

New Brunswick, Seal of, v, 283, 284.

Newby, Mark, i, 419.

Newcastle, Duke of, Letter from, to the Lords of Trade, relative to instructions for Jonathan Belcher, appointed Governor of New Jersey, vii, 1; Reply to the same, 2; Instructions for Governor Belcher inclosed to, 4; Referred to, 67, 100; Officers who had served in the expetition to Canada, recommended to, 102; Succeeded as Secretary of State by the Duke of Bedford, 137.—Referred to, ix, 15.

New Castle, Governor Andros to Commanders and Justices at, i, 189; Meeting of Commander and Justices, 190, 191; Private court held at, 192; Letter from the authorities to the Council of New York relative to John Fenwicke, 200; Meeting of Commander and Justices of, 201; Letter to the same from the Council of New York relative to John Fenwicke, 201; Letter from the same to John Fenwicke, 203; Order to, from Governor Andros, 204; Court held at, relative to the conduct of John Fenwicke, 274; Order and letter to the Court at, respecting John Fenwicke, from Secretary Nicolls, 278, 279, 280; Meeting of the Court, 281; Letter from the authorities of, to Captain Matthias Nicolls, relative to John Fenwicke, 282; Justices at, ordered

to protect the inhabitants on the East side of the River in the possession of their lands, 285; Referred to, 347, 348.

Newcomb, Joseph, x, 531.

Newcomb, Silas, Lieutenant, ix, 185, 186—x, 531.

Newell, James, i, 283.

Newell, James, Deposition of, viii, Part I, 48.—Referred to, x, 302.

New Hampshire, ii, 123; Its Lieutenant-Governor and several of its inhabitants notorious illegal traders, 362.—Quota of, for the defence of
New York, viii, Part I, 195.

New Jersey, Patent for, to the Duke of York, i, 3; Lease for, to John,
Lord Berkeley, and Sir George Carteret, 8; Release to the same, 10;
Philip Carteret's commission as Governor of, 20; Robert Vauquillin's
commission as surveyor, 26; Concessions and agreements to and
with the settlers, 28; The Lords Proprietors' true intent and meaning of their concessions, 99, 101; Inhabitants of towns in petition to
the Council of New Netherlands for confirmation of their privileges,
155; Number of families in, in 1665, 183; Divided by Quintipartite
Deed into East and West Jersey, 205; Sir John Werden, on the extent of the authority granted to the Proprietors of, 289; Visit to,
from Governor Andros, 299.—Report of Solicitor-General Trevor, on
the grant of, ii, 100; Connection with illegal trading, 122; Letter
from the Lords of Trade, relative to Ports in, 201; Proclamation of
Governor Bellomont of New York, against the establishment of
Courts in New Jersey, 218; Documents relative to the Ports, 247;
Disorders in, 327; Letter from the Lords of Trade relative to the
boundary between it and New York, 367; Letter to the Lords of
Trade from New York Council, relative to the conditions of, 368;
The disorders in, 398; Surrender of the Government of, to the
Crown, 452; Letter from the Governor of Maryland relative to irreg-
ularities in, 462; Petition from the Proprietors of, that Andrew
Hamilton be appointed Governor of the Province, 469; The Lords of
Trade recommend to the Queen that some one not connected with
its affairs be appointed Governor, 484; Council for, recommended
by the Earl of Nottingham, 486; Lord Cornbury commissioned Governor of, 488, 489; Lord Clarendon's letter concerning the Council
of, with enclosure, 501; Letter from the Lords of Trade concerning
the same, 502; Letter from Lewis Morris relative to the difficulties
in, 504; Letter from Robert Quary, relative to the troubles in, 544.—
The pretentions and injustices of the Proprietors of, iii, 18; Bills
affecting the interests of the Proprietors of, 29; Objections of the
Proprietors to two of the Council of, 35; Difficulties attending the
raising of troops in, 53; Commissioners for, 64; Rights of the Proprietors of, in fines, escheats, etc., 108; Speech of Lord Cornbury to
the Assembly of, 165; Petition of the Assembly of, relative to the
difficulties of Lord Cornbury's Government, 171; Remonstrance of
the Assembly of, against certain evils to which Lord Cornbury was

subjecting the Province, and his reply, 173, 180; Address of the Governor and Council of, to the Queen, congratulating her on the success of Her Magesty's Arms, 239; Answer of the Assembly of, to Lord Cornbury's reply to their remonstrances, 242; Several members of the Assembly of, reported by Lord Cornbury as not qualified, 269; Documents explanatory of the difficulties in, 274; Proeedings of the Assembly of objected to by the Council, 286; Minutes of the Assembly of, from the 5th to the 12th of May, 1708. 291; Speech of the Governor to the Assembly of, 293; Lord John Lovelace appointed Governor of, 298; Objections of some of the Proprietors of, to several of the members of the Council, 300; Order of the Council of, relative to Receiver-General Barclay, 332; Speech of Lord Lovelace to the Assembly of, 361; Reply to the same, 362; Address of the Lieut.-Governor and Council of, to the Queen, 364; Address of the Assembly of, to Governor Lovelace, in relation to said address to the Queen, 368; Defence of the Council of, 372; The Assembly of, complain of Peter Sonmans to the Governor, 374; Address of, to the same, relative to Peter Fauconnier, 379; Address from the same, to the Queen, relative to the address of the Council complaining of the Assembly, 385; Address of the Council of, to Lord Lovelace, relative to the proceedings of the Assembly of, 390; Answer of Peter Sonmans to the complaints of the Assembly against him, 416; Petition to the Assembly of, against Peter Sonmans, 445; Report of the said committee upon the said petition, 447; Memorial from several Proprietors asking for a change in the Council, 497.—An intended meeting of the Assembly of, iv, 11; Relative to the place of said meeting, 16; Address of the Council of, to Governor Hunter, 17; Minutes of the Assembly of, 19, 22; Representation of the Assembly of, relative to the administration of Governor Cornbury, 24; Complaints of the Assembly of, against William Hall, 79; Memorial of the same, relative to the perversions of justice in the courts of law, 87; Petition of several of the members of the Assembly of, to Lord Cornbury, 110; Address of the Assembly of, to the Queen, 134; Troops and money raised by, for the Canadian expedition, 138; Memorial of the Proprietors of, in England, relative to the disputes between the Council and the Assembly of, 140; Letter from Governor Hunter relative to changes in the Council of, 149; Action of the Lords of Trade in relation to the Council of, asked by Governor Hunter, 151; Persons recommended to fill vacancies in the Council of, 152; The Bishop of London invited to assist the Lords of Trade in selecting Councillors for, 168; Communication from, to the Queen, relative to changes in the Council of, 169; Governor Hunter's reply to Lord Clarendon's objection to apply £999 for the support of the government of, 211; Speech of Governor Hunter to the Assembly of, 249; Address of the Council and Assembly of, to the King, upon the defeat of the Scotch rebellion, 252; Disorders in, 297; Address

of the House of Representatives of, to Governor Hunter, 303; New
seal for, 332; Message and speech of Governor Hunter to the Assembly of, 364, 365; Neglect of the Assessors of some of the counties in,
400; Memorial of the Proprietors of, relative to the survey of the
boundaries between it and New York, 408; Petition of the inhabitants of New York relating thereto, 433; Letter of Lewis Morris relating thereto, 439; Caveat of Daniel Coxe, 444; Answer of Governor
Hunter to queries relating to, 449; Proceedings of the Council of
West Jersey Proprietors relating to the boundary line, 452.—Assembly
of, dissolved by Governor Burnet, v, 8; Condition of, in 1721, 20; Addresses of the Assembly of, and speeches of Governor to, 24–27;
Report on proposed alterations in the Constitution of, 72; Opinion as
to the ownership of gold and silver mines in, 74; Address of the
Assembly of, to the King, 77; Report on acts of the Assembly of,
79; Respecting the manner of electing representatives to the Assembly of, 83; Instruction to Governor Burnet relative to the same, 84;
Negroes imported in, 152; Value of the paper money of, in New
York, 153; Value of the same in Perth Amboy, 154; Letter from the
Lords of Trade, relative to the same, 156; Census of the population
of, 1726, 164; Address of the Grand Jury of, to the King, 185;
Address and memorial of the Council of, to President Morris, on the
death of Governor Montgomerie, 296; A separate governor for,
desired, 303, 314; Petition of the Assembly and Council of, for a
separate government, 441; Petition of Richard Partridge for a separ-
ate Governor of, referred to the Lords of Trade, 448; Sir William
Keith's memorial on the same subject, 450; Reasons for appointing a
separate governor received from Mr. Partridge, 451; Minute of the
Council of, 463; Report of four of the Council of, on the claim of
Lewis Morris to the Presidency thereof, 474; The difficulties in, 479;
Lord Dela-Warr appointed Governor, 490; Lewis Morris made Governor, 511.—Address of the Council and Representatives of, to the
King, thanking him for giving New Jersey a separate Governor, vi,
58; Memorial of the Proprietors of, relative to the line between it
and New York, 138; Representation of the Council and Assembly of,
to Governor Morris, relative to encouragement for the making of
iron, 140; Address of the Eastern Council of Proprietors of, to
Governor Morris, relative to the line between it and New York, 144;
Disturbances on the northern boundary of, 163; Memorial of the
Proprietors of the Eastern division of, concerning the partition line,
216; Several acts of the Assembly of, rejected by the Council of, with
reasons therefor, 219; Certificate of Governor Morris concerning the
surrender of the government of, by the Proprietors, 234; Population
of, in 1837–38, and in 1745, 242–244; Minutes of the House of Representatives of, 246; Publication of the Proprietors of the eastern
division of, relative to the riots, 297; Commissioners appointed to run
the line between the eastern and western divisions, 352; Letter from

the Proprietors of the eastern division of, to a committee of the sub-
scribers to a proposal sent to the Governor, 353; Notice from the
Proprietors of the eastern division of, stating their willingness to
appear in Court, to test their rights, 365; Minutes of the Council of,
367–378; Proceedings of the Council of, March 19, 1746, 424; Proceedings of the Council of, May 6th and 7th, 1747, 435.—Proceedings
of the Council of, on the arrival of Governor Belcher, ;vii, 11;
Address of the same, to Governor Belcher, 13; Reply thereto, 14;
Address of Governor Belcher to the Council and Assembly of, 19;
Answers to the same, 23–29; Message from the same, to the same, 67;
Address of the Council of, to Governor Belcher, 81; Proceedings of
the same, relative to the riots, 86, 88; Message of Governor Belcher
to the Council and Assembly of, relative to the expedition to Crown
Point, 94; Letter from the Council of, to the Duke of Newcastle,
recommending sundry officers who had served in the expedition to
Canada, 102; Message from Governor Belcher to the Assembly of,
103; Legislature of, prorogued by Governor Belcher, 104; Address of
the Council of, to Governor Belcher, 110; Acts of the Assembly of,
transmitted by Governor Belcher, 137–140; Message to the Council
and Assembly of, from Governor Belcher, 149; Communication from
the members of the Council of, to Governor Belcher, 185; Address
of the same, to the King, 189; Address of the same, to the Duke of
Bedford, relative to the riots, 191; Petition from the Council of Proprietors of the eastern division of, to the King, in relation to the
riots, 193; Letter from the Council of, to the Lords of Trade, relative
to the riots, 236; Report of the Attorney-General and Solicitor-General upon certain acts passed in, 305; Proposals of the Lords of
Trade with regard to the disturbances in, 311–316; Proprietors of
West Jersey pray relief from the riots, etc., in, 316; Power of attorney from Proprietors of East Jersey, to Robert H. Morris, to act for
them in matters relating to the riots, 318; Letter from J. Alexander
in relation to reuniting the Province of, to New York, 331; Message
from Governor Belcher to the Legislature of, 332; Proceedings of the
Council of, relative to arrears due the family of the late Governor
Morris, 335; Address of the House of Assembly of, to Governor
Belcher, 345; Petition of the same, to the King, relative to the condition of the Province, 351; Centention between the Assembly and
the Council of, 356; Letter from F. J. Paris respecting the junction
of the Province of New York with, 360; Letter from Governor Belcher respecting the proceedings of the Assembly of, 361; From
Richard Smith respecting the same, 365; Affidavits showing the state
of the Province, 369–379; Complaint against the Assembly of, for
not paying the arrears of salary due the late Governor Morris, 401;
Letter from six of the Council of, to Governor Belcher, relative to
the state of the Province, 452; Representation of the Assembly of,
relative to arrears of salary due to the late Governor Morris, 459;

Petition of the Assembly of, to the King, 462; Representation of the
Lords of Trade, on the state of the Province of, 466; Memorial of
the Council of, to the King's Privy Council, relative to the riots, 537;
Minutes of the Council of, 541–550; Message from Governor
Belcher, to the Council and Assembly of, 580, 583; Assembly
of, dissolved, 587; Messages of Governor Belcher to the Council and new Assembly, 591, 615, 625, 634; Acts transmitted, 646.—
Memorial relative to the disturbances in, viii, Part I, 1; Message to
the Legislature of, from Governor Belcher, 12; The Constitution of
the Council of, 13; Memorial relative to, 18; Message of Governor
Belcher relative to a bill for the support of the Government of, 21;
Report of the Lords of Trade on some of the proceedings of the Assembly of, 28; Extracts from the minutes of the Council, relative to
the riots at Perth Amboy, 43; Order in Privy Council, relative to the
riotous proceedings in, 53; Report upon the draft of a commission for
inquiring into the grievances of, 90; Minutes of the Council of, 103;
Opinion of the Lords of Trade on the boundaries between New
York and, 128; Letter of Robert Charles, relative to the same, 135;
Argument that the forks of the Delaware are the true northern limits
of, 139; The act of 1747 relative to, 144; Petition of the Proprietors
of the eastern division of, to the King, relative to the repeal of the
Boundary Act of 1747, 160; Petition of the Assembly of, for making
current £60,000 in bills of credit, 183; Disputes between the people of,
and those of New York for want of a dividing line, 190; Quota of
assistance of, to the defence of New York, 195, 196; Bill for the
issue of £60,000 recommended by the Lords of Trade, 196; Bond of
indemnification by the Council of the Proprietors of the eastern
division to William Alexander and John Smyth, 200; Memorial of
the Council of Proprietors of the eastern division of, relative to the
boundary line, 202; Memorial of the Proprietors of both divisions to
Governor Lewis Morris, 244; Proceedings of the Council and Assembly of, transmitted to the Lords of Trade, 287.—Petition of the Assembly of, relative to the bill for making current £70,000, viii, Part
II, 14; Unsatisfactory proceedings of the Assembly of, 24; Action of
the same upon various subjects, 26; Bill for making current £70,-
000, 36; Queries relating to the present condition of, with answers
by Governor Belcher, 78; Message to the Assembly of, from Govern-
or Belcher, 93; Action of, thereupon, 94; Representation of the
Lords of Trade to the King in relation to bills of credit, 100; Messages to the Council and Assembly of, from Governor Belcher, 119,
128, 162; Governor Belcher directs a meeting of the Assembly of, to
be called, 181; Message of Governor Belcher to Council and Assembly of, 193, 198, 201; The services of, in defending the country commended by the Lords of Trade, 206; Petition of the Proprietors of
the eastern division of, relative to the boundary line, 225; Council
and Assembly summoned to meet, 249.—Address of the Council of,

to Lieutenant-Governor Pownall, ix, 4; Assembly of, prorogued, 126 ; Vacancies in the Council of, 127; Message from the Assembly of, to Governor Bernard, 129; Speeches of the Governor to the Legislature of, 159, 291; Reply of the same, 222; Use of former seal of, continued, 239; Imputed illegal trade in, 240; Amicable proceedings of the Assembly of, 248; Defective post arrangements in, 249; Action of the Assembly of, in relation to raising additional troops, 260, 261; Post routes in, 265; Address of the representatives of, to Governor Boone, 287; Certain acts of the Legislature of, recommended to be disapproved, 331; Duties on negroes imported in, 345; Ordinance for holding the Supreme Court for the Province of, 434; Lists of instruments used in the Courts, etc., of, 480; Illicit trade in, 484; Marriage licenses in, 504; The seditious spirit aroused in, by the Stamp Act, 505, 507, 524; Minutes of the Council of, 509; Address from the Council and Assembly of, to the King, and the repeal of the Stamp Act, 558, 560; Council of, congratulates Governor Franklin on the repeal of the Stamp Act, 562; Robbery of the treasury of the eastern division of, 564; Votes of the Assembly of, transmitted to the Lords of Trade, 567, 568; Conduct of the people of, during the late disturbances approved by the King, 570; Henry Wilmot appointed agent of, 571; Annual salaries granted to the officers of, 579; Fees taken in the different offices of, 592; Salaries of Governor and Judges of, 620; The King's displeasure with the Assembly of, 636.—Petition of the Assembly of, against taxation for revenue purposes, x, 18; Civil establishment of, 50; Proceedings of the Assembly of, in connection with the bill for issuing £100,000 in bills of credit, 60; Laws of, printed, 97, 102; The Lords of Trade recommend that the act of the Assembly of, for issuing £100,000 be disallowed, 106; Act disallowed, 115, 196; Riots in Monmouth and Essex Counties, 172, 180; Council of, 198; Displeasure of the Assembly of, at the disallowance of the Paper Money Act, 200; Message from Governor Franklin to the Assembly of, relative to supplies for the troops, 203; Answer to the same, 204; Report on certain acts of the Legisture, 233; Assembly of, refuse to provide for the King's troops, 237; Speech of Governor Franklin to the Assembly and Council of, 238; Answer to the same, 242; Message of Governor Franklin to the Assembly of, 243; Reply to, 251; Rejoinder, 256; Supplies for the troops still refused by the Assembly of, 297; An agent for appointed, 320; Arrears due to the troops, and debt incurred during the late war to be paid, 321; Minutes of the Council of, 351, 419; Message of the Governor, relative to the resignation of the Treasurer of the eastern division of, 420; The present state and condition of, 433–454; Speech of Governor to the Council and Assembly, 538; Reply of the Council to the Governor's speech, 541; List of the members of the Council of, 561; Provincial Congress of, 639; Congress of, assumes command of the militia, 656; No gentleman will accept a seat in the

Council of, 662; Its quota of the $3,000,000 issued by the Continental Congress, 670; The submission of, to the Continental Congress gives the King great concern, 675; Ships taken from, to be seized, 711; Message of Governor Franklin to the Legislature of, 719.

Newman, Walter, ii, 326.

New Netherlands, Director and Council of, Patent to Samuel Godyn and Samuel Bloemmaert, i, 1; Minutes of, 122; Petition to, from the inhabitants of towns in New Jersey, 155.

New York, Name of, given by Governor Nicolls, i, 47; Capture of, by the Dutch, 121; Affidavit of William Hayes, relative to the taking of, 152; Proceedings of the government of, relative to the jurisdiction of John Fenwicke, 188, 196, 200, 278, 280, 283; Court of Assizes at, for the trial of Governor Carteret, 303; Letter to Governor and Council of, relative to the ownership of Staten Island, from Governor Carteret and Council, 349; Province suffering from loss of East and West Jersey, 491; Line between New Jersey, 518; Report on the Province of, 524.—Minutes of the Council of, relative to the boundary line between New York and East Jersey, ii, 106; Quota of troops from other Colonies for its defence, 134; Duties on the Hudson trade to be paid in, 200; Minutes of the Council of, relative to the clearance of a vessel from, to Perth Amboy, 237; Report on the harbor of, 252; Boundary line between it and the Jerseys, 367; Three of the Council of, to the Lords of Trade, relative to the condition of the Jerseys, 368.—Commissioners for, iii, 64.—Assembly of, authorize the running of the partition line, iv, 365; Report of Council of, on Jarratt's petition about boundary line, 406; Petition to Council, relative to survey of the line, 433.—Memorandum relating to, v, 511.—Opinion of the Lords of Trade, on the boundaries between it and New Jersey, viii, Part I, 128; Quota of assistance to its northern frontier, 194; Report of the Committee of the Assembly of, on border disturbances, Part II, 20; Extracts from the minutes of the Assembly of, relative to border disturbances, 28.

New York and Elizabeth Town Committees of Observation, Proceedings of, x, 561-568 ; New York and Massachusetts, boundary line between, 660.

Nicholls, Matthias, i, 197, 201, 239, 282, 287, 304, 307.

Nicholson, Colonel Francis, iii, 461, 462.—Letter from, to the Lords of Trade, relative to the Quakers in New Jersey and Pennsylvania, 464. —Referred to, 471—iv, 37, 118.

Nicholson, Samuel, i, 227, 269, 414.

Nicholson, Governor of South Carolina, on protection against the Indians, v, 113.

Nicolls, Captain, i, 76, 334, 336.

Nicoll, William, ii, 106—vii, 43.

Nicolls (Nicholls), Richard, Application to, for the Elizabethtown grant, i, 15; Confirmation by, of the purchase of the Elizabethtown tract

from the Indians, 17; Grant from, for lands at Sandy Point (Sandy Hook) and on Raritan Bay, 43; Letter to the Duke of York, relative to the grants to Berkeley and Carteret, 46; Letter from, relative to the same, 54; Referred to, 88, 98, 108; Legal opinion on his patent for Elizabethtown, 272; Referred to, 301, 429, 437—ii, 108, 109, 125, 126, 322, 347—iii, 18, 30, 31, 56—vi, 208—vii, 269—ix, 229.

Nicolson, Mr. (General), iv, 220, 224, 225.

Nightingale, Samuel, ii, 339.

Nightingall, Simon, Grand Juror, Essex County, iii, 496,

Nilly, John, iv, 185.

Nix, John, x, 718.

Noble, Joseph, viii, Part II, 71, 235.

Noble, Richard, i, 227, 414.

Non-resident debtors, Acts relating to, x, 300, 325–329, 337.

Norris, Henry, ii, 129, 326.

Norris, Henry, Jr., ii, 326.

Norris, Captain Matthew, v, 328.

North Carolina, Resort for pirates, ii, 120, 359.

North, Lord, x, 492.

Northey, Edward, Attorney-General, ii, 432—iii, 108, 155—iv, 330—v, 338, 345.

Northumberland, Earl of, ix, 621.

Norton, Fletcher, Solicitor-General, ix, 397.

Norton, James, x, 717.

Norton, John, ii, 42-62, 66, 74, 79; Signs the surrender of the government, 456–460; Asks the appointment of Andrew Hamilton as Governor, 470.—Referred to, iii, 82, 95, 498—iv, 95; Affidavit of, 98; Signs as a Proprietor, 141.

Nottingham, Earl of, Recommends to the Lords of Trade, a Council for New Jersey, ii, 486; Letter to, from the Lords of Trade, relative to the Council of New Jersey, 502.—Communication to, from Peter Sonmans, relative to Jeremiah Basse, iii, 23.

Nox, James, x, 717.

Nugent, Sir George, ix, 450.

Nuttman, James, ii, 336.

Nys, Philip, i, 138.

O.

Oake, William, x, 471, 588.

Odell, Rev. Jonathan, x, 302.

Officers of Government, Moneys paid to, viii, Part I, 67–72, 76–79, 105.

Ogborne, John, Jr., iv, 98.

Ogborne, William, iv, 98.

Ogden, Amos, Lieutenant-Colonel, ix, 186.

Ogden, Benjamin, ii, 129, 334, 339, 396.

Ogden. Benjamin, Contributes to a supposed Cornbury Fund, iii, 199; Affidavit thereto, 201.

Ogden, Benjamin, Jr., ii, 334.—Grand Juror for Essex County, iii, 496.

Ogden, David, i, 50—ii, 339.

Ogden, David, vi, 293, 294, 314, 315, 318, 334, 349, 355, 393, 395, 396, 412; Letter from, to President Hamilton, transmitting affidavits respecting the riots, 426; Notice of. 427.—Referred to, vii, 48-51; Letter to, from James Alexander, relative to the rioters, 53, 288; Letter from, to J. Alexander, relative to the titles of the rioters, 343; To the same, respecting the riot at Horseneck, 364, 368; Letter to, from J. Alexander, relative to the trial of the rioters, 430; Referred to, 527; Recommended by the Lords of Trade. to be made a member of the Council, 578; Appointed, 588; Referred to, 609, 628, 629, 649 —viii, Part I. 43. 293; Part II, 268—ix, 217, 274; Named as one of the Commissioners for trying pirates, 283; Mr. Ashfield claims precedence over him in the Council, 430; Precedence given to him, 447; Referred to, 449; Notice of, 451; In Council, 509, 518; Observations of, on the resumption of business under the Stamp Act, by the Attorneys, 531.—Stable and out-houses of, burned by the rioters, x, 149, 183; Resigns his seat in the Assembly, 306; The dispute relative to his resignation, 334; Report on the claim of the Assembly to order an election to supply his place, 369; Commission of, as Supreme Court Justice, 372; Notice of, 372; Referred to. 413, 427; Salary of, 450; Member of Council, 561.

Ogden, Isaac, x, 467.

Ogden. John, i, 18, 50, 82, 84, 122; His appointment as a civil officer by the Council of New Netherlands, and his acts as such, 128-130, 137, 138, 141, 149, 155; Referred to, 300, 334—ii, 326—vi, 208, 210.

Ogden, John, Jr., i, 50.

Ogden, Jonathan, i. 50—ii, 129, 326, 339, 397—iii, 486.

Ogden, Jonathan, Jr., ii, 129, 334, 339, 396.

Ogden, Joseph, ii, 395.

Ogden, Josiah, iv, 253, 370—v, 146, 150, 155—x, 372.

Ogden, Lewis, Surrogate, ix, 360.

Ogden, Robert, viii, Part I, 83; Part II, 151.—Surrogate, ix, 360; Letter from, to Cortlandt Skinner, advising that the Colonies unite in keeping off the threatened blow of imposing taxes, duties, etc., 449; As Speaker of the House of Assembly, replies to a letter from the Assembly of Massachusetts, respecting late acts of Parliament, 496; Referred to, 518; Burned in effigy, 525.

Ogden, Samuel, vi, 351—vii, 457.

Ogden, Uzal, vii, 223, 445, 446—ix, 360.

Ogilvie, Rev. John, x, 313.

Oldale, Samuel, i, 269.

Olden, William, ii, 396.

Oldman's Creek and Salem, Titles to plantations between. i, 109-119.

Olive, Anthony, ii, 336, 339.

Olive (Olave), Thomas, i, 239, 288, 291, 522, 523—ii. 65—iii, 221.

Oliver, Andrew, One of the Commissioners selected to settle the boundary line. ix, 390, 447, 582, 591, 624, 631, 632.

Oliver, Peter, x, 375, 377.

Oliver, Mr., of Boston, Letter to, from Governor Belcher, vii, 76.—Nephew of Governor Belcher, viii, Part II, 131, 175.

Ollice, Thomas, i, 268.

Olliver, William, i, 50, 65.

Oraton, Indian Sachem, Letter to, from Governor Carteret, relative to the Newark tract, i, 55, 56.

Orme, Mr., Aide-de-Camp to General Braddock, viii, Part II, 120.

Ormston (Orminston), Charles, i, 530—ii, 187-193, 199; Disbursements by, on account of East Jersey, 205, 416; Signs the surrender of the government, 456-460; Recommends Andrew Hamilton for Governor, 470.

Ormston, John, iii, 161, 446.

Ormston, Joseph, i, 527—ii, 171, 177, 186-193, 198, 199, 213, 257, 263 376, 408, 411, 416; Signs the surrender of the government, 456-460 Recommends Andrew Hamilton for Governor, 470.—Referred to, iii 48, 161; Memorial of, against Peter Sonmans, 310, 312; Did not sign is commission, 314, 316; Signs as a Proprietor, 498.—Referred to, iv, 141: Authorizes James Alexander to collect his quit rents, 241.

Osborne, Sir Danvers, Copy of instructions to, viii, Part I, 194.

Osborne, Edward, ii, 396.

Osborne, Jeremiah, ii, 129, 325.

Osborne, John, ii, 129, 327.

Osborne, Richard, ii, 363.

Osbourne, Jeremy, i, 50.

Osburne, Joseph, i, 50.

Osburne, Stephen, i, 65.

Ossawath, Indian grantor, i, 115.

Oswald, Mr., viii, Part I, 128.

Otter, George, Letter from, relative to an island between Burlington and Bristol, ix, 337.

Otto, Gerrett, i, 195, 201, 282.

Oulver, William, iv, 9.

Outhout, Fop, i, 111; Permit to take up a piece of land, 113; Justice of New Castle, 190; Declarations of, concerning John Fenwicke, 194, 195; Justice, 203; Name signed to concessions, 268; Deposition of, 274; Letter from, to John Fenwicke, 281; To be one of the Court, 284.

Overton, Benjamin, A Commissioner of Customs, ii, 179, 254.

Oxenford, John, viii, Part I, 118, 119.

Oysters, Act for the preservation of, v, 80.

P.

Paca, William, x, 530.

Pacheco, Rodrigo, Letter to, from James Alexander, vi. 77.—Memorial of, to the Lords of Trade, relative to the purchase of lands from the Indians, 142.

Packa-go-nack, Lands at, sold by John Fenwick, i,414.

Packe, George, i, 50, 83, 84—ii, 325.

Packet-Boats, The establishing of, between England and America, viii, Part II, 138, 144, 146.—Discontinued between England and North America, x, 666.

Page, Anthony, i, 269.

Page, John, ii, 397.

Page, John, Jr., ii, 397.

Pagit, His authority as Constable denied, iv, 214.

Paice, Joseph, ii, 42-62, 66-74, 79—iv, 344, 345.

Paine, John, i, 269, 270.

Paine, Robert Treat, x, 529.

Paine, Timothy, x, 615,

Palmer, Captain (Judge), i, 305, 306, 498, 527; Petition of, to King, 532.

Palmer, Thomas, i, 288—ii, 417.

Palmer, President of Pennsylvania Council, complains of the pilots of Delaware River, vii, 70; Reply of, to a letter from Governor Belcher, 131.

Pancoast, John, i, 270.

Paper Money, Project of William Pinhorne for raising money by paper bills, iv, 269; Table illustrating the interest arising from, 272.— Acts concerning, v, 75, 87; Value of, in New York, 153; Value of, in Perth Amboy, 154; Letter from Lords of Trade, relative to, 156; Opinion of Governor Montgomerie respecting, 168; Counterfeits of, 191; The Lords of Trade upon, 200; Reference to, 305.—Proposal of William Wood relative to, vi, 51; Report of the Lords of Trade on, 73; List of papers relating to, 80; State of, in the British Plantations, 82; Argument of Richard Partridge, relative to, 91; Scarcity of, 103; Scheme for putting it on a better footing, 111; List of papers relating to, 125; Letter from Governor Morris, relative to, 131-137; Observations of the New Jersey Council on, 225; Order in Council respecting, 363: Representation of the Lords of Trade, respecting, 433.—Value of, vii, 27; Extracts from letters of the Lords of Trade, relative to, 172; Referred to, 272, 339; Examination into the state of, 357.—Petition to the King, relative to making current £60,000 in bills of credit, viii, Part I, 183; The bill recommended by the Lords of Trade, 196; Petition of the Assembly relative to the bill for making current £70,000, Part II, 14; Bill for the same, 36; Opinion of Counselor Belcher as to bills of credit being made legal tenders in New Jersey, 87; Memorial of Richard Partridge, relative

to bill for making current £70,000, 95; Representation of the Lords of Trade to the King, relative to, 100; Remarks of, concerning, to Governer Belcher, 124; Referred to, 162.—Petition for emitting £60,000 in bills of credit, ix, 11; Report of the Lords of Trade on the same, 34; Petition for emitting £89,000 in bills of credit, 107; Report upon the same by the Lords of Trade, 113; Message from the Assembly to the Governor, relative to, 129; Observations of the Governor respecting, 131; Bills of credit outstanding, and amount sunk each year, 143-146; Representation from the Lords of Trade, relative to a law for issuing bills of credit, 147; Draft of instruction to Governor Bernard, relative to, 156; Observations of Governor Bernard upon, 170; Observations of Governor Franklin upon, 385; Representation of the Lords of Trade, relative to, 405.—Governor Franklin refuses assent to a bill for striking $100,000 in bills of credit, x, 48; Proceedings of the Assembly in connection therewith, 60; Governor Franklin gives further reasons for issuing £100,000 in bills of credit, 99; Letter from the Earl of Hillsborough, relative to the same, 103; The Lords of Trade recommend the disallowance of the act for issuing £100,000, 100; Act disallowed, 115, 196; Henry Wilmott in relation to, 142; Observations of Govsrnor Franklin on the act for striking £100,060 in bills of credit, 150; Displeasure of the Assembly at the disallowance of said act, 206; Proposed repeal of the act authorizing the emission of, 315; Act for striking £100,000 and emitting the same on loans, 461; Report upon the same, 509; Order in the Privy Council relative to the same, 549; The Earl of Dartmouth in relation to the same, 557.

Papists, Not permitted liberty of conscience, ix, 66.

Parant, John, ii, 396.

Parat, Henry, ii, 396.

Pardon, Thomas, i, 149.

Pardon, William, i, 65, 72, 76, 81, 82; Difficulty with William Meaker, 85, 86; Letter from Lords Berkeley and Carteret, relative to his difficulty with William Meaker, 104; Note relative to his arrest by Captain James Carteret, 104; Case of William Meeker against, 334; Petition of Governor Andros, 335; Letter from, to Captain Nicolls, 336; Referred to, 337.

Paris, Ferdinand J., i, 524.—Recommended by Thomas Penn as agent for New Jersey, v, 293; Letter to, from James Alexander, 327; Autograph, 405; Referred to, 431, 434—vi, 76; Letter from, to James Alexander, 422; Autograph, 424; Notice of, 424; Referred to, 474—vii, 10; Letter from, to James Alexander, 12; Autograph of, 13.—Letters to, from James Alexander, relative to the boundary line between New York and New Jersey, 119, 125, 131, 152; Letters from, to James Alexander, relative to the New York and New Jersey line, 156, 167, 176; Letter to, from J. Alexander and R. H. Morris, relative to the New Jersey riots, 197; Petition of, relative to the

division line between New York and New Jersey, 226; Letter from'
to J. Alexander, relative to action against the rioters, 234; Letter
from, to J. Alexander, commenting on Governor Belcher's proceedings, 238; Letter to, from J. Alexander and R. H. Morris, concerning Governor Belcher and the rioters, 251; Letter from, to J.
Alexander, relative to business before the Lords of Trade, 260; Letter
to, from J. Alexander and R. H. Morris, relative to the New York
and New Jersey division line, 262; Letter from, to J. Alexander,
relative to the condition of New Jersey affairs in London, 271; Letter
to, relative to the New Jersey rioters, 272; Transmits papers relating
to the rebellion in New Jersey, 273, 275; Letter from, to J. Alexander, relative to his proceedings in London, 294; To the same, in
regard to the division line between New York and New Jersey, 297;
Letter from, to James Alexander, concerning the riots, 301, 304;
Letter from, to the same, relative to granting pardons to those
accused of treason, 308; Letter from, to the same, containing sug-
gestions for remedying the difficulties in the Province, 310; Incloses
letter to the Lords of Trade, relating to the riots, 328; Letter from,
to J. Alexander, respecting the junction of the Provinces of New
York and New Jersey, 360; Referred to, 525, 526—viii, Part I, 137,
145; Letter from, to Robert H. Morris, relative to the boundary line
between New York and New Jersey, 152; Reply to the same, 157;
Further letter from, on the same subject, 182; Referred to, 218, 219;
Letter to, from James Alexander, relative to the boundary line, Part
II, 89; Memorandum of, relative to commissioners for determining
the boundaries, 242; Referred to, 244, 247—ix, 342, 445.

Park, James, vii, 533–536.

Parke, Roger, iii, 165.

Parker, Elisha, ii, 487.—Affidavit of, relative to the supposed Cornbury
Fund, iii, 217; Member of the Assembly, 295—iv, 10; Recommended
for the Council, 63, 153, 154; Referred to by Rev. Jacob Henderson,
157; Recommended for the Council, 169, 171, 182; Dead, 326; Notice
of, 326; Payments due, 370, 372.

Parker, Elisha, Commissioned to run the line between East and West
Jersey, vi, 352; Letter from, acting for the Proprietors of East Jersey, to the committee making the proposals, under date of August
11, 1746, 392; Affidavit of, relative to legal proceedings of the committee of the rioters, 395; Notice of, 397.—Address of, to the Speaker
of the Council of New York, vii, 141, 155.

Parker, Henry, i, 113.

Parker, James, Number of men in his company, vi, 425.—Referred to,
vii, 114—viii, Part I, 200.—Petition of, as a Proprietor, Part II,
228.—Recommended for appointment as member of Council of New
Jersey, ix, 366, 427, 442, 444; Notice of, 446; Acknowledges the receipt of His Majesty's mandamus to be of the Council of New Jersey,

483; Referred to, 501; In Council, 509.—Referred to, x, 137, 195, 561, 604.

Parker, James (Printer), x, 98.

Parker, John, i, 50—ii, 327, 397.—Recommended as a member of the Council, iv, 331; Notice of, 333; One of the commissioners to try pirates, 340; Appointed a member of the Council by Governor Hunter, 363, 373, 374, 394.—One of Governor Burnet's Council, v, 3, 34; Money received from, on account of bills of credit, 134; Money paid to, 137, 146, 147, 150; Certificate of, 155; Letter from, to Rev. William Skinner, relative to the seal of the city of New Brunswick, 283; Signs memorial, 301.—Referred to, vii, 428.

Parker, Colonel John, Return of stores at Schenectady, ix, 10; Notice of, 10; Letter from, to Lewis Johnson, referring to the co-operation of the Indians, 172.

Parker, Joseph, i, 50—ii, 397—iii, 212.

Parker, Nathaniel, Contributes to the supposed Cornbury Fund, iii, 212.

Parker, Peter, i, 51, 59, 62, 177.

Parker, Samuel, x, 588.

Parker, Thomas, ii, 397.

Parker, Thomas, Jr., ii, 397.

Parkins, Samuel, vi, 351—vii, 457.

Parkhurst, Benjamin, ii, 395.

Parlaman, John, x, 718.

Parmeter, Joseph, Indicted, iii, 496.

Parmyter, John, ii, 239, 240.

Parrent, William, ii, 397.

Pars, John, ii, 327.

Parsons, Ann, i, 186.

Partition Lines, See Boundary Lines.

Partridge, Richard, v, 289, 293; Comments of, on the desire of the people of New Jersey for a separate government, 303; Memorial of, to the Lords of Trade, relative to New Jersey bills, 304; Letter to Secretary Popple, relative to export duty on copper ore, 406; Reply of, to the objections of Solicitor Sharpe to the New Jersey act for making £40,000 in bills of credit, 416 ; Petition of, for a separate Governor for New Jersey, referred to the Lords of Trade, 448; His reasons for a separate Governor for New Jersey, 451. —Arguments of, relating to the paper currency in America, vi, 91; Memorial of, to the Lords of Trade, relative to the purchase of lands from the Indians, 142 ; Order in Council upon his petition to the King, relative to the emission of £40,000 in bills of credit, 361, 362; Representation of the Lords of Trade respecting his said petition, 433; Referred to, 474.—Letters to, from Governor Belcher, relative to private affairs, vii, 59, 75; Letter to, as agent of New Jersey, from Governor Belcher, 100; From the same, relative to the action of the Legislature, 106; Re-

ferred to, 138, 139, 169, 176; Letter from, to Richard Smith, Jr.,
    relative to the riots, 242, 268; Letter to, from Richard Smith, re-
    specting the proceedings of the Legislature, 365; Referred to, 525,
    526, 527; Letters to, from Governor Belcher, relative to the proceed-
    ings of the Legislature, etc., 553, 573; Letter to, from Governor
    Belcher, on personal matters, 592; Defence of the character of Will-
    iam Morris, addressed to the Lords of Trade, 602; Referred to, 606;
    Letter to, from Governor Belcher, relative to Lewis M. Ashfield, 614.
    —Memorial of, relative to the Council of New Jersey, viii, Part I,
    18; Referred to, 29; Letters to, from Governor Belcher, 36, 52, 61;
    Referred to, 102.—Memorial of, relative to the bill for emitting £70,-
    000 in bills of credit, Part II, 95; Letters to, from Governor Belcher,
    190, 197; Warrant to, 232.—Petition of, for the emission of £60,000
    in bills of credit, ix, 12; Referred to, 9, 17; Memorial of, respect-
    ing bill for emitting £89,000 in bills of credit, 107; Report of the
    Lords of Trade on the same, 113; Referred to, 445.
Partridge, William, ii, 123—vii, 1—ix, 445.
Pate, William, ii, 148.
Patent to Samuel Godyn and Samuel Bloemmaert for Cape May County,
    i, 1; To James, Duke of York, for New Jersey, 3.
Patterson, Edward, i, 51.
Paul, Philip, ii, 380.
Paulson, Cornelius, iv, 189.
Pauncfort (Pausford), Edward, ii, 42-62, 66-74, 79.
Pauncfort, Tracy (Francis), ii, 42-62, 66-74; Signs the surrender of the
    government, 456-460; Recommends Andrew Hamilton for Governor,
    470.
Paxson, Henry, viii, Part II, 151-153, 233, 234—x, 358, 417, 479.
Paxton, Charles, ix, 622.
Payne, William, i, 72.
Paynter, Richard, i, 50.
Peace, Joseph, v, 132, 134, 136, 138—vii, 339.
Peachee, William, i, 268, 288, 421.
Peacher, Thomas, iii, 165.
Peacock, Captain James, i, 464, 466.
Peagram, John, Appointed a member of the Council, v, 347.—Surveyor-
    General of Customs, vi, 15.
Pear, John, x, 718.
Pearce, James, i, 268, 414.
Pearce, John, ii, 326.
Pearson, Isaac, iv, 113—v, 282—vi, 202.
Pearson, Joseph, v, 187.
Pearson, Theophilus, ii, 313, 333, 335, 336, 338—iii, 307, 351, 352; Jus-
    tice of the Peace for Essex County, 495.
Pearson, Samuel, ii, 336.
Pearson, Thomas, i, 242, 530.

Peck, Joseph, ii, 336.

Pedrick, Rodger, i, 269, 414.

Peer, Abraham, x, 718.

Peer, John, x, 718.

Peirce, Daniel, i, 155.

Peirce, Edward, v, 187.

Peirce, Thomas, i, 268, 413.

Peirson, Jonathan, vi, 346, 350, 361, 367—vii, 64, 74.

Peiterson, Walter, i, 269.

Pemberton, Rev. Mr., Letter to, from Governor Belcher, relative to the new college, vii, 118; Referred to, 618—viii, Part I, 9, 11.

Pemhake, i, 1.

Pemrepogh, Relations with Bergen, i, 145, 146, 151.

Pendleton, Edmund, x, 530.

Penford, John, i, 239, 268, 271, 291.—One of the first commissioners to buy and lay out lands, iii, 221.

Penn, John, x, 574, 650, 651.

Penn, Richard, viii, Part I, 200.

Penn, Thomas, Governor of Pennsylvania, Letter to, from Governor Belcher, vii, 147.—Referred to, viii, Part I, 137, 154, 158; Bond of Indemnity, 200.

Penn, William, Quintipartite deed to, from Sir George Carteret, i, 205; Instructions from, and others, to their commissioners in West Jersey, 219; Letters from, and associates, 230, 235; Signed concessions, etc., to settlers in West Jersey, 268; Resident of Salem, 283; Grant to him and others from the Duke of York, 324; Referred to, 347; Letter to, from Sir John Werden, 348; Grant to, from trustees of Sir George Carteret, 366; Deed to, from John Fenwicke, for half of New Jersey, 370; Letter to, from James Nevill, 381; Named among the twenty-four East Jersey Proprietors, 383; Appointments by, as Governor of Pennsylvania, 395; Commissioners to treat with West Jersey appointed by, 415; Letters from, to the Governor and Council of West Jersey, 417, 419; Proclamation of, against Thomas Mathews, 422; Signs as Proprietor, 437; Letter to, from Governor Dongan, 437; Referred to, etc., as Proprietor, 442, 499; Agreement between, and the executors of John Fenwicke, 507; Referred to, 529—ii, 5, 14, 15, 16, 22; Named as Proprietor, 26; Referred to, 49, 62; Observations of, on the proceedings of Governor Fletcher, 132; Petition of, as a Proprietor, to the Commissioners of Trade, 164; Named as a Proprietor, 186; Disbursements by, on account of East Jersey, 205; Signs as Proprietor, 263; Referred to, 279, 281; Letter from, to Samuel Leonard, 318; Offences charged upon him by Edward Randolph, 360; Referred to, 388, 463, 475, 480—iii, 53, 234; Letter from, to William Popple, respecting Messrs. Revell and Leeds, 303; Certificate from, 305; Signer of Peter Sonmans' commission, 313; Referred to, 329, 345.—Named as a commis-

sioner for trying pirates, iv, 239.—Extracts from grants of, v, 17; Referred to, 30—ix, 395—x, 574.

Pennsylvania, Minutes of Council, relating to letters sent from East Jersey to England, i, 394.—Illegal trading with, ii, 120; Quota of troops for the defence of New York, 134; Offences committed in, by persons in authority, 360.—Proceedings of the Council of, on the approaching departure of Governor Hunter for England, iv, 393. —Excommunication of a Quaker Chief-Justice, vi, 173.—Proceedings of the Provincial Council of, vii, 120; Quota of assistance of, to the defence of New York, viii, Part I, 194, 196.

Pensbury Island, v, 42.

Penton, William. i, 118, 269, 283, 284, 292, 414.

Pepperell, Sir William, Appointed Colonel, viii, Part II. 17, 19, 111.

Pequanock, Association of the freeholders and inhabitants of, to sustain the action of the Continental and Provincial Congresses, x, 716.

Percival, Hon. Spr., ix, 621.

Pere (Pierce), Mr., i, 62.

Peregoe, Ezekiel, ii, 326.

Perin, Thomas, Recommends Ferdinand John Paris as agent for New Jersey, v, 293.

Perry, Benjamin, vi, 351—vii, 458.

Perry, Frederick, vii, 375.

Perry, Michaiah, iv, 131.

Perte, John, ii, 396.

Perth Amboy, i, 427, 428; Instructions for laying it out, 434, 449, 461, 474; Markets and fairs at, 451; Opposition to, as a port, by Governor Dongan, 525; Seizure of vessels at, for not entering at New York, 535; Erected into a port of entry, 540, 543.—Instructions of the Commissioners of Customs to the Surveyor-General of Customs, relative to the port of. ii, 178; Situation of, 183; Proclamation of Governor Basse, establishing it as a port, 227; Reasons of the Attorney-General of New York, why it should not be a free port, 231; Seizure of a vessel at, 238; Letter from Secretary Popple to Mr. Lownds, relative to the port of, 244; Note on, 246; Report of the Commissioners of Customs, relative to the settlement of a port at, 251-254; Proprietors' claims of a port at, to be tried at Westminster Hall, 266, 267; Letter from, condemning Governor Basse, 273; Letter from the Lords of Trade to the Earl of Bellomont, relative to the port at, 302; Memorial to the Lords of Trade, insisting upon establishing it as a port of entry, 308; Depth of water between it and Elizabethtown, 355; Proprietors wish it recognized as a port, 405; Markets at, desired, 406.—Transportation between it and Burlington, iii, 176, 186, 250, 327.—As a place of meeting for the Assembly, iv, 12, 40—v, 11; Number of Assemblymen from, 12; Lands in, given to voters, 61; How represented, 83; Seal of, 284.—A poor, inconsiderable place, vi, 108; Riots at, 463; Affidavits relating to riots at, 465.

—Reception at, of Governor Belcher, vii, 15, 17.—Riots at, viii, Part I, 38, 39, 43, 52.—Address of Corporation of, to Lieutenant-Governor Pownall, ix, 6, 8.—Exports from, x, 454; Removal of the seat of government to, 457, 468.

Perth, Earl of, one of the Proprietors of East Jersey, i, 383, 412, 425, 433, 434, 437, 439, 441, 446, 448, 451, 454, 460, 462, 463, 474, 482, 483; Letter to, from Governor Dongan, 483; Signs as Proprietor, 490, 504; Instructions from, and other Proprietors, to Andrew Hamilton, 508.—Named as a Proprietor, 528—ii, 26, 32; Disbursements by, on account of East Jersey, 202; Referred to, 389, 422.

Perth, Town, See Perth Amboy.

Peters, Richard, viii, Part II, 228.

Peters, Samuel, Intercepted letter from, x, 616.

Peters, William, ix, 622.

Petersen, Hessel, iv, 370—v, 147.

Petersen, Mones, i, 50.

Petersen, Johannes, ii, 327.

Pettinger, John, iv, 293.

Pettinger, Richard, iv, 293.

Pettinger, Sicha, iv, 293.

Pettit, Benjamin, vii, 426.

Pettit, Charles, Deputy Secretary of New Jersey, x, 132; Notice of, 133; Referred to, 210, 216, 358, 450.

Petty, John, i, 269.

Petty, William, Jr., iii, 165.

Pew, William, Jr., Lieutenant, ix, 185, 187.

Philips, Adolphus, iv, 340.

Philips, Theodore, vii, 606.

Philipse, Ad., viii, Part I, 237.

Philipse, D., iv, 408.

Philipse, Frederick, viii, Part I, 239, 248.

Phillips, Abraham, vii, 364; Affidavit of, respecting the state of the Province, 370; Referred to, 375, 407; Affidavit of, relative to the riots, 444; Referred to, 446, 515.

Phillips, Ambrose, iv, 254, 293-295, 305, 328, 336, 338.

Phillips, John, vii, 628.

Phillips, Lidia, vii, 374, 444.

Phillips, Mary, vii, 374.

Phillipse, Frederick, ii, 105, 106—iv, 412, 434—v, 329, 333-335, 344.

Phillipse (Phillips), Matthew, vii, 281, 371-373.

Phipps, Thomas, ii, 42-61, 65-73, 79.

Phrase, Joseph, i, 50.

Pictor, Lucas, i, 115.

Pierden, William, ii, 397.

Pierson, Bethune, vi, 351.

Pierson, Daniel, vii, 344; Affidavit of, as to the riots, 436; Referred to, 439; Signs, 445, 446.

Pierson, John, x, 718.

Pierson, Joseph, vi, 245—vii, 436, 457.

Pierson, Methuel, Newark rioter, vii, 178, 179, 435, 436, 458.

Pieterse, Marcilis, ii, 326.

Pietersen, Christian, i, 49.

Pietersen, Paules, i, 49.

Pike, Charles, iv, 10.

Pike (Pyke), John, i, 50, 81, 89, 134, 150, 177.—Contributes to the supposed Cornbury Fund, iii, 200; Petition of, to the House of Representatives against said fund, 202; Petitions the Assembly in relation to the East Jersey records, 220; Member of Assembly, 483.—Signs, iv, 10; Affidavit of, 16.

Pike, John, Jr., iii, 446.

Pike, Thomas, iii, 351; Grand Juror, 486, 487.

Pinhorne, John, Appointed Clerk of the Assembly, iii, 227; Signs as Clerk, 298, 446; Affidavit of, respecting the proceedings of Peter Sonmans, 450.—Referred to, iv, 122, 147; Salary, 185, 368.

Pinhorne, William, ii, 106, 386; Recommended for Council, 417, 429, 431; Objected to as a member of Council, 488; Remarks concerning, 502; Appointed member of the Council, 507; Announces the death of Governor Andrew Hamilton, 541.—One of Governor Cornbury's Council, iii, 2, 64, 155, 160, 290; Proposed as a member of Lord Lovelace's Council, 299; Notice of, 299; Appointed a member of Council, 317; Signs addresses, 367, 373, 415, 473; The Proprietors ask that he may be left out of Governor Hunter's Council, 397.—Member of Governor Hunter's Council, iv, 2, 19; Referred to, 40, 44, 48; His removal from the Council recommended by Governor Hunter, 61; Referred to, 75, 77, 101, 115, 130, 141; Removed from his Judgeship, 129; His removal from the Council urged by Governor Hunter, 149, 153; Referred to by Rev. Jacob Henderson, 156; Further reference to, 164, 169, 175, 182; Project of, for raising money by paper bills, 269.

Pintard, Anthony, ii, 332, 364; Recommended for Council, 417.

Pirates and Piracies, ii, 150-155, 277, 285, 304, 310, 358-362, 366.—Report of the Attorney and Solicitor Generals on the effect of the proclamation for pardoning, iv, 329; Commissioners named for the trial of, 339—v, 196, 197.

Piron, Joseph, iv, 309.

Pisbrou, Henry, i, 128.

Piscataway, The land of, to be patented to particular persons by Governor Carteret, i, 62; Directions as to the payment of arrears of quit rents of, i, 106; Relations with the Council of New Netherlands, 122, 124, 126, 129, 130, 133, 134, 137, 149, 150; Differences between, and Woodbridge, 154; Petition of the inhabitants of, to the Council

of New Netherlands, 155, 159; Appointments at, approved by the Council of New York, 319.

Pitcher, James, Commissary of the musters, viii, Part II, 76.

Pitt, William, Circular letter to Governors, urging the raising of additional troops, viii, Part II, 241, 258.—Referred to, ix, 9, 17, 110, 112, 159, 161, 162, 169, 170, 211, 221, 223; Urges preparation for the invasion of Canada, 149; Orders the use of the former seal, to be continued, 239; Is informed by Governor Boone in regard to the imputed illegal trade in New Jersey, 240; Also as to the raising of additional troops, 261; Referred to, 263, 278.

Planbord, Josias, ii, 397.

Plantations, Scheme, or treatise relating to, iv, 345.

Pledger, John, i, 268, 414.

Plese, Turrse, i, 268.

Plowman, Matthew, Collector of Customs at New York, instructions to, 543.

Plum, Samuel, ii, 327.

Plumstead, Clement, An East Jersey Proprietor, i, 366, 374, 383, 424, 433, 434, 437, 442, 446, 451, 454, 457, 460, 462, 474, 482, 483, 490, 499, 500, 504, 530—ii, 26, 186-193, 198; Disbursements by, on account of East Jersey, 205; Signs name, 213-263, 376, 408, 411, 431; Referred to, 437; Signs the surrender of the Government, 456-460.—Signs Peter Sonmans' commission, iii, 313.

Pocock, Thomas, i, 366.

Pofen, Henry, iv, 9.

Pokahake, i, 1.

Pollexssen, Henry, Opinion of, on Elizabethtown Patent, i, 272.

Ponnereau, Mrs., ix, 307.

Pope, Joseph, i, 522, 523.

Pope, Nathaniel, iii, 165.

Pope, Thomas, i, 50.

Popple, William, ii, 138; Letter from, to Mr. Basse, inclosing form of bond to be entered into by the Proprietors of the several plantations in America, 141; Letters to, from Mr. Basse, in relation to pirates and piracies, 150, 154, 157; Letter from, to Mr. Basse, in answer to the above, 155, 162; Letter to, from Secretary Lownds, transmitting documents, 163; Letter from, to Secretary Lownds, 168; Letter from, to the Attorney-General and Solicitor-General, 174; Letter to, from Governor Basse, 214; Letter from, to Governor Basse, 243; Letter from, to Mr. Lownds, relating to the Port of Perth Amboy, 244; Letter from, to Secretary Sansom, transmitting documents relative to the ports of New Jersey, to the Commissioners of Customs, 247; Letter to the Attorney-General, relative to the eligibility of Andrew Hamilton to the office of Governor, and the answer thereto, 250; Letter to, from Secretary Sansom, transmitting report concerning port at Perth Amboy, 251; Letter to, from Andrew Hamilton, relative to his

appointment as Governor of New Jersey, 259; Letter from, to Wm.
Dockwra, relative to the port of Perth Amboy, 266; Letter to, from
Governor Basse, relative to pirates and illegal traders, 286; Letter
from, to William Dockwra, inquiring as to the operation of the act
against fraud, etc., in East and West Jersey, 306; Answer to the
same, 306; Letter from, to Attorney-General Trevor, asking his
opinion respecting a new mode of approving Proprietary Governors,
307; Letter from, to William Dockwra, 340; Letter from the same, to
the same, asking for the transmission of the proposed surrender of
the government of East Jersey, 353; Letter to, from Lewis Morris,
relative to the surrender of the government of East and West Jersey,
412; Letter from, to Sir Thomas Lane, 428; Letter from, to Attorney-
General Northey, relative to the surrender, 432; Letter from, to Sir
Thomas Lane, transmitting papers relative to Andrew Hamilton, 473.
Popple, William, Jr., Letter from, to Wm. Sloper, relative to Lord Corn-
bury's salary, iii, 144.—Letter to, from William Penn, respecting
Messrs. Revell and Leeds, 303; Letters to, from Secretary Lownds,
relative to the petition of John Keble, 341, 347; Letter to, from
Thomas Cockerill, relative to the death of Governor Lovelace, 466.—
Letter to, from Edward Richier, iv, 115; Letter to, from William
Dockwra, transmitting papers, 116; Letter from, to the Bishop of
London, relating to the proposed New Jersey Councillors, 168; Letters
to, from Governor Hunter, 211, 218, 223; Letter from, to Governor
Hunter, 229; Letters to, from Governor Hunter, 242, 258, 294, 295,
297, 305, 326, 333, 376, 387.—Letter from, relative to the islands in
the Delaware, v, 6; Letter to, from Governor Burnet, 163; Letter to,
from Governor Montgomerie, 291; Letter to, from James Alexander,
360; Letter to, from Richard Partridge, relative to export duty on
copper ore, 406; Letter from, to John Hamilton, relative to vacancies
in the Council, 454.
Population of New Jersey, viii, Part II, 84; Of the Colonies in America,
132.—Of New Jersey in 1772, x, 445.
Population, See Census.
Porter, Joseph, x, 717.
Post, Capt. Adrian, i, 66—ii, 327.
Post Offices, ix, 249, 265.
Poswhelse, Martin, ii, 327.
Pot and Pearl Ashes, Manufacture of, proposed, iii, 304, 329, 341-349.—
Letters from Thomas Lowndes and Sir William Keith, respecting the
manufacture of, in the Plantations, v, 245, 246.
Potter, Marmaduke, i, 50.
Potter, Samuel, ii, 315, 334, 395—iv, 147.
Potter, Sarah, iii, 485.
Potter, Thomas, ii, 396.
Potts, Henry, Letter from, relating to the post routes in New Jersey,
ix, 265.

Potts, Thomas, iv, 98, 305.

Poulisen, Dirk, ii, 326.

Poulse, Johannis, ii, 327.

Povey, John, ii, 169, 200.

Powel, Robert, i, 269, 288.

Powell, Richard, ii, 292.

Powell, Rodrick, i, 50.

Pownall, John, ix, 2; Letter from, to James West, relative to the seizure of a vessel engaged in illicit trade, 306; Desires Sir Matthew Lamb to draft a bill for the punishment of murder, within the Admiralty jurisdiction in the Plantations, 351; Transmits letter asking for removal of Governor Hardy, 360; Query from, as to the right of aliens to hold lands in America, 382, 397; Incloses to Governor Franklin, order relative to Peter Gordon's lottery, 487; Referred to, 529, 530; Receives from Governor Franklin votes and laws, 567; Writes to Henry Wilmot, relative to the boundary commissioners, 622.—Recommended by the Lords of Trade as Lieutenant-Governor of New Jersey, viii, Part II, 102; Notice of, 102; Commission of, 106; Congratulated on his appointment by Governer Belcher, 118; Letter of thanks from, to the Lords of Trade, 134; Congratulated by Governor Belcher, 139; Informed by the same of the movement of the troops, 160; Referred to, 167, 169; Requested by Governor Belcher to attend a convention of the Governors at New York, 170; Referred to, 183; To be deputed to attend meetings of the Governors in case of the inability of Governor Belcher, 215; Referred to, 246; Notified of the death of Governor Belcher, 257; President Reading gives to him reasons for not assuming the chief authority, 260; Reply of, to Mr. Reading, 261; Mr. Reading's rejoinder, 262; Gives an account of the death of Governor Belcher to the Lords of Trade, 266.—Letter from, to the Lords of Trade, ix, 1; To John Reading, on leaving the government in his hands, 2; Notice of, 2; Address to, from the Council, 4; Answer to the same, 6; Address of the corporation of Perth Amboy to, 6; Answer of, 8; To President Reading, relative to the invasion of Canada, 111; Appointed Governor of South Carolina, 188; Named as one of the commissioners for trying pirates, 283.

Pratt, Benjamin, ix, 283.

Pratt, Mr., viii, Part I, 145.

Prayers for the Royal family, ix, 302, 375.

Preijers, Andryas, ii, 327.

Presbyterian Clergy of New Jersey, Petition of, for a charter incorporating "The New Jersey Society for the better support of the widows, and education of the children of deceased Presbyterian ministers, x, 339–349; Opinion of David Ogden on said charter, 350; Opinion of Cortlandt Skinner on the same, 353; Governor Franklin, in relation to the petition of, 400; The Earl of Dartmouth, in relation to the

same, 404, 407; Permission given to the Governor to pass their charter; 409.

Preston, Isaac, x, 531.

Price, Benjamin, i, 50, 65, 306—ii, 315, 326—iii, 201, 295, 486, 495—v, 187.

Price, Benjamin, Jr., ii, 129, 326, 397.

Price, Daniel, ii, 129, 327, 334.

Price, Edward, v, 187.

Price, Ephraim, ii, 129, 315, 326, 334.

Price, Joseph, License to, as Branch pilot, ix, 18; Authorized to impress vessels to transport troops to New Jersey, 246.

Price, Philip, Jr., x, 718.

Price, Robert F., x, 251, 458, 479.

Price, Samuel, vi, 455—vii, 206, 458—x, 718.

Price, Thomas, x, 717.

Price, William, x, 718.

Pridmore, John, vii, 622.

Princeton, Building of a college at, vii, 58.

Pringle, Thomas, ii, 290.

Prior (Pryyer), Corsparus, vii, 402; Affidavit of, relative to the riots, 429; Referred to, 510.

Prisoners to be delivered up, vii, 549.

Prit, Benjamin, ii, 129.

Prite, Thomas, ii, 129.

Proclamation money, vii, 393–400.

Produce of New Jersey, x, 444.

Proprietors of East Jersey, Lease to, from Lady Elizabeth Carteret and Trustees, i, 366; Agreement as to the benefit of survivorship, 373; Commission from, to Thomas Rudyard, as Secretary and Register, 376; Commission from, to Samuel Groom, as Receiver-General, 378; Commission from, to Gawen Lawrie, as Deputy Governor, 423; Instructions from, to Deputy Governor Lawrie, 426, 459; List of, in 1683, 441; Regulations of, for taking up lands, 452, 470, 492, 499; Seal of, 488; Quo warrantos against, authorized, 501; Appointment of William Dockwra as their agent, 506; Deputy Governor Lawrie's powers revoked by, 531; Petition of, to the King, relative to the entering of their vessels at New York, 533; Representation of, to the King, relative to customs, or desiring that East Jersey be made a distinct government, or be joined with West Jersey, 535.

Proprietors, See also New Jersey, East Jersey, West Jersey, and Berkeley and Carteret.

Provincial Congress of New Jersey, Resolution, Association and circular letter of, x, 639.

Provost, David, iv, 340—v, 153.

Provost, William, Recommended for the New York Council, v, 70; Money received of, 142, 144, 149; Money paid to, 146; Commissioned to try

pirates, 197; Recommended for Council, 318, 323; Appointed, 346; Referred to, 456; Report on claims of Lewis Morris, 478.—Referred to, vi, 14, 15—vii, 646.

Pummerent, Claus Jansen, i, 82.

Purdy, William, ii, 327.

Putland, Heron, v, 155.

Pyle, Sarah, i, 414.

Pyles, William, i, 65.

Q.

Quakers in New Jersey in 1699, ii, 305; Allowed to affirm instead of taking an oath, 522.—Their admission to office, without taking an oath, iii, 2; Favored by Colonel Hamilton, 13, 15; Complaints against, by Lord Cornbury, 66, 83, 84; Excluded their right of voting, 153; Remarks of Lord Cornbury concerning, 229; Colonel Quary's opinion of, 235, 273; Opinion of Lord Cornbury's Council in regard to them, 394, 413, 414; Not allowed to serve on juries in criminal cases, 345–443, 448; Their objections to raising troops, 461, 462, 465, 466; Complaints against them made by Lieutenant-Governor Ingoldsby and his Council, to the Queen, 470—iv, 20; Harrassment of, under Lord Cornbury, 25; Remarks of the Assembly upon them, 42; Remarks of William Dockwra upon, 121, 129, 133; Representation respecting them by Rev. Jacob Henderson, 155, 156; Their position, etc., 196, 232, 236–240; Two speeches relating to Daniel Coxe, 243, 246; Form of affirmation appointed, 259; Threats against, 302; Lords of Trade recommend that they be allowed to affirm, 334; Petition against allowing them to affirm, 342; Representation of the Lords of Trade, relative to the same, 366.—Numbers in New Jersey, v, 21; Number of, in the Assembly, 234, 235.—Against the Council, vi, 65; Claim to be exempt from military duty, 104, 105; Account of the excommunication of a Chief-Justice in Pennsylvania, 173.—Governor Belcher's treatment of, vii, 121, 133; Referred to, 629.—Plan of protection against the Indians proposed by, ix, 118.

Quary, Colonel Robert, Letters from, to the Lords of Trade, concerning pirates, ii, 277, 280; Notice of, 280; Referred to, 286, 291, 464, 473; Letter from, to the Lords of Trade, adverse to Andrew Hamilton, 479; Objected to as a member of Council, 488; Appointed member of the Council, 507; Letter from, to the Lords of Trade, concerning the trouble in New Jersey, 544.—One of Governor Cornbury's Council, iii, 2; Letter from, to the Lords of Trade, desiring to succeed Mr. Randolph as Surveyor-General, 7; Letter to the same, relative to New Jersey affairs, 13; Referred to, 37, 45; Letter from, to the Lords of Trade, 52; Commissioner for New Jersey, 64; Referred to, 103, 132, 155, 160; Letters from, to the Lords of Trade, relative to

New Jersey affairs, 234, 271; Objected to as a member of the Council, 301; Appointed a member of Lord Lovelace's Council, 317; Signs addresses, 373, 415, 473.—Member of Governor Hunter's Council, iv, 2, 19; Letter from, to John Pulteny, 6; Complimented by Governor Hunter, 61; Referred to, 85, 123, 131, 157, 159; Dead, 175, 216; Referred to, 324.

Quigg, Hugh, x, 717.

Quintin, William, Sr., Commissioner of Customs. 254.

Quintipartite Deed between Sir George Cartaret, William Penn, Nicholas Lucas, Gawen Lawrie and Edward Byllyinge, Dividing the Province of New Jersey into East and West Jersey, i, 205.

Quit-rents, Selling of, forbidden, i, 477.—Instructions respecting, ii, 84–86; George Willocks authorized to receive them, 186; Rip Van Dam likewise authorized, 194.—Governor Franklin, in relation to, ix, 586.

R.

Radler, John, ii, 334.

Rahl (Rall), Colonel, x, 272.

Raleigh, Sir Walter, i, 272.

Raleman, Jane, ii, 327.

Ralph, Moses, iv, 303.

Rambo, John, ii, 146, 380.

Rambo, P., i, 183.

Randall, ———, ix, 251.

Randolph, Edmund, ix, 326.

Randolph, Edward, ii, 49; Memorial from, to the Commissioners of Customs, 116; Memorial from, to the Lords of Trade, 131; Letter to, from the Commissioners of Customs, relative to the ports of Perth Amboy and Burlington, 178; One of the Council of West Jersey, 209; Referred to, 215, 228, 235, 243, 248, 252; Letter from, to the Lords of Trade, relative to East and West Jersey, 356; Crimes and misdemeanors charged by him upon the Governors of the Proprietary Governments in America, 358; Referred to, 473, 476, 480; Letter from, to the Lords of Trade, adverse to Andrew Hamilton, 481.

Randolph, John, ix, 622.

Randolph, Joseph Fitz, ii, 326.

Randolph, Peter, One of the commissioners selected to settle the boundary lines, ix, 390, 447, 582, 591, 624, 631, 632.

Randolph, Peyton, One of the commissioners selected to settle the boundary line, ix, 390, 447, 582, 591, 625, 631, 632.—Letter from, to the Speaker of the House of Representatives of New Jersey, x, 25.

Randolph, Richard, vii, 109.

Raper, Caleb, viii, Part I, 69.

Raper, Thomas, ii, 148.

Rarlemon, Jacob, ii, 326.

Ramlinson, Thomas, iii, 153.

Read, Bowes, x, 149.

Read, Charles, vi, 368—vii, 125, 128, 139, 150; On the state of the paper currency, 357; Collector of Customs at Burlington, 381; Clerk, 542–550; Referred to, 650—viii, Part I, 38; Letter to, from Governor Belcher, relative to the riots at Perth Amboy, 39; Referred to, 45, 75, 106; Letter from, to Robert Hunter Morris, 186.—To agree with printer for printing bills of credit, Part II, 71; Letter to, from Governor Belcher, relative to the defeat of General Braddock, 117; Warrants to, 150–155, 232–234; Colonel of Burlington militia, 158; Informs Lieutenant-Governor Pownall of the death of Governor Belcher, 257.—Recommended for the Council, ix, 127; Bearer of message to the Governor, 129; Appointed a member of the Council, 151, 153; Notice of, 151; Certifies, 205; Referred to, 217, 237; Member of Council, 274; Named as one of the commissioners for trying pirates, 284; Referred to, 342; Commissioner to purchase lands of the Indians, 356; Appointed Surrogate, 359, 360; Referred to, 387; Commission of, as Chief-Justice, 424, 425, 427; In Council, 509—x, 7, 17, 28; Commissioned with others to take charge of the seals, 54; Referred to, 133, 231, 279; In Council, 351; Warrant to, 357; Removal of, to St. Croix, 426; Notice of, 426; Referred to, 427, 455.

Read, George, x, 529.

Read, Israel, x, 345.

Read, Joe, viii, Part I, 123.

Read (Reed), John, iii, 498—iv, 215, 326, 334, 375, 377.

Read, Mr., Intrusted with letters from Mr. Dockwra, and died on the passage, iv, 116, 117.

Reader, Jeremiah, iii, 446.

Reading, Elizabeth, ix, 3.

Reading, John, ii, 146, 380, 486.—Summoned by Lord Cornbury, to show his authority as one of the Council of West Jersey, iii, 158; One of the Council, 221.—Notice of, iv, 62; Judge of the Supreme Court, 140; Recommended for the Council, 153, 154, 169, 170, 182; Died, 333; Payments due him, 370, 372; Referred to, 452, 453.

Reading, John (2d), One of Governor Burnet's Council, v, 2, 3; Money paid to, 135, 141; Commissioner to try pirates, 197; Signs, 443; Referred to, 456; Reports on the claim of Lewis Morris, 478.—Named as one of Governor Morris' Council, vi, 14, 15, 109; Signs as a Proprietor, 139; Speaker of Council, 142, 232; Letter from, to the Lords of Trade, announcing the death of President Hamilton, 462.—Member of Governor Belcher's Council, vii, 6, 11, 98, 103, 237, 644—viii, Part I, 16, 105; Part II, 150; Objects to assume the chief authority on the death of Governor Belcher, 259; States his objections in a letter to Lieutenant-Governor Pownall, 260; Governor Pownall's reply, 261; Rejoinder of, 262; Opinion of the Attorney-General as

to his authority as President of the Council, 264; Referred to, 267.—
Letter to, on receiving the government from Lieutenant-Governor
Pownall, ix, 2; Notice of, 5; Referred to, 7; Letter from, to William
Denny, 110; Letter to, from Governor Pownall, relative to the invasion of Canada, 111; Asks leave to resign as a member of the Council, 127; Charles Read appointed in his stead, 151; Referred to,
184, 207.

Reading, Joseph, x, 352.

Reading, Thomas (John?), Referred to by Rev. Jacob Henderson, iv, 157.

Reap, Widow, Contributes to the supposed Cornbury Fund, iii, 212.

Reape, William, i, 44.

Receivers-General, Crown rules and instructions for, ix, 289-299.

Redford, John, vi, 373.

Redman, John, x, 227.

Redford, Thomas, iv, 9.

Reed, Andrew, x, 5.

Reed, Joseph, x, 428.

Reed, Joseph, Jr., Deputy Secretary of the Colony of New Jersey, x, 5,
7; Surrogate, 8; Referred to, 133-135, 681.

Reeve, John, iv, 81, 85.

Reeve, Mark, i, 186, 269, 413, 414.

Reeves, John, iii, 376, 423, 424, 427, 447, 452.

Reformed Christian religion, to be maintained in the Province of New
Jersey, i, 135.

Register of Scotland, Letter from, to Sir John Werden, i, 379; Answer to
the same, 380.

Regnier, Mr., iv, 102, 103, 132.

Reid, James, i, 512.

Reid, John, i, 448, 464, 465, 467, 468; Notice of, 510; Referred to, 511-513,
523; Award of, relative to the settlement of the line between East
and West Jersey, 523.—Referred to, ii, 16, 17, 33; Commissioned
Surveyor-General in the case of the disability of John Barclay, 81;
Signs as Proprietor, 113; Referred to, 186, 190, 195-197; A Grand
Juror, 332.

Renowewan, Indian chief, i, 182.

Representatives, Method of choosing, vi, 19.

Ressey, Joseph, ii, 397.

Revell, Thomas, i, 260, 284—ii, 146, 147, 209, 384; Recommended for
Council, 417, 429, 486; Objected to, 488; Appointed member of the
Council, 507.—One of Governor Cornbury's Council, iii, 2, 64;
Objects to certain representatives in the General Assembly, 88, 112,
137, 150; Referred to, 155, 160, 172, 178, 279; Notice of, 290;
Objected to, as a member of the Council, 300; Letter from William
Penn concerning, 303; Removal of, from the Council, recommended
by the Lords of Trade, 309; Signs address, 367; Referred to, 463—
iv, 41.

Revenues and fines from December, 1704, to December, 1708, iii, 350.

Revolutionary disturbances, King's message to Parliament, relative to outrageous proceedings in Boston, x, 431; Resolution of the House of Lords in reply, 432; The same, of the House of Commons, 433; Comments on the events in Boston, by the people of Essex County, 459; Resolves of the Freeholders of Essex County, 465; Pamphlet entitled "Argument on both sides in the dispute between Great Britain and her Colonies, etc.," 478; The importation of arms and ammunition into the Colonies forbidden by the King, 497; The King determines to withstand every attempt to weaken his authority over the Colonies, 513; Destruction of tea at Greenwich, 530; Seizure of arms and ammunition imported without license, 548; Earl of Dartmouth expresses hopes of a restoration of the public tranquility, 553; News of the affair at Lexington and Concord, 587; Lawyers agree to prevent all unnecessary litigation on account of, 589; Proceedings of the King's troops at Concord, 590; The affair at Weymouth, 606; At Halifax, 608; The King's bust disfigured at Montreal, 610; Affidavits relative to the affairs at Lexington and Concord, 612–615; Respecting prisoners made at Ticonderoga and Crown Point, 641; Movement of troops in New Jersey, 644; The King determines to crush the rebellion, 645; War declared by Congress and preparations in progress for it, 652; Fears of the Tories, 654; Lord Stirling (William Alexander) appointed a colonel by the Provincial Congress, 662; No one will accept a seat in the Council, 662; Troops and money raised in New Jersey, 669; General belief that Congress will have the assistance of France, 676; Vessels authorized by Congress to obtain from foreign ports gunpowder and military stores, 684; Oath imposed on the inhabitants of Newport, Rhode Island, by General Lee, 685; An act passed in Connecticut for punishing persons inimical to the Colonies, 686; Notes of what Mr. Dickinson said before the Assembly of New Jersey, 689; Articles of confederation and perpetual union, 691–697; Arrest of Governor Franklin, 698–702; Lord High Admiral of England, to seize all ships taken from the Colonies, 711; Association of the inhabitants of Pequanock, to sustain the action of Congress, 716.

Reynolds, John, i, 369.

Reynolds, John, of Morris County, x, 717.

Reynardson, Samuel, x, 3.

Rhode Island, Connected with illegal trading, ii, 123; Quota of troops of, for the defence of New York, 134; A retreat for pirates, 361.—Assistance from, for New York, viii, Part I, 194, 195.—Oath imposed on the people of Newport, x, 685.

Richards, Paul, v, 400, 402, 409, 410.

Richards, Thomas, x, 673.

Richardson, Joseph, x, 413.

Richardson, John, x, 717.

11

Richier, Edward, ii. 42–62, 66–74. 76, 79. 95, 257, 258, 300, 302, 376, 408, 411, 416; Signs the surrender of the government, 456–460; Asks the appointment of Andrew Hamilton as Governor, 470.— Signs as a Proprietor, iii, 38, 82, 95, 302; Did not sign Sonmans' commission, 314; Signs as a Proprietor, 498.—Letter from, to Secretary Popple, iv, 115; Signs as a Proprietor, 141; Recommends certain persons for the Council, 153; Referred to, 242—v, 6.

Richmond, Duke of, Circular letter from, relative to penalties incurred under the Stamp Act, ix, 553; Acknowledgment to, from Governor Franklin, 568.

Ricketts, Colonel, vii, 528.

Rickie, Israel, vi, 455—vii, 458.

Rickie, John, vi. 455, 465—vii, 458.

Riddell (Riddle), Walter, ii, 186–193; Disbursements by, on account of East Jersey, 202; Signs name, 213.

Riddle, William, Summoned by Lord Cornbury to show his authority to act as one of the Council of West Jersey, iii, 158.

Rig, Ambrose, Disbursements by, on account of East Jersey, ii, 205.

Rigg, Ambrose, An East Jersey Proprietor. i, 266, 373. 383. 425, 433, 434, 529.

Riggs, Joseph, x. 467.

Right, R., i, 269.

Righton, William, ii, 121, 122.

Riker, Hendrick, vii, 372–375, 444.

Riker, John, vii, 372–374.

Riley, John, Captain, ix, 184, 186.

Rillingworth, Thomas, Judge in Salem County, a scandalous person, iii, 152.

Ringo, Cornelius, vii, 606.

Ringo, Philip, vii, 606.

Riots, In Monmouth County, x, 148; In Essex and Monmouth, 172, 192.

Rioters, List of, vi, 245; Communication from, 292; Speech of Samuel Nevill in answer to their petition, 323; Petition from, to the House of Assembly, 348; Member of Council, 369, 370; Affidavit of Elisha Parker, relative to legal proceedings of, 395; State of facts about the riots, 397; Affidavits respecting, 427–432; Numbers of, increasing, 446.—Answer of, to the publication of the Proprietors and speech of Samuel Nevill, vii, 30; James Alexander, relative to, 53; Petition from, to Governor Belcher, 71; Referred to, 82, 86; Proceedings of the Council, relative to, 86; Letters from James Alexander, relative to, 113, 122, 154, 161; Affidavits relative to, 178–182; Address from the Council of New Jersey to the King, relative to, 189; Address of the same to the Duke of Bedford, relative to, 191; Petition from the Council of Proprietors of East Jersey, to the King, relative to, 193; Letter from James Alexander and Robert T. Morris, relative to, 197; State of facts concerning, 207; Proposal of, relative to instituting

suits, 233; Letter from the Council of New Jersey, relative to, 236; Governor, to the Lords of Trade, concerning, 249; J. Alexander and R. H. Morris, to F. J. Paris, relative to, 251; Richard Partridge, relative to, 268; Timber destroyed by them near Newark on the Passaic River, 272; List of papers relating to, 274; Affidavits and other documents relating to, 275–288; J. Alexander on the trial of, in Essex County, 288; Letter from Governor Belcher to the Lords of Trade, relative to, 293; Letters from F. J. Paris, concerning, 301, 304; Proprietors of West Jersey pray relief from, 316; Letter from J. Alexander, relating to, 328; Letter from David Ogden, relative to the titles of, 343; From the same, respecting the Horseneck, 364, 368; Affidavits relative to, 369–378; Petition of R. H. Morris, respecting, 379; Proclamation of Governor Belcher, relative to, 382; Additional facts, affidavits, examinations and other documents relating to, 402–456; List of those indicted in Essex, Middlesex and Somerset Counties, 456; Representation of the Lords of Trade, concerning, 467; Memorial of the Council, relative to, 537; Not convicted of treason, 574,—Memorial, responsive to representations made by them, viii, Part I, 1; At Perth Amboy, 38, 39, 43, 52; Order in the Privy Council, relative to, 53; Letters from Governor Belcher, relative to, 60, 61; Report of the Lords of the Committee of Council, relating to, 90; Letters of Governor Belcher, referring to, 90, 102; His speech in Council concerning, 103.

Ritchie, John, ii, 186.

Ritger, Abraham, vi, 245.

Robeards, Luman, x, 718.

Roberts (Robards), Amos, One of the rioters in Essex County, vi, 351, 403, 455, 465—vii, 156, 178, 180, 181, 207, 210, 223–225, 231, 232, 283, 310, 457, 458, 471, 489, 497, 505.

Roberts (Roberdes), John, i, 269—iv, 276, 281, 283, 369—v, 187.

Roberts, Joseph, One of the rioters, vii, 178, 179, 405, 444, 512.

Robeson, Andrew, ii, 22, 24, 146; Disbursements by, on account of East Jersey, 204; Signs, 380.

Robeson, John, Sr., x, 717.

Robeson, John, Jr., x, 717.

Robeson, Dr. William, Disbursements by, on account of East Jersey, ii, 202.

Robinds, Peter, x, 718.

Robins, Aaron, ii, 397.

Robins, Daniel, ii, 396, 397—iv, 310.

Robins, Moses, ii, 396.

Robins, Nathaniel, ii, 396.

Robins, Richard, ii, 397—iii, 353.—Affidavit of, against Jeremiah Basse, iv, 74.

Robins, Robert, iv, 215.

Robinson, Andrew, Surveyor of West New Jersey, i, 517, 521—vi, 148, 149—viii, Part I, 205, 227, 249.

Robinson, John, x, 229.

Robinson, Thomas, An East Jersey Proprietor, i, 474, 490, 529.

Robinson, Sir Thomas, viii, Part I, 93; Letter from, to Governor Belcher, relative to the hostile attempts of the French on the Ohio, 292; From the Lords of Trade, with a plan for the defence of the Colonies, Part II, 1; Circular letter from, to the Governors in America, urging enlistments, 17; Letters to, from Governor Belcher, relative to the conduct of the Assembly, 24, 76; Letter to, from James Alexander, relative to the action of New York Council in regard to the boundary line, 89; Circular letter from, to Governors, relative to augmenting the regiments in America, 93; Letters to, from Governor Belcher, relative to military matters, 105, 135; From the Lords of Trade, relative to establishing packet-boats between England and the Colonies, 138; From Governor Belcher, relative to military affairs, 148; Referred to, 209.

Robinson, William, i, 530—ii, 327—iv, 188.

Robison, Patrick, ii, 122.

Robison, Richard, i, 269.

Robs, John, x, 711.

Rockhill, Edward, iii, 165.

Roddam, Colonel Robert, Correspondence relating to the accidental killing of a maid-servant of Colonel Ricketts of Elizabethtown, by a shot from the ship Greyhound, vii, 528–537.

Rodman, Dr. John, Recommended for the Council, v, 294, 366, 402, 446, 454, 469.—Member of Governor Morris' Council, vi, 14, 15, 109, 369, 370, 435.—Referred to, vii, 5; Member of Governor Belcher's Council, 6, 86, 88, 97, 237, 541, 644.—Referred to, viii, Part I, 16; Dead, Part II, 236.

Rodney, Cæsar, x, 529.

Roe, Azel, x, 345.

Roeloste, Helemock, ii, 326.

Roemer, Col. W. W., Report of the Earl of Bellomont, on the harbor of New York, ii, 354.

Rogers, Jabez, ii, 336, 339.

Rogers, John, i, 288—iv, 98.

Rogers, Joseph, x, 717,

Rogers, Nathaniel, vii, 421, 424.

Rolf, Henry, iv, 188, 190.

Rolph, Benjamin, iv, 189.

Rolph, John, Affidavit of, relative to the riots, vii, 438.

Rolph, Joseph, ii, 217.

Rolph (Rolfe), Moses, iv, 186, 187—v, 142, 144, 147, 149.

Romer, Wolfgang William, iii, 64.

Ronal, James, x, 717.

Roosevelt, John, v, 153.

Rose, Joseph, vii, 542; Affidavit of, against John Coxe, 543.

Rose, William, x, 717.

Ross, George, i, 65—ii, 397.

Ross, George, x, 529, 574.

Ross, George, Jr., ii, 129, 334.

Ross, Isaac, x, 718.

Ross, John, ii, 129, 326, 334, 396—vii, 439.

Ross, Major John, ix. 355.

Ross, William, x, 717.

Rosse, George, ii, 397.

Rowe, George, i, 320.

Rowleson, Aaron, v, 151.

Royal Mines in New Jersey, Articles of association to work, ix, 318.

Royce (Royse), John, ii, 255, 270, 325, 348, 437, 439, 441, 486, 487, 502.—
    Contributes to the supposed Cornbury fund, iii, 211; Affidavit rela-
    tive to the same, 217.—Referred to, 429, 459, 480, 482, 484, iv, 107,
    111.

Roydon, William, i, 268.

Roye, John, Nominated as Justice of the Peace, viii, Part I, 105.

Ruckman, John, ii, 326, 365.

Rudderow, John, ii, 384.

Rudvores, John, iv, 310.

Rudyard, John, iv, 9; Statement of, respecting Peter Sonmans, 15;
    Referred to, 136.

Rudyard (Ruddiard), Thomas, i, 268; An East Jersey Proprietor, 366,
    373; Commission of, as Secretary and Register of East Jersey, 376;
    Note on, 376; Among the twenty-four East Jersey Proprietors, 383,
    410, 432; Referred to, 438, 442, 447, 460, 462, 481; Censured by the
    Proprietors of East Jersey, 492; Referred to, 529; Disbursements by,
    on account of East Jersey, ii, 203; Referred to, 232, 388.

Rufane, General, ix, 277.

Ruggles, Mr., ix, 451.

Rumsey, William, i, 269.

Runyon (Rugnion), Vincent, i, 85—ii, 325.

Runyen, William, ii, 396.

Rush, Benjamin, x, 430.

Rushout, Sir John, viii, Part I, 23.

Russell, Chambers, One of the Commissioners selected to settle the
    boundry line, ix, 390, 582, 591, 624, 631, 632; Admiralty Judge, 622.

Russell, Charles, vii, 379.

Russell, Samuel, ii, 63, 72.

Russell, Mr., viii, Part I, 176.

Rutherfurd, John, vi, 397—x, 422.

Rutherfurd, Walter, vi, 397—x, 137, 195, 502.

Rutledge, Edward, x, 530.

Rutledge, J., x, 530.

Rycroft, David, Letter from, to John Parker and Andrew Johnston, v, 183.

Ryder, D., Attorney-General, Report upon certain acts passed in New Jersey, vii, 305.—Report on the riots in New Jersey, viii, Part I, 54.

Ryerson, Joseph, ix, 5.

Ryerson, Martin, vi, 154, 158.

Ryerson, May, ix, 5.

Ryker, Abraham, vii, 457.

Ryker, Hendrick, Jr., vii, 444.

Ryker, Isaac, vii, 444.

Ryley, Mark, x, 531.

S.

Sabine, James, x, 375.

Sabrengh, Jacob, ii, 326.

Sacket, Mr., Director of the Tar-work, iv, 223.

Sackett, Joseph, Jr., In relation to the titles of the Common lands in Bergen County, in possession of Edward Earle, ix, 451.

Sackville, Edward, Affidavit of, as to the number of families in New Jersey in 1665, i, 184.

Sacoock, i, 1.

Sadler, Richard, i, 142, 143.

Sadloe, Thomas, ii, 48.

St. Clair, Sir John, Deputy, Quater-Master-General, viii, Part II, 105; Letter to, from Governor Belcher, on the necessity of driving the French from America, 133; Referred to, 140.

St. Johns, James, ii, 41-61, 65-73, 76, 79, 88, 90, 95.

St. Megill, Sloop captured, vi, 380-292.

Salaries of Public Officers, iii, 120, 144—iv, 22, 185—ix, 579—x, 51.— Fees in compensation for deficiency of, 389; Governor Franklin's observation on, 405, 448; Order in Privy Council respecting, 549; Referred to, 558, 697.

Sale, Obadiah, ii, 129, 334, 397.

Salem, Court held at, i, 118; Appointments at, by John Fenwicke, 275; Names of persons at, 283; Overseers at, Commissioned by Governor Andros, 284; Memorial from, to Governor Jennings, 421; Visited and described by Lord Cornbury, iii, 80.—Address from inhabitants of, to Governor Hunter, relative to payment of taxes and the election of a new County representative, iv, 112.—County taxes, 368, 369.—Number of representatives from, v, 12; To be restrained from sending representatives, 74; In relation to representatives from, 83-85.—Manufacture of glass at, vi, 98.—Imports and exports, vii, 587.

Salem County, Population of, in 1699, ii, 305.—Taxes of, iv, 368, 369.— Money received from, by the Treasurer, v, 132, 133.—Money received from Collector of, viii, Part I, 66-68; From Commissioners, 71; Interest moneys from, 73, 74.

Salem and Old Man's Creek, Titles to lands between, i, 109, 119, 508; Lands at, sold by John Fenwick, 414.

Salisbury, Silvester, Affidavit of, as to the number of families in New Jersey in 1665, i, 183.

Salmon, Captain John, ix, 184, 185.

Salsbury, Evan, i, 50.

Salsbury, Jonathan, x, 717.

Saltar, Ebenezer, Affidavit of, relative to the riots, vii, 450.

Saltar, Elisha, vii, 621, 622.

Saltar, Richard (2nd), In charge of beacon on Neversink Highlands, vi, 374; Referred to, vii, 169; Order in Privy Council approving the appointment of the Council of New Jersey, 175; Referred to 177; Recommendation of, for Council commented upon by Governor Belcher, 247; Referred to, 259; In Council, 335, 343.—Referred to, 644, viii, Part I, 16, 41, 187, 201.—viii, Part II, 150–153, 191, 232–234, 268; ix, 274; Named as one of the commissioners for trying pirates, 283; Commissioned Third Justice of the Supreme Court, 340; Notice of, 341; Reappointed Third Justice, 345; Commissioner to purchase lands of the Indians, 356; Death of, 386; Referred to, 442.

Salter, Henry, i, 414.

Salter, Richard, ii, 327, 328; Presented by Monmouth County Grand Jury, 332; Arrested for contempt of court, 364; Fined, 365.—Lord Cornbury complained of for making him a Justice of the Peace, iii, 93–118, 128. 152, 156; Referred to, 198, 199; Collecting money, supposed to be for Lord Cornbury, 199–218, 277.—Referred to, 393. iv, 3.

Saltonstall, Mr., Chosen Governor of Connecticut, iii, 271.

Samuels, Christian, x, 515.

Sanders, Christopher, i, 268.

Sandford (Samford), William, President of a special court held at Elizabethtown, i, 65; Member of Council, 110; Affairs with the Council of New Netherlands, 125, 131, 140, 145, 149, 150; Named by Governor Carteret to succeed Capt. Berry, 296; Before the New York Council, 297; Referred to, 300, 301, 303.—President of Essex County Court, ii, 313; Note on, 314; Ill-treatment of him in Court, 333; Signs petition to the King, 373; Signs, 386; Recommended for Council, 417, 429, 431, 486, 487; Appointed member of the Council, 507.—One of Governor Cornbury's Council, iii, 2, 64, 155, 160, 290; Proposed as a member of Lord Lovelace's Council, 299; Appointed as such, 317; Signs addresses, 367, 373, 415, 473; Justice of the Peace for Essex County, 495; The Proprietors ask that he be left out of Governor Hunter's Council, 497.—Member of Governor Hunter's Council, iv, 2; Expelled from the Assembly, 22, 125; Re-elected, 125, 126. 133.

Sands, Thomas, ii, 46.

Sandwich, James, Earl of, ii, 388.

Sandyland, James, i, 181, 183.

Sandy Point (Sandy Hook), Grant for lands at, i, 43, 220; Fortifications at, 292, 294, 525, 526.

Sansom, John, Secretary to the Commissioners of Customs, Letter to, with documents relative to the ports of New Jersey, ii, 247; Letter from, to Secretary Popple, transmitting a report of the Commissioners of Customs, relative to Perth Amboy, 251.

Santen (Santon), L., i, 458, 526.

Sargeant, Jonathan, Jr., ii, 336.

Sargeant, William, i. 67.

Sarjent, Samuel, x. 202.

Sarjeant, Thomas, vi, 245, 401—vii, 210, 457.

Salterthwait, James, Salary as doorkeeper of the Assembly, iv, 185, 368, 369.

Sawowouwe, i, 1.

Sayre, Daniel, ii, 129.

Sayre, David, iv, 215.

Sayre, Thomas, ii, 397.

Sayro, Francis, ii, 326.

Saxton, Nehemiah, x, 273.

Scanck, Garrat, v, 146, 150.

Scattergood, Joseph, vii, 642.

Scattergood, Thomas, viii, Part II, 235.

Schermerhorn, John, Indicted, vii, 458.

Schermerhorne, Robert, vii, 64.

Schoolmaster to be supported, i, 140.—How licensed, ix, 68.

Schooly, John, v, 187.

Schooley, Thomas. i, 270.

Schuyler, Arent, Journal of a visit of, to the Minisink country, ii, 103.—Referred to, vii, 166.

Schuyler, Gertrude, ix, 641.

Schuyler, John, Recommended for the Council, v, 318, 374, 402, 446, 454, 469.—Member of Governor Morris' Council, vi, 14, 15; Discharged at his own request, 105, 237; Orders to, from Governor Belcher, 182 —viii, Part II, 158, 174. 177, 180; Referred to, 252—x, 387.

Schuyler, Peter, iv, 340; Letter from, to the Lords of Trade, relating to Surveyor Jarratt, 431; Letter from, to the same, inclosing petition, 438; Letter to, from Lewis Morris, relating to the boundary between New York and New Jersey, 446, 448.—Appointed Colonel of the forces in Canada, vi, 378; Number of men in the several companies under his command, 425; Letter to, from Governor Clinton, of New York, 441; Letter to, from President Hamilton, 447; Referred to, 451-453.—Recommended by Governor Belcher, vii, 93, 102.—President of the New York Council, viii, Part I, 136; Petition of Allan Jarrat to, 233; Report to, on the same, 235; Petition to, of inhabitants of New York, relative to boundary line, 237.—Letter to, from Governor Belcher, viii, Part II, 11; Referred to, 121, 127, 183, 185,

200, 201, 204, 230, 258, 259.—Recommended for the Council, ix, 127; Commands the New Jersey Regiment, 174, 184-186.

Schuyler, Philip, iv, 370—v, 147—x, 114.

Scotch Rebellion, Defeat of, iv, 252.

Scott, Benjamin, i, 239, 268, 271, 291.—One of the commissioners to lay out lands, iii, 221.

Scott, Charles, ix, 318-321.

Scott, John, ii, 148, 380—iii, 213—iv, 10.

Scott, John Morin, ix, 179.

Scovenoven, Isaac, vi, 167.

Scritchfield, John, vii, 378.

Scrutall, Jan, i, 49.

Scudder, Nathaniel, x, 345, 559.

Sdmodt, Ma'tys, ii, 326.

Seabrooke, James, ii, 397.

Seafer, Richard, iv, 189.

Seals, Of New Jersey, under Berkley and Carteret, i, 27; Of Governor Philip Carteret, 60: Of the twenty-four Proprietors, 488.—Of the Province, iv, 332, 373.—Warrants for new, v, 180.—Of the several Colonies, ix, 243, 247; Of New Jersey, 239, 247, 618, 640.—Defacing of in Council, x, 13.

Sealton, John, ii, 397.

Seamans, Colonel, x, 671.

Sears, Daniel, Grand Juror for Essex County, iii, 496.

Sears, Isaac, x, 362.

Sebering, Jacob, iv, 147.

Secaucus (Sekakus), Common lands in the island of, ix, 451; Note on, 452: Opinion of Wm. Samuel Johnson in relation to, 454.—Patent of the island of, x, 169.

Seeley, Ephraim, x, 531.

Seely, Joseph, ii, 488.

Seeres, David, ii, 339.

Septennial Elections, x, 142.

Sesson, Thomas, i, 530.

Severns, Theodore, vii, 542, 544, 606, 607, 643.

Severns, Theophilus, Surrogate, ix, 359.

Seymour, Robert, Executed for the murder of an Oneida Indian, ix, 578.

Shaddock, Samuel, i, 51.

Shaddock, William, i, 413.

Shallet, Arthur, ii, 42-61, 65-73, 78.

Shamgungoe, Bash, i, 51.

Shammit, George, ii, 396.

Shane, James, x, 718.

Sharp (Sharpe), Anthony, i, 530—ii, 187-193, 257—iv, 256, 370.

Sharp, Elizabeth, iii, 452.

Sharpe, Horatio, Governor of Maryland, viii, Part II, 173.

Sharp, Isaac, Affidavit of, against Jeremiah Basse, iv, 74; Referred to, 107, 108, 109, 253—v, 58–60, 133, 139.

Sharpe, John, ii, 327—iii, 164—v, 410.

Sharp, Thomas, ii, 332—iv, 243, 246, 296.

Sharp, William, iv, 10.

Sharper, John, iv, 174.

Shaw, John, ii, 146, 384.

Shaw, Thomas, Lieutenant-Colonel, ix, 184, 185.

Sheate, Stephen, ii, 397.

Shelburne, Earl of, Circular letter from, relative to murdering the Indians, ix, 569; Imparts to Governor Franklin the King's approval of the conduct of the people of New Jersey, 570; Inquires into the annual charges of maintaining the several Provinces, 573; Informed by Governor Franklin, respecting violences done to the Indians, 574, 578; Petition to, from Peter Hasenclever, 583; Informed by Governor Franklin, respecting annual charges for the government, and the fees of different offices, 586, 592; Transmits seals to the several Colonies, 618; Announces the King's displeasure with the Assembly of of New Jersey, 636; Letters to, from Governor Franklin, 640, 642.— Referred to, x, 87.

Shelley, Captain Giles, ii, 286, 287; Letter from, 289; Referred to, 291.

Shelton, Sampson, iii, 64.

Shennock, Andrew, i, 269.

Shepheard, Dickersons, iv, 370—v, 137.

Shepherd, David, ii, 486.

Sheppard, Joseph, x, 531.

Sherd, William, x, 273.

Sheriffs, Act of the New Jersey Legislature, obliging them to give security, vii, 296, 329.

Sherman, Roger, x, 539.

Sherrard, Robert, vii, 416, 417.

Sherwood, Joseph, x, 28.

Sherwood, John, ix, 445.

Shields, Robert, vii, 64.

Shin, Thomas, vi, 202.

Shinar, Edward Earle, High Sheriff of Bergen County, iv, 142.

Shinn, John, iii, 165.

Shipman, Jacob, vi, 455, 465—vii, 458.

Shippoy, John, iv, 190.

Ships, Entered and cleared at the ports of Burlington and Perth Amboy, vii, 381.—Report on the act concerning, ix, 628.

Shirley, William, Governor of Massachusetts, vii, 67, 68, 101; Letter to, from Governor Belcher, 135; Referred to, 310, 386–400—viii, Part I, 27, 94.—Appointed Colonel, viii, Part II, 17, 19.—Letter from, to Sir Thomas Robinson, relative to military matters, 111; Referred to, 127; Succeeds General Braddock, 148; In command at Albany, etc.,

159; Referred to, 167; Letter to, from Governor Belcher, relative to military affairs, 168; Referred to, 170; Letter to, from Governor Belcher, relative to councils of war, 182; A letter from, to Governor Belcher, 198, 203; Referred to, 201, 206.

Shoemaker, Benjamin, vii, 130.

Shoemaker, Conrad, x, 512.

Short, William, iv, 113.

Shotwell, Abraham, i, 50.—Affidavit of, relative to the riots at Newark and Perth Amboy, vii, 179; Referred to, 181.

Showen, Ada, x, 717.

Shreave, Thomas, iv, 310.

Shreve, Joseph, v, 187.

Shrewsbury, Proclamation of the Governor and Council, relative to the inhabitants of, i, 58; Confirmation to, of certain privileges, 88; Relations with the Council of New Netherlands, 123, 125, 130, 134, 135.—Meeting of inhabitants called to choose a committee in accordance with the recommendation of Congress, x, 333; Proceedings of the inhabitants, 600; Proceedings of the Committee of Correspondence of, 666.

Shute, William, Ensign, ix, 187.

Sibley, Robert, i, 289.

Sibly, Thomas, i, 289.

Silk, Bounties for the culture of, ix, 490.

Silk, Lawrence, v, 139.

Simkins, Joseph, iv, 215.

Simpkin, Michall, i, 50.

Simpson, Henry, viii, Part I, 299.

Sinclair, Mr., iv, 163.

Singletary, John, i, 130; Arrested by the Dutch authorities, 131; Fined, £500, 132.

Singleton, Thomas, i, 470.

Sinnicka, Andrew, i, 413.

Sinnicks, Thomas, x, 471.

Sirwo, James, ii, 326.

Skeene, Major Philip, x, 608; Arrest of, 648; Parole of, 649; Letter from, to John Penn, 649; Referred to, 658.

Skene, John, Deputy Governor of West Jersey, i, 517, 522, 523—ii, 4, 19, 65.

Skenoye, Thomas, ii, 396.

Skermerhorn, John, vi, 456, 465.

Skillman, Thomas, i, 50.

Skinner, Courtland, Nomination of, as Attorney-General of New Jersey, viii, Part I, 293.—Notice of, 293; His appointment favored by Governor Belcher, 298; Letter from Governor Belcher to Lord Halifax, concerning, viii, Part II. 200.—Petition of, as a Proprietor, 228; Warrants to, 233, 234; Answers queries submitted to him by

the Council, relative to the authority of Mr. Reading as President, 264.—Referred to, ix, 317; Notice of, 449; Letters to, 449, 451, 573; Referred to, 641.—Speaker of the Assembly, x, 21, 59, 97, 99, 103, 139, 193, 215; Gives his opinion as Attorney-General, on the proceedings of the Magistrates at Cape May, 216, 217; Opinion on the charter petitioned for by the Presbyterian clergy, 353, 359; Warrant to, 358; Asks from the Crown an adequate salary as Attorney-General, 383; Relative to the proceedings of the Assembly in regard to the Treasury, 412, 414, 415; Representatives from Burlington County instructed not to discharge him from his liabilities as Treasurer, 417; Resignation of, as Treasurer, 421; Salary of, 450; Referred to, 603, 604; House of, entered, 700; Took refuge on board of a man of war, 706.

Skinner, John, ix, 16.

Skinner, Stephen, recommended for appointment as Treasurer of East New Jersey, ix, 366; Robbing of the Treasury, 565.—Affidavit of, relative to the robbing of the East Jersey Treasury, x, 37; Notices of, 37, 144; Appointed member of the Council, 139, 143; Error in regard to his christian name corrected, 147; Referred to, 191, 414; In Council, 351; Warrant to, 357; Act to authorize a suit against him for the recovery of the sum alleged to have been stolen from the Treasury, 510; Of the Council, 561.

Skinner, Thomas, ii, 41–61, 65–73, 79, 187–194, 376, 408, 411; Signs the surrender of the Government, 456–460; Asks the appointment of Andrew Hamilton as Governor, 470.—Referred to, iii, 82, 95, 314 —vii, 326.

Skinner, Rev. William, Letter to, relative to the seal of New Brunswick, v, 283; Answer to the same, 284; Letter from, to Sir William Keeth, announcing the death of Governor Cosby, and urging him to apply for the vacant position, 435; Notice of, 436.—Referred to, 473, viii, Part I, 293—Part II, 178, 228, 252.—Letters to, from his son, ix, 8, 14.—Referred to, 449, 641, x, 144.

Skinner, Capt. William, Notice of, viii, Part II, 178, 252; Letter to his father William Skinner, 252; Letter from, to his brother Cortlandt Skinner, 258; Commissioned as Lieutenant in Cornwallis's regiment, ix, 8, 14; Gives an account of the assault and landing upon the island of Belle Isle by the English forces, 277; Referred to, 449; Writes to James Parker that the Stamp Act will probably be repealed, 548; Referred to, 641.

Slaney, John, ii, 42–62, 66–74, 79—iii, 498.

Slater (Slaughter), Edward, i, 307, 319, 320, 355—ii, 217, 316, 326, 328, 486, 502—iii, 480, 481, 487.

Slater, Samuel, iv, 189.

Slaughten (Sloughten), William, ii, 123, 431.

Slaughter, Edward, See Slater.

Slaves, An act relating to, recommended by the Lords of Trade to be

repealed, iii 473.—Duty on importation of, iv, 196.—Bounty upon, x, 229.

Slocum, John, i, 51—ii, 332.

Sloper, William, Agent of, Lord Cornbury answers the complaints of the West Jersey Proprietors, iii, 133; Letter from, to Wm. Popple, Jr., relative to Lord Cornbury's salary, 144.

Slot, Jacobus, ii, 326.

Slouby, Henry, iii, 358.

Small, ———, x, 113.

Smalley, Isaac, ii, 397—iii, 446.

Smart, Isaac, i, 269.

Smeeman, Herman, i, 49.

Smith, Alexander, Jr., iv, 215.

Smith, Andrew, i, 288.

Smith, David, i, 269.

Smith, Daniel, iv, 253, 370—v, 137—viii, Part I, 74.

Smith, Daniel, Jr., Commissioned Surveyor-General of West Jersey, x, 15; Notice of, 16.

Smith, Emanuel, iv, 267.

Smith, Isaac, Newark rioter, vii, 179—x, 471, 487, 588.

Smith, James, iv, 371.—Secretary, Fees to, v, 4; Referred to, 12; Recommended for the Council, 34; Appointed a member of Council, 52, 71; Referred to, 103; Money paid to, 135, 137, 139, 143, 147, 148; Commission to try pirates, 197; Memorial of, relative to his fees as Secretary of New Jersey, 198; Referred to, 281, 454; Signs memorial, 301; Dead, 320.

Smith, James (2nd), vi, 465, 466—vii, 109.

Smith, Jeremiah, iv, 113.

Smith, Capt. John, viii, Part I, 137.

Smith, John, i, 50, 134, 227, 268, 284, 414, 508.

Smith, John, viii, Part I, 106—Part II, 40.—Recomended for the Council, ix, 127; Appointed, 151, 274; Named as one of the commissioners for trying pirates, 284; Referred to, 387. — Commis_ sioned with others to take charge of the seals, x, 54; Dead, 230; Notice of, 231.

Smith, Jokabad, Grand Juror on Woodbridge riot, iii, 486, 487.

Smith, Jonathan, iv, 113.

Smith, Jonathan (2nd), x, 531.

Smith, Joseph, vii, 180, 542—x, 139.

Smith, Peter, i. 184.

Smith, Ralph, vii, 542; Affidavit of, respecting John Coxe, 544; Referred to, 546.

Smith, Richard, i, 268—iv, 215.

Smith, Richard (2nd), Recommended for the Council, v, 317, 366, 402, 446, 454, 469.—Member of Governor Morris' Council, vi, 14, 15, 109; Vote on the Militia Act, 202, 203; In Council, 369, 370—vii, 5;

Member of Governor Belcher's Council, 6, 86, 88, 90, 97; Comments upon, by James Alexander, 121; Letter to, from Richard Partridge, 242, 268; Letter from, to Richard Partridge, respecting the proceedings of the Legislature, 365; Referred to, 525; In Council, 541; Dead, 585.—Referred to, ix, 356, 394—x, 231, 256, 358, 471, 530, 546, 698.

Smith, Robert, ii, 335, 337—iii, 496.

Smith, Robert (2nd), viii, Part II, 155.

Smith, Samuel, iv, 253.

Smith, Samuel (2nd), Recommendation of, for the Council condemned by the Lords of Trade, vii, 586; Letters relative to, from Governor Belcher, 600, 607; Referred to, 628.—Accounts of, as Treasurer, viii, Part I, 65, 73, 106.—Part II, 150, 155, 228-235.—Recommended for Council, ix, 387; Appointed, 394; Notice of, 394.—Referred to, x, 54, 231, 351, 357, 450, 561, 665.

Smith, Jamuel J., ix, 395.

Smith, Seth, iv, 215.

Smith, Thomas, i, 268, 413, 414.

Smith, Thomas (2nd), v, 187; Asks to be appointed Governor of New Jersey, 278.

Smith, Widow, i, 414.

Smith, William (of New York), ii, 369—iii, 64.

Smith, William (2nd, of New York), Named as one of the commissioners for trying pirates, ix, 283.

Smith, William, ii, 363,

Smith, William, v, 398, 404—vi, 169, 171, 393, 396.

Smith, William, Jr., viii, Part II, 265.

Smith, Wm. Lovett, x, 231.

Smith, William P., x, 345, 467.

Smith, Rev. Dr., x, 341.

Smoke, Petrus, ix, 179, 181.

Smyth, Andrew, Surrogate, ix, 360—x, 420.

Smyth, Frederick, Proposed as a member of the Council of New Jersey, ix, 442; Recommended for the office of Chief-Justice, 444; Commission of, as such, 475; Notice of, 475; Commission issued, 486; Referred to, 489; In Council, 509.—Affidavit before, x, 37, 56; Complains of the insufficiency of his salary, 62, 144, 146; Resigns his seat in the New Jersey Council, 220; Salary of, made adequate, 261; Referred to, 375; Writes to the Earl of Hillsborough, in relation to the robbery of the Treasury of East Jersey, 379; To the Earl of Dartmouth, relative to the schooner Gaspée, 395; Of the Council, 561.

Smyth, John, vii, 413, 415.—Board of Indemnification to, from the Council of Proprietors of East Jersey, viii, Part I, 200; Certifies, Part II, 228; Money due to, 234.—Surrogate, ix, 360; Recommended for Council, 366; In Council, 509.—Referred to, x, 420, 450.

Smyth. Laurence, vi, 309, 361—x, 422.

Snake Hill, i, 19.

Snell, Captain, i, 130, 132.

Snelling, William, ii, 470—iii, 95.

Snow, Joseph, i, 134.

Snowden, John, i, 270.

Sobrisco, John (Zabriskie, probably), Surrogate, ix, 360.

Society for the Propagation of the Gospel in foreign parts, Proposition from, to establish a library for the use of New York and the neighboring Colonies, v, 237.

Society for Propagating Christian Knowledge, Missions of, viii, Part I, 140.

Solomons (Salmon), John, ix, 185.

Somers, Richard, x, 685.

Somerset County, Taxes in, iv, 368, 369.—Jail of, broken open, vi, 417; List of rioters in, 455.—Petition of the land-holders in, viii, Part I, 54–56.

Somerset, Duchess of, viii, Part I, 84.

Sonmans, Arent, An East Jersey Proprietor, i, 383, 424, 433, 434, 448; Interested in goods shipped to East Jersey, 466; Notice of, 527; Referred, 528—ii, 32; Disbursements by, on account of East Jersey, 202.—Referred to, iii, 161, 162, 310, 312, 314.

Sonmans, Johanna, i, 437.

Sonmans, Peter, i, 437, 442, 457—ii, 32, 149, 164, 165, 171, 177, 186-193, 198, 257, 263, 431; Signs the surrender of the Government, 456–460; Petition of, to the Queen, 466; Note on, 467; Memorial from, to the Lords of Trade objecting to Hamilton's appointment as Governor, 470; Reply of the Proprietors to his complaints against Mr. Hamilton, 475.—To the Earl of Nottingham, relative to the appointment of Jeremiah Basse as Secretary of New Jersey, iii, 23; His indebtedness to Mr. Basse, 27; Several of the Proprietors of New Jersey object to his becoming a member of the Council, 35; His answer to the same, 39, 48; His petition relative to the title to Staten Island, 61, 62; Memorial of, with others, to the Lords of Trade, relative to affairs of New Jersey, 82; Proposed for the Council, 101; Reference to said proposition, 125; East Jersey Proprietors ask for his appointment to Council, 129; Referred to, 141, 154, 160, 161, 162, 177, 189, 192; A petition relative to his carrying away of the public records, 219; Referred to, 253, 254, 259, 261; Objected to as a member of the Council, 301; Memorial of to Governor Cornbury, against John Harrison, Judge of the Court of Common Pleas, 306; Objected to as a member of the Council by Joseph Ormston, 310, 312; Lists of the Proprietors who signed, and who did not sign the commission of, 313, 316; Appointed a member of Lord Lovelace's Council, 317, 328, 329; Referred to, 331, 339; Complaints against, by the Assembly, to the Governor, 374; Letter from, to the Governer, relative to said com-

plaints, 379; Answer of, to the complaints of the Assembly, 416; Petition to the Assembly against, by the Grand Inquest of Middlesex County, 445; Report of the committee on said petition, 447; Petition of, to Governor Lovelace, 449: His answer to the Assembly, ordered by Lieutenant-Governor Ingoldsby to be printed, 460; Signs, 473; Referred to, 488; The Proprietors ask that he be left out of Governor Hunter's Council, 497.—Member of Governor Hunter's Council, iv, 2, 19; Petition against, from Middlesex County, 8: Referred to, 14; Statement concerning his conduct at Woodbridge, 15; Charges of the Assembly against, 38, 39, 43, 45, 48; His removal from the Council recommended by Governor Hunter, 61; Referred to, 64; Indicted for perjury and adultery, 88; Referred to, 93, 94, 101-103, 115, 119, 130, 131, 141, 145; His removal from the Council urged by Governor Hunter, 149, 153; Referred to by Rev. Jacob Henderson, 157; Further reference to, 164, 169, 171, 172, 175, 182, 216, 228, 261, 266, 293, 294, 298, 315, 390—v, 103; Proclamation against, 124; Letter relating to, from James Alexander, 202; Referred to, 263.

Sonmans, Rachel, i, 437.

Sons of Liberty, Address of, to the gentlemen of the law of New Jersey. ix, 547.—Referred to, x, 192.

Sooleys, Robert, ii, 48.

Sospanninck, Indian Grantor, i, 111,

Southall, Robert, Commissioner of Customs, ii, 131

South Carolina, A retreat for pirates, ii, 119, 359.—Resolves of the Assembly of, x, 130, 146.

Southwell, Edward, ii, 275, 276.

Sower, Christopher, x, 227.

Spain, Declaration of war against, ix, 363.—The war with, x, 221, 274.

Spencer, Elisha, Petition of, x, 342; Notice of, 343.

Spencer, William, iv, 310, 313.

Spicer, Jacob, Removed from the judgeship in Gloucester County, iv. 129; Recommended for the Council, 133; Payments to, 370.—Referred to, v, 137—viii, Part 1, 74; Part II, 150, 153, 230, 233—ix, 129, 356.

Spicer, Samuel, i, 44—ii, 146.

Spier, Francis, vi, 215, 355, 356—vii, 248, 414.

Spier, Gerard, vii, 374.

Spiers, Hendrick, i, 151.

Spinage, Humphrey, i, 50.

Spire, Tunis, viii, Part I, 6.

Spotswood, Governor of Virginia, On protection against the Indians, v. 113.

Spragg, Mr., ii, 271.

Spragge, J., 517, 518.

Spratt, John, vii, 322.

Springer, Benjamin, ix, 356, 357.

Springett, Jr., Harbt., i, 369, 376.

Spry, Dr. William, ix, 621.

Squibb, Robert, ii, 47.

Squire, Jonathan, vi, 245—vii, 457.

Stacy, Henry, i, 268, 419.

Stacy's Island, v, 39, 42—x, 512.

Stacy, Mahlon, i, 242, 268, 522, 523—ii, 148, 380.

Stacey, Mahlon (2nd), v, 141; Recommended for Council, 317.—Signs. vi, 139.

Stacy, Robert, i, 239, 268; Matiniconck Island leased to, 286; Magistrate, 291.—Commission, iii, 221.

Stakes, Dr., ix, 9.

Stamp Act, Resolution of the House of Commons, relative to, ix. 448; Instruments used in the courts, etc., of the Province that will bear the highest duty, 480; Letters relating to, from Gov. Franklin and others, 492–503; Its effect upon the business of the courts, 506; Increasing disturbances occasioned by it, 507, 524; List of papers relating to the riots in America growing out of, 527; Meeting of the lawyers called, in relation to resuming business under, 531; Attitude of the lawyers of New Jersey towards, 536, 540, 546; Probability of its repeal, 548; Bill brought into Parliament for the repeal of, 549, 550; Persons who have incurred penalties under to be indemnified, 553; Congratulations on the repeal of, 555–562.

Stancliff, Samuel, ii, 31; Disbursement by, on account of East Jersey, 205.

Stark, John, iv, 309.

Staten Island, Letter from Governor Carteret and Council to the Governor and Council of New York, relative to the ownership of, i, 349; Surrender of, demanded by Governor Carteret, 350; Proclamation of Governor Carteret to the inhabitants of, 350; Ownership of, 484, 485.—Petition, relative to the title of, iii, 62.

Stathem, Philip, iv, 215.

Stathem, Thomas, iv, 215.

Stathem, Zebulon, iv, 215.

Stearndall, John, ix, 318–321.

Stebbins, Elizabeth, vii, 531.

Steele, Benjamin, ii, 42–62, 66–74, 79; Signs the surrender of the Government, 456–460; Asks the appointment of Andrew Hamilton as Governor, 470.

Steel, James, iv, 399.

Steenhuis, Engelbert, i, 49.

Steenmeets, Johannes, iii, 485.

Steenwyck, Cornelis, i, 72, 142, 143, 144, 148, 149.

Stelle, Gabriel, Recommended for the Council, v, 319.

Stelle, John, vi, 465, 466.

12

Stelle, Pontius, Member of the House of Assembly, vii, 89.

Stenmets, Gasper, i, 49, 82, 132.

Stephani, Johan Sebastian, ix, 318-321.

Stephenson, John, ii, 79, 80.

Stephenson, John (2d), vii, 318.

Stephenson, Jonathan, vii, 377.

Stevens, Captain Campble, Number of men in his company, vi, 425.

Stevens, John, Signer of bills of credit, viii, Part II, 39; Petition of, as a Proprietor, 228.—Recommended for the Council, ix, 127; Appointed thereto, 335; Notice of, 335; Commissioner to purchase lands of the Indians, 357; Referred to, 511; Announces the arrival and names of a commission for settling the boundary line between New York and New Jersey, 581.—Referred to, x, 137, 186, 195, 422, 502, 561.

Stevens, Joseph, v, 155.

Stevens (Stephens, Stivans), Nicholas, ii, 327, 363, 366, 396.

Stevens, Richard, x, 701.

Stevens, Samuel, vii, 457.

Stevenson, Thomas, Member of the Council of West Jersey Proprietors, iv, 152.

Stevenson, William, iii, 164.

Stewart, Charles, ix, 582, 590, 591, 624, 631, 632.

Stewart, John, ii, 333—v, 187.

Stiles, Moses, x, 718.

Stillman, Charles, iv, 188.

Stillwell, Captain, iii, 213.

Stillwell, Jeremiah, ii, 332.

Stillwell, Nicholas, x, 210.

Stillwise, Daniel, iv, 10.

Stirling, Earl of, See William Alexander.

Stivers, Samuel, vi, 245.

Stock, Henry, x, 717.

Stockton, John, iv, 98.

Stockton, Richard, Recommended for the Council, ix, 426—x, 44, 58; Appointed as such, 59; Renders an opinion that the Governor of New Jersey, for the time being, is authorized to hold, and preside in, a Court of Chancery, 155; Member of a corporation, 345; In Council, 351; Commission of, as Associate Justice of the Supreme Court, 427; Notice of, 427; Salary of, 450; Of the Council, 561.

Stockton, Robert, x, 352.

Stoker, Thomas, iii, 165.

Stokes, John, iii, 165—v, 187.

Stokes, Joseph, v, 187.

Stokes, Thomas, i, 269.

Stout, Abraham, x, 273.

Stout, Andrew, x, 273.

Stout, Benjamin, ii, 326; Presented by Monmouth County Grand Jury, 332.

Stout, Benjamin (2d), x, 273.

Stoutt, David, ii, 326; Presented by Monmouth County Grand Jury, 332.

Stout, Hezekiah, x, 273.

Stout, James, Presented by Monmouth County Grand Jury, ii, 332, 363, 397.

Stout, John, Contributes to the supposed Cornbury Fund, iii, 212.

Stout, John, Sr., ii, 396.

Stout, Jonathan, ii, 326, 363.

Stout, Jonathan, Ensign, ix, 187.

Stout, Joseph, Colonel of the militia of Hunterdon County, viii, Part II, 156, 158, 174, 177; Orders to, from Governor Belcher, 182.

Stout (Stoot), Peter, ii, 326, 396.

Stout, Richard, i, 44—ii, 326.

Stout, Richard, vii, 543.

Stout, Samuel, vii, 606.

Straughen, David, iii, 356.

Straybearn, William, ii, 129, 397.

Streat, Mr., iv, 266.

Strettell, Robert, vii, 130.

Stringham, Charles, viii, Part I, 215.

Stringham, Peter, i, 288.

Strong, James, ix, 179.

Street, Col., Governor of New England, on protection against the Indians, v, 113.

Stuart, Charles, x, 717.

Stuart, Mr., viii, Part I, 154.

Stubbens, Henry, i, 269.

Stuyvesant, Governor, ix, 456.

Styles, John, Affidavit of, relative to the riots at Newark and Perth Amboy, vii, 178; Referred to, 223, 350; Affidavit of, relative to the riots in Essex County, 433.

Sulen, Daniel, iv, 188.

Sullivan, John, x, 529,

Sunderland, Earl of, Letter from, to the Lords of Trade, relative to Lewis Morris, iii, 328; Reply to the same, 328.

Supreme Court, See Courts.

Surrege, John, i, 268.

Surrogates, Commissions for, ix, 359.

Sussex County, Iron in, viii, Part II, 79; Drowned lands in, 80; Proclamation of Governor Belcher, relative to the defence of, 182; When set off, x, 298.

Sutton, Ambrose, i, 505, 506.

Sutton, John, iv, 189.

Stuton, Jud., ii, 396.

Sutton, Richard, ii, 326.
Sutton, Thomas, ii, 326, 397.
Swaine, Capt. Samuel, i, 134.
Swamp Town, or Salem, i, 283.
Swarths, John, vii, 377.
Swartwont, Jacobus, ix, 179.
Swartwont, Philip, ix, 178-182; Petition of, relative to the Northern
    boundary, 250; Referred to, 254.
Swartwoots, Thomas, viii, Part I, 207, 208, 224, 228, 231, 273.
Sweetable, John, ii, 42-61, 65-73, 79.
Swift, John, iii, 165.
Swift, Mr., Appointed Collector at Perth Amboy, iv, 49.
Swift, ———, x, 219.
Swinton, J. S., i, 376.
Swinney, John, ii, 396.
Sykes, Anthony, x, 417.

T.

Tagnitz, Jonathan, iv, 189.
Talbot (Talbutt), Rev. John, iv, 13, 158; Complaints against, by Governor
    Hunter, 209, 218-220, 223-226; Referred to, 228, 229; Further com-
    plaints against, by Governor Hunter, 230, 234, 255, 274; Letter
    relative to, from George Willocks, 290; Letter from, to Governor
    Hunter, 291; Referred to, 294, 295, 298; Deposition of George
    Willocks, relative to, 301; Referred to, 323.
Talmage, Daniel, x, 717.
Tankerville, Lord, viii, Part I, 93.
Tapan Creek, Point of partition on Hudson's River, i, 522.
Tapan Patent, viii, Part I, 275.
Tappan (Tappin), Jacob, iv, 107, 215.
Tarbat (Tarbutt), i, 466, 500, 528.
Tarbet, Viscount, ii, 32; Disbursements by, on account of East Jersey, 202.
Tashiowycam, Indian murderer, i, 73.
Tathan, John, i, 509—ii, 41, 146, 209, 349—iii, 223—iv, 13.
Taylor, Abraham, vii, 130.
Taylor, Charles, i, 394.
Taylor, Christopher, i, Deputed by Governor Penn, to go to East Jersey,
    395; Appointed a commissioner to treat with West Jersey, 415, 419.
Taylor, Daniel Jr., vi, 351—vii, 457.
Taylor, Edward, x, 458, 459.
Taylor, George, ii, 146, 384, 486.
Taylor, Jacob, iv, 390.
Taylor, John, ii, 148.
Taylor, John, x, 459.
Taylor, Jonah, iv, 371.

Taylor, Mary, iii, 358.

Taylor, Parson, vii, 54.

Taylor, Thomas, Presented by Monmouth County Grand Jury, ii, 332; Signs petition, 396.

Taylor, William, Proceedings against, i, 313, 314, 322.

Tayne, Isaac, Assignment of lands to Michael Lecroa, i, 116.

Taxation for Revenue, Petition of the Assembly of New Jersey to the King against, x, 18; The King has no design to tax the Colonies for purposes of revenue, 109.

Techepewoya, i, 1.

Teller, Andrew, v, 153.

Temple, John, ix, 582, 590, 624, 631, 632.

Tenbrook, John, Captain, ix, 184, 186.

Tenecunk Island, v, 43, 44, 46.

Tennent, Rev. William, vii, 62—viii, Part I, 95; Part II, 198—x, 345.

Tep, John, ii, 327.

Terry, John, x, 531.

Terwilliger, Matthew, ix, 180, 181.

Tew, Thomas, A pirate, ii, 123.

Thackery, Thomas, ii, 148, 380.

Thanksgiving, Day of, ordered, i, 139.—General, on the defeat of the French in Canada, ix, 183, 209; For the conclusion of peace, 391.

Tharp, James, x, 717.

Thomas, Edward, x, 202.

Thomas, Captain George, vi, 102.

Thomas, Captain James, ii, 417—iii, 306.

Thomas, John, ii, 129, 327, 396.

Thomas, Jonathan, viii, Part II, 151.

Thomasse, Thomas, ii, 327.

Thomas, General, x, 606.

Thomaston, Johannes, ii, 327.

Thomlinson, Captain John, Scheme of, for putting the paper currency in America on a better footing, vi, 111.

Thompson, Charles, x, 574.

Thompson, Isaac, i, 269.

Thompson, James, iv, 98.

Thompson, John, i, 268, 381—ii, 129, 148, 326, 334, 339, 380—iii, 496.

Thompson, John (2nd), viii, Part I, 42.

Thompson (Tomson), Moses, i, 50—ii, 326, 334, 397.

Thompson (Thomson, Tomson), Thomas, i, 50, 149—ii, 129, 339, 397—iii, 351, 352, 496.

Thompson, William, Opinion of, on Elizabethtown Patent, i, 272,

Thompson, William (2nd), ii, 42-61, 65-73, 79.

Thomson, James, vi, 465, 466; Affidavit of, relative to the riot at Perth Amboy, 468.

Thomson, William, iv, 10, 330.

Thong, Thomas, v, 153.

Thorp, George, ii, 326.

Throckmorton, Joseph, x, 600.

Throp, Samuel, ii, 397.

Tice, Peter, x, 718.

Tilghman, Mat., x, 529.

Tillman, William, vii, 283.

Tilton, John, i, 44.

Tindall, Richard, i, 413, 414, 508.

Tindal, Thomas, x, 367.

Tinker, John, viii, Part I, 27.

Titus, Richard, viii, Part I, 201.

Tolmash, Colonel, ii, 430.

Tom's River, 74.

Tom, William, i, 72, 73; Letter to, from Governor Lovelace, relative to the Indian murders at Matiniconk Island, 74; Justice of New Castle, 190; Estate of, 197, 201.

Tomesen, Jillis, i, 269.

Tomkins, John, vii, 457.

Tomkins, Micah, vii, 32.

Tomkins, Seth, ii, 336.

Tomlinson, ———, Appointed Judge in Gloucester County, iv, 129.

Tompkins; Ichabod, Nominated as Justice of the Peace, viii, Part I, 105.

Tompkins, John, vi, 245.

Tompson, Hurr, i, 82, 85.

Tomson, John, Contribntes to a supposed Cornbury Fund, iii, 199.

Tonkin, Keziah, x, 367.

Tooker, Charles, ii, 397.

Toshack, David, i, 460—ix, 337.

Towle, Percival, i, 268.

Townley, Effingham, vii, 33.

Townly, Colonel Richard, ii, 109, 486, 487, 502.—Proposed for the Council, iii, 51, 78, 115; Notice of, 115; Appointed a member of the Council, 125; Referred to, 130, 155, 160, 201; In Council, 290; Proposed as a member of Lord Lovelace's Council, 299; Appointed as such, 317; Signs addresses, 367, 373, 415, 473; Referred to, 479; Justice of the Peace for Essex County, 495; The Proprietors ask that he be left out of Governor Hunter's Council, 497.—Member of Governor Hunter's Council, iv, 2, 19, 48; Dead, 61; Referred to, 101, 129, 130, 133, 153; Referred to by Rev. Jacob Henderson, 157; Further reference to, 164.

Townsend, Charles, viii, Part I, 62.

Townsend, John, Sr., i, 506.

Townshend, Lord, Transmits to the Lords of Trade a discourse by Sir William Keith on the state of the Plantations, v, 214.

Townsend, ———, Appointed Judge in Cape May County, iv, 129.

Trade of the British Empire in America, vi, 83; Value of goods shipped
from Great Britain and Ireland to the Plantations, 87, 88.

Trade and commerce, x, 442–444, 454.

Traile, George, ix, 318–321.

Trapnell, John, vii, 547.

Treasurers of the Eastern and Western Divisions, Accounts of, viii, Part
I, 65–83; Part II, 150–155, 171, 223, 228–235.

Treasury of East Jersey, Proclamation of the Governor of New York,
relative to the robbery of, ix, 564.—Affidavit of S. Skinner, relative
to the robbery of, x, 37; Proclamation of Governor Moore, regarding
the same, 39; Chief-Justice Smyth in relation thereto, 379; Cortlandt
Skinner in relation to, 412, 414, 415; Representatives from Burlington County instructed not to discharge the Treasurer from his liabilities, 417; Resignation of the Treasurer, 420.

Treat, Captain, i, 52, 56.

Treat, John, ii, 313—iii, 484; Justice of the Peace for Essex County, 495.

Treat, Robert, i, 65, 81—ii, 122.

Trelawny, Edward, viii, Part I, 27.

Trenchard, Surrogate, ix, 359.—Referred to, x, 362, 363, 364.

Trent, Maurice, ii, 121, 481.

Trent, William, Chief-Justice, iv, 13, 296—v, 77; Notice of, 77; Chosen
Speaker of the Assembly, 77; Death of, announced, 97; Money paid
to, 133, 139, 143, 147, 148; Grand Juror, 187; Referred to, 344, 374
—x, 97, 111; Notice of, 112; Letter to, from Governor Franklin, 227.

Trenton, Named after Chief-Justice Trent, v, 77.—A library at, viii, Part
I, 32.

Trevor, Thomas, Solicitor-General, Report on the Charter of Connecticut,
and on the Grant of New Jersey, ii, 100; Letter from, to Secretary
Popple, inclosing form of bond for Deputy-Provincial Governor, 138;
Enquired of, as to the authority of the Proprietors of East Jersey to
constitute ports of entry to their province, 174; Answer to said
inquiry, 176; Opinion of, as to the eligibility of Andrew Hamilton
to the office of Governor, 250; His opinion asked as to a new mode
of approving proprietary governors, 307.

Tripartite Indenture, settling the North partition point between New
Jersey and New York, iv, 394.

Troops, See Military Affairs.

Trough, William, v, 187.

Trott, Nicholas, Governor of the Bahama Islands, ii, 119.

Trotter, Wm., i, 50.

Trumbull, Governor, x, 616, 619.

Trumbull, Mary, ix, 226.

Tryon, Governor William, Letter from, to the Earl of Dartmouth, relative to the boundary line, x, 393; Referred to, 658, 766.

Tucker, Charles, i, 50.

Tucker, Charles, Jr., ii, 334, 339; Grand juror of Essex County, iii, 496.

Tucker, Samuel, Deposition of, as to the character of William Morris, vii, 636; Certificate as to his character, 639; Instructions to him from his constituents, x, 269; Notice of, 270; Referred to, 458, 471, 479, 587, 588, 720.

Tudeyscung, King of the Wyoming Indians, ix, 121, 125.

Tullie, Robert, iv, 215.

Tunisber, John, iv, 3.

Tunisen, Derrick, i, 49.

Tunnisen, Hendrick, i, 49—ii, 396.

Turin, John, 90. (See Jurin.)

Turner, Joseph, vii, 377, 515; Certificate of, 560.

Turner, Robert, i, 186; An East Jersey Proprietor, 384, 412, 424, 433, 434, 437, 442, 451, 530; Disbursements by, on account of East Jersey, ii, 205.

Turnout, John, ix, 179.

Tuttell, Henry, ii, 397.

Tuttle, Ebenezer, x, 717.

Tuttle, Col. Joseph, viii, Part II, 158, 174; Letter to, from Governor Belcher, relative to the defence of the frontier, 179; Order to, from Governor Belcher, 182.

Tuttle, Moses, x, 717.

Tuttle, Nathaniel, i, 50.

Twigg, Thomas, iv, 215.

Tyll, Capt. Abram, v, 122.

U.

Upham, William, x, 717.

Urmston, Rev. John, iv, 224.

V.

Vadoon, Jacob, ii, 396.

Vallean, Mrs., 415.

Vanaken, Abraham, Petition of, relative to disturbances on the northern boundary of the Province, vi, 163, 168.—Justice of the Peace, viii, Part I, 212, 226, 268.—Referred to, ix, 180, 181.

Vanaken, Jacobus, ix, 180, 181.

Vannatta, Anthony, Constable, viii, Part I, 225.

Vanbrunt, Nicholas, x, 600.

Van Buskerk, Lawrence, vi, 202.

Van Campica (Van Cam, Van Camp, Van Kemper), Abraham, Colonel of the regiment of militia and Judge of the County of Sussex, viii, Part II, 35, 158, 177.

Van Cock, Richard, x, 717.

Van Cortlandt, Anne, ix, 641.

Van Cortlandt, Elizabeth, ix, 641.

Van Cortlandt, Stephen, i. 45^, 518—ii, 106, 237—ix. 641.

Van Courtlai.d, Jacobus, v, 368.

Van Dorn, Richard, v, 153.

Van Dorn, Rip, Authorized to collect quit-rents from George Willocks, ii, 194.—Referred to, iii, 64—iv, 340, 408; Notice of, 408.—Certifies to the value of Jersey money, v, 153; Commissioner for trying pirates. 197; As President of the New York Council informs the Lords of Trade of the death of Governor Montgomerie, 294; Referred to, 324, 332–336, 360, 395, 402, 408, 410, 431, 439—vi, 73, 74—viii, Part I, 237.

Vandelinda, Paul, ii, 327.

Vanderbeck, Burgher, Indicted, vii, 458.

Vanderburgh, Cornelius, i, 320.

Van der Linde, Joost, 146, 151.

Vanderpool, David, x, 717.

Vanderspiegel, Henry, v, 153.

Vanderveer, Cornelius, x, 600.

Vandeventer, Jacob, vii, 428.

Van de Vorst, Cornelis, ii, 326.

Vandike, Lieutenant John, ix, 185.

Vandorn, Jacob, ii, 326; Presented by Monmouth County Grand Jury, 332.

Van Duyne, Isaac, x, 717.

Vanduyne, Jacob, x, 718.

Vane, Stephen, ii, 397.

Van Este, Peter, iii, 483.

Van Etten, Anthony, ix, 253.

Van Faerling, Floris, v, 153.

Van Faerling, Nicholas, v. 153.

Van Giesen, Renier, i, 49—ii, 326.

Vangezen, Isaac, v, 146, 150—vi, 293, 311—vii, 41, 457.

Vanhighst, Abraham, i, 269.

Van Hooren, Ruth, ii, 326.

Van Horn, Abraham, Recommended for the New York Council, v, 70; Governor Burnet married his daughter, 70; Signs certificate, 153; Commissioner to try pirates, 197.

Van Horn, Cornelius, v, 153, 166, 197, 443, 456, 478—vi, 14, 15; Discharged from the Council at his own request, 106, 237.

Van Horne, Garret, v, 153.

Van Horne, James, vii, 621.

Van Horne, John, v, 153.

Vanhorn, Major, viii, Part I, 123—Part II, 158; Orders to, from Governor Belcher, 182.

Van Houten, Henry, x, 718.

Vanhurst, Reneare, i, 268.

Van Jimmen. Johannes, Declaration of, concerning John Fenwicke, i, 194.

Van Jumne, Ganet, i, 268.

Van Kirk, Henry, x, 273.

Van Middleswart (Van Middleswardt, Van Middlesworth), John. vi. 202 —vii, 502.

Vannest, Peter, ii, 270—iv. 111.

Van Quelen, Robert, See Vauquillin Robert.

Van Ranslaer, Killian, iii, 64—iv, 340.

Van Ruyven. Cornelis, i, 142, 143, 144, 148.

Vantuyl, Walter, Lieutenant, ix, 187.

Van Uleck (Vleck), Isaac, i, 49.

Van Vechten, Derrick, vi, 202.

Van Vechten (Van Weghtie, Van Veigty), Michael. ii, 315.—Difficulties with Peter Sonmans, iii, 377, 430, 448, 455.—Moneys paid by, v, 142, 144, 149.

Vanwinkle, Abraham, vi, 456, 465—vii, 458.

Vanwinkle, Johannes, vi, 245—vii, 457.

Varlet, Nicholas, x, 169, 170, 189.

Vaughan, Edward, iv, 174; Certificate of, relating to the character of Thomas Gordon, attacked by Jacob Henderson, 180.

Vaughan (Vahhan), John, ii, 326, 363.

Vanquillin, Robert, Commission as Surveyor-General of New Jersey. i, 26; Took oath of allegiance, 50; At Council meeting. 76; Court at Elizabethtown, 81; Removed goods from Governor Carteret's house, 130; Arrested by the Dutch authorities, 131; Banished by the same. 133; Referred to, 350.

Veltscheerder, Peter, x, 515.

Verety, William, ii, 396.

Verlant, M , ii, 327.

Verlett, Captain Nicholas, i, 49.

Vernon, Henry, iv, 238.

Vesey, William, ix, 337.

Vesey, Rev. Mr., iv, 163; Governor Hunter's comments upon, 216–219, 223–226; Appointed Commissary by the Bishop of London, 218; Referred to, 228, 229.

Vessels, Number of, trading with the Colonies, vi, 84, 85, 86; Value of, 86, 87.

Vetch, Colonel Samuel, iii, 461: Letter from. to the Lords of Trade. relative to the Quakers in New Jersey and Pennsylvania, 464; Referred to, 471—iv, 27.

Vicary, James, i, 269.

Vice and immorality, Proclamation of Governor Basse for the suppression of, ii, 206.—Instructions to Governor Burnet relative to, v, 159, 161.

Vinblin, Norman Ali, a pirate, ii, 159.

Vincent, John, vi, 245—vii, 435, 457.

Vincent, Larmes, Indicted, vii, 457.

Vincent, Levi, vi, 245.

Vincent, Levy, Jr., vii, 457.

Vincent, Livines, vi, 351.

Virginia, Quota of troops for the defence of New York, ii, 134, viii, Part I, 194.—Union of the Colonies advocated by the House of Burgesses of, x, 21; Resolves of the Assembly of, 146; Committee of Correspondence appointed, 458.

Vreeland, Coon, x, 718.

Vreeland, George, vi, 202, 203.

Vreelandt, Michael, vi, 346, 367.

Vrelant, Abraham, ii, 327.

W.

Waddell, John, ix, 18.

Waddell, Henry, x, 459.

Wade, Benjamin, Sr., ii, 129, 326, 334.

Wade, Benjamin, Jr., ii, 334, 339—iii, 496.

Wade, Edward, i, 118, 227, 284, 414.

Wade, Robert, i, 227, 414.

Wad, Samuel, i, 26—ii, 148—iv, 113.

Wadman, Lieutenant Arthur, x, 233.

Wager, Sir Charles, Notice of, vi, 60; Referred to, 77.

Waghackemack, Patent, viii, Part II, 75.

Waites, Elizabeth, i, 186.

Waley (Wooley), Robert, ii, 270.

Walker, Alexander, iii, 377, 431, 432, 448, 453.

Walker, Francis, Grand Juror on Woodbridge riot, iii, 486, 487.

Walker, Samuel, ii, 270, 317, 325, 396; Recommended for Council, 429, 431, 487; Appointed member of the Council, 507.—One of Lord Cornbury's Council, iii, 2, 65; Dead, 78; Referred to, 483.

Walker, Thomas, x, 352.

Wall, Garret, ii, 363—iii, 212.

Wall, Jarad, ii, 326.

Wall, Jarrett, Affidavit of, relative to the riot at Perth Amboy, vi, 467.

Wall, Walter, ii, 327, 395.

Waller, John, Jail-keeper, viii, Part I, 37, 43, 47.

Waller, William, vii, 599.

Walley——, viii, Part I, 11.

Wallop, Richard, Opinion of, on Elizabethtown patent, i, 272.

Walpole, Horatio, viii, Part I, 128.

Walpole, Robert, ix, 630.

Walter, John, v, 153.

Walter, Robert, One of the commissioners to run partition line, iv, 340, 383, 394, 429, 435—v, 197, 323—viii, Part I, 209, 239, 264.

Walton, Jaçob, x, 114.

Walton, Mark, x, 717.

Walton, William, ix, 283.

Wamdall, J., i, 299.

Wankle, Benjamin, x, 718.

Wansick, Thomas, i, 51.

Ward, Abel, vi, 351—vii, 458.

Ward, Caleb, vi, 351—vii, 457.

Ward, Edward, i, 284, 292.

Wardil, Eliakim, i, 128.

Ward, Elihu, vi, 245—vii, 178, 179.

Ward, John, i, 128, 134, 310, 320—vi, 135, 146.

Ward, Nathaniel, ii, 271, 275.

Ward, Robert, vi, 245—vii, 457.

Ward, Samuel, ii, 336.

Ward, Samuel (2nd), x, 529.

Wardell, Joseph, Contributes to the supposed Cornbury Fund, iii, 212.

Ware, Joseph, iv, 113.

Ware. Capt. Nathaniel, Number of men in his company, vi, 425—vii, 102.

Warne, Joseph, i, 268.

Warne, Thomas, An East Jersey Proprietor, i, 383, 442, 460; Referred
　　to, 481, 499, 530.—Signs as a Proprietor, ii, 2, 113, 270; Surrenders
　　the Government of East Jersey, 387; Signs the surrender, 456-460;
　　Recommended for Council, 487; Member of court, 479, 482-486.

Warner, Edmund, Instructions from, and others, to their commissioners in
　　West Jersey, i, 219; Complained of by John Fenwicke, 225; Grant
　　to him and others from the Duke of York, 324; Referred to, ii, 50.

Warner, William, i, 268—iii, 351, 352.

Warrell, Joseph, Recommended for Council, v, 410, 454.—Referred to,
　　vi, 166.—Attorney-General, vii, 613, 614; Certificate of, to the
　　character of Samuel Tucker, 639.—Salary, viii, Part I, 106; Notes of,
　　as Attorney-General, upon the trial of Lewis M. Ashfield, 112; Resig-
　　nation of, and nomination of Courtland Skinner as his successor, 293,
　　298; Warrants to, 151; Referred to, ix, 257.

Warren, Admiral, vii, 646.

Warren, John, i, 319; Letter from, to Governor Andros, 337.

Warren, Lady, viii, Part II, 253—ix, 15, 17.

Warren, Sir Peter, viii, Part I, 93—ix, 641.

Warren, Susan, ix, 641.

Warrington, Henry, v, 187.

Warsan, Richard, i, 269.

Wase (Wasse), James, Instructions to as one of the commissioners in West
　　Jersey appointed by William Penn and others, i, 219, 227; Lands
　　sold to, 414; Signs the surrender, ii, 456-460.

Washington, General George, ix, 339—x, 429, 530, 669, 670.

Watts, John, ix, 178, 283, 460.

Watt, Michael, II, 41–61, 65–73, 79, 258, 276, 300, 302, 376, 408, 411, 416; Signs the surrender of the Government, 456–460; Asks the appointment of Andrew Hamilton as Governor, 470.—Referred to, iii, 95.

Watts, Rev. Robert, Certificate of, sustaining the character of John Anderson against the attack of Jacob Henderson, iv, 179.—Referred to, vii, 78.

Watson, John, ix, 17.

Watson, Luke, i, 15, 18, 50, 82, 83, 85, 155, 504-506—vi, 207, 210.

Watson, Matthew, iii, 105.

Watson, Peter, i, 465, 512.

Watson, Thomas, i, 269, 413, 414.

Watson, William, iv, 215.

Wawayanda Patent, viii, Part I. 220, 223, 224, 274, 278, 281, 290—Part, II, 20, 28.

Wayne, John Waynes, i, 50.

Webb (Web), Edward, i, 186, 268, 413, 414.

Webb, Colonel, of New York, viii, Part II, 221, 222.

Webley, Thomas, ii, 332.

Webster, Nathan, i, 50.

Webster, Robert iv, 9,

Weeks, Zach., v, 143, 146.

Welch, Nathaniel, ii, 460.

Welch, William, i, 421.

Wells, John, Recommended for the Council, iv, 326; Appointed to the same, 331; One of the commissioners to try pirates, 340; Referred to, 373, 374.—One of Govenor Burnet's Council, v, 3; Commissioner to try pirates, 197; Superannuated, 316, 446.

Wells, John (2nd), vi, 351—vii, 457.

Wells, Phillip, i, 517.—Engaged to run the line between New York and East Jersey, 518, 521—ii, 22, 23, 24—iv, 412-414—vi, 148, 149—viii Part I, 205, 227, 247, 249.

Welshear, Thomas, x, 718.

Wenham, Thomas, iii, 64.

Wentworth, Benning, Governor of New Hampshire, Instructions to, viii, Part I, 27.—Referred to, ix, 529, 628—x, 521.

Wentworth, John, ix, 622.

Wentworth, Mark, ix, 390.

Werden, Sir John, Secretary to the Duke of York; Letters to Governor Andross, i, 332, 179, 230; To the Secretary of State, on the extent of the authority granted to the Proprietors of New Jersey, 289; The Duke of York's orders to, 323; Letters from, to Governor Andross, 345, 347; Letter from, to Wm. Penn, 348; Letter to Sir Allen Apsley, relative to customs, 353; Letter to, from the Register of Scotland, 379; Letter from, to the Lord Register, 380; Witness, 394; Letters

to, from Governor Dongan, 457, 485; Letter to, from the Mayor of New York, 491.

West, Ben, i, 369.

West, Edward, ii, 42-62, 66-74, 79.

West, James, ix, 306.

West, John, ii, 332.

West, Joseph, ii, 363, 396.

West, J., i, 299.

West, Richard, Report of, on several acts of the New Jersey Assembly, v, 79.

West, Robert, An East Jersey Proprietor, i, 51, 366, 383, 412, 529—ii, 26, 48, 49.

West, Robert, Jr., i, 51.

Westbrook, Suit against Abraham Vanaken, viii, Part I, 267, 268.—Referred to, ix, 180, 181.

Westbrook, Anthony, ix, 179.

Westbrook, Johannes, Jr., vi, 166, 167.

Westcott, Richard, x, 684.

Wester, Casper, Erects a glass manufactory in New Jersey, vi, 98; Notice of, 98.

Westfall, Cornelius, viii, Part II, 13—ix, 180, 254.

Westfall, Jacob, viii, Part II, 13—ix, 180, 181, 251, 254.

Westfall, Nathaniel, ix, 251.

Westfall, Petrus, viii, Part II, 13.

Westfall, Simon, ix, 180, 181, 251.

Wesfall, Uryon (Jurian), viii, Part II, 13—ix, 117, 180, 181.

Westfalls, ———, viii, Part I, 208, 224, 228, 231.

West Jersey, Quintipartite deed to William Penn and associates, i, 205; Instructions from Penn and associates to their commissioners in, 219; Agreement for first settlement of, 225; Letter from the Proprietors of, to Richard Hartshorne, 227; Letter from the same, to those proposing to settle in West Jersey, 231; Permission to settle in, asked by the passengers of the ship "Kent," 239; The concessions and agreements of, 241; Charter or Fundamental laws of, 252; Letter from Governor Andros to commissioners of, 271; Appointments for, by John Fenwicke, 275; Proclamation to claimants of land in, 276; Order of Governor Andros to protect the inhabitants of, 285; Petition from persons in England for land in, 289; Names of the magistrates of, 291; Grant of, to William Penn and his associates by the Duke of York, 324; Commissioners to, appointed by Governor Penn, 415; Instructions to them, 416; Letters from Governor Penn, to the Governor and Council of, 417, 419; Memorial to the Governor and Council of, from the people of Salem, 421; Quo warranto against, 501; Minutes of New York Council, relative to the line between it and East Jersey, 517; Obligation of the authorities of, to abide by the determination of the arbitrators on the division line, 522; Award,

respecting the division line, 523.—Commissioners from the Proprietors of East Jersey, to confer with Governor thereof, ii, 1; Letter to the Council of Proprietors of, from Daniel Coxe, 4; Minutes of the West Jersey Proprietors, respecting running the line between the Provinces, in accordance with the award of Reid and Emley, 24; Agreement between the Governor of, and the Governor of East Jersey, in regard to the partition line 34; Release of, from Daniel Coxe and wife, to the West Jersey Society, 41; Grant of the government of, to the West Jersey Society, 64; Andrew Hamilton commissioned to be Governor of, 87; Letter from the Proprietors of, to Governor Fletcher, 89; Instructions to the Deputy-Governor of, 93; Letter from Proprietors in England to Jeremiah Basse, 97; Letter to the Proprietors of, from the Lords of Trade, 134; Letter to the Proprietors of, from the King, relating to the Plantation trade, 140; Agreement of the authorities of, to support the King, 145; Address of the Governor and Council of, to the King, on his escape from the attempts of assassins, 146; Agreement of the Quaker members of the House of Representatives of, to support the King, 147; Memorial of the Proprietors of, asking the appointment of Jeremiah Basse as Governor, 149; Petition of the Proprietors of, relative to customs, 163, 165; Order in Council, relative thereto, 169; Opinion of the Attorney-General and the Solicitor-General in the premises, 177; George Willocks authorized by the Proprietors to receive quit-rents, 186; Rip Van Dam likewise so authorized, 194; Letter from the Council of, to the Proprietors in England, 207; Memorial from the Proprietors of, asking the appointment of Andrew Hamilton as Governor, 257; Petition to the same effect, 276; Commission to Andrew Hamilton to be Governor of, 301; Account of the inhabitants of in 1699, 305; A retreat for pirates, as charged by Edward Randolph, 360; Memorial of the Proprietors of, to the Lords Justices, asking the approval of the appointment of Andrew Hamilton as Governor, 374; The same to the King, from the Council and Representatives, asking his confirmation, 377; Address of the inhabitants of, asking to be taken under the King's immediate government, 380; Memorials of the Proprietors of, relative to the surrender of their government of, 404, 415; Names of persons proposed for Governor and Council, by the Proprietors of, 429; Surrender of the government of, to the Crown, 452; Reply of Proprietors of, to complaints against Andrew Hamilton by Mr. Dockwra and Mr. Sonmons, 475.—Petition of the Proprietors of, to the Lords of Trade, relative to the proceedings of Lord Cornbury, iii, 81; Memorial from the same, to the same, complaining of Lord Cornbury and asking for the restoration of Lewis Morris to the Council, 85; Observations of the Lords of Trade on said memorial, 117; Answer of Wm. Sloper, agent of Lord Cornbury, to said complaints, 133; The Council of, commanded by Lord Cornbury to show their authority for acting as a Council of the Proprietors, 158; Petition

from the proprietors and purchasers of, to Lord Cornbury, relative to granting warrants, etc., 164; Answer of the Proprietors of, to certain questions of Lord Cornbury, 220.—Protest of Daniel Leeds against the proceedings of the Council of Proprietors of, iv, 146; Election of a new Council by the Proprietors of, 151, 152; Minutes of the Council of, March, 1716-17, appointing James Alexander Surveyor-General, 288; Proceedings of the Council of, relating to the line of partition between the two Provinces, 452.—Letter from the Council of Proprietors of, to James Alexander, v, 67; Account of the money received and paid by the Treasurer of, 132; Proceedings of the Council of Proprietors of, relative to the appointment of a Surveyor-General, 211; Memorial of James Alexander relative to the same, 273; Answer of the Council of Proprietors of, to said memorial, 278; Quota of, for the defence of New York, viii. Part I, 196.

West Jersey Society, Release of West Jersey to, from Daniel Coxe and wife, ii, 41; Grant of the Government of West Jersey to, 64; Agreement of, for the managing and improving of their lands, 73; Commission from members of, in England, to Jeremiah Basse as their agent, 91; Letter from, to Rev. Thomas Bridges, 94; Commission from to Andrew Hamilton, to be its agent, 299; Commission from, to the same, to be Governor of West Jersey, 301.—Referred to, 434—iii, 49; Apply to Parliament to vest all their lands in trustees to be sold, v, 508.—Letters to, from Governor Belcher, vii, 57, 145, 150; Referred to, 213; Petition of, to the Lords of Trade, for relief from the riots and disturbances in New Jersey, 316; Instructions of a committee to agents, 320.

Westland, Nathaniel, ii, 98, 146, 147, 299, 384—iii, 351, 352—iv, 184.

Westphale, Juriam, Petition of, relative to disturbances on the Northern boundary of the Province, vi, 163, 168.

Wetherby, Pockayne Terry, ii, 63.

Wetherhill, John, iv, 275, 277, 319.

Wetherill, Christopher, Summoned by Lord Cornbury to show his authority for acting as one of the Council of West Jersey, iii, 158; One of the Council, 221.

Wetherill, John, Inspector of the Press, viii, Part II, 70, 230.—Referred to, ix, 120—x, 458.

Wetheril, Thomas, iv, 9—v, 211—x, 358.

Whales, As royal fishes, ix, 65; Duty upon the fins of, 405.

Whandrick, William, ii, 396.

Wharton, Joseph, x, 97, 375.

Wharton, Samuel, x, 97, 113.

Wheate, Benjamin, ii, 148.

Wheaton, John, x, 531.

Wheavens, William, ii, 396.

Wheeler, Nathaniel, vi, 346, 351, 361, 365, 367—vii, 64, 74, 435.

Wheeler, Robert, ii, 384—iv, 13; Recommended for the Council, 63, 227; Justice of the Peace, 75; Referred to, 375; Dead, 377.

Whillden, James, x, 207-212, 281, 282.

Whitacar, Richard, i, 227.

White, Anthony, Surrogate, vii, 543—ix, 360; Appointed Judge of the Admiralty, 377; Notice of, 379.

White, Anthony Walton, ix, 379.

White, Christopher, i, 269, 414.

White, Daniel, Indicted, vii, 458.

White, Dennis, i, 50.

White, John, i, 269, 299—iii, 459.

White, John (2d), x, 717.

White, Thomas, Contributes to the supposed Cornbury Fund, iii, 213.

White, William, ii, 397—v, 133, 135.

Whitefield, George, Letter to, from Governor Belcher, viii, Part I, 84; Referred to, 87; Letter to, from Governor Belcher, Part II, 146, 195.

Whitehead, Captain, i, 300.

Whitehead, G., iii, 158.

Whitehead, Isaac, i, 50, 86, 133; Letter to Captain Nichols, 334; Referred to, 129, 326.—Affidavit of, iii, 201; Indicted, 480, 486.

Whitehead, Isaac A., Sr., i, 320.

Whitehead, Isaac N., i, 305, 309, 311.

Whitehead, James, ii, 324, 395—iii, 496.

Whitehead, Joseph, i, 335—ii, 326, 334, 395.

Whitehead, Nathaniel, ii, 327, 397.

Whitehead, Samuel, i, 15—ii, 129, 271, 273, 327, 338, 339, 397—iii, 496.

Whitehead, Samuel, Jr., ii, 326, 334.

Whitehead, Stephen, iii, 413.

Whitehead, Timothy, Nominated as Justice of the Peace, viii, Part I, 105.

Whitehead, William, ii, 339, 397—iii, 496.

Whitlock, John, ii, 396.

Whitham, Ffra, i, 369.

Whiting, John, ii, 79; Signs the surrender of the Government, 456-460; Asks the appointment of Andrew Hamilton as Governor, 470.—Signs as Proprietor, iii, 38, 82.—Memorial of, iv, 141.

Whitlock, Thomas, i, 134.

Wickham, William, x, 194.

Wicknaminck (Weinamink), Indian grantor, i, 111.

Wiggins, Gersham, x, 717.

Wiggins, Thomas, x, 587, 588.

Wightman, William, ii, 42-61, 65-73, 76, 79, 88, 90, 95, 96.

Wilcocks, John, ii, 42-62, 66-74, 79, 300; Signs the surrender of the government, 456-460; Asks the appointment of Andrew Hamilton as Governor, 470.

Wilcocks, Mr., viii, Part I, 253.

Wild, Daniel, ii, 460.

13

Wildigos, Joseph, ii, 470.

Wileman, Henry, vi, 145—viii, Part I, 211, 215, 270, 271.

Wilkes, John, x, 28.

Wilkeson, William, ii, 326.

Wilkins, Constantine, x, 512.

Wilkins, Thomas, ii, 380—iii, 165.

Wilkinson, Richard, i, 268.

Wilkinson, William, i, 186, 269.

Willard, Mr., Secretary, Letter to, from Governor Belcher, vii, 61.

Willcox, Thomas, An East Jersey Proprietor, i, 366, 374.

Willes, E., ix, 629.

Willes, Lord Chief-Justice, viii, Part I, 23.

Willets, John, vi, 202.

Willett (Willit), Samuel, ii, 326, 362, 363, 397.

Williams, Amos, ii, 336.

Williams, Daniel, vi, 245—vii, 457.

Williams, James, ii, 481.

Williams, John, ii, 397—iii, 212.

Williams, Joseph, ii, 129—vi, 351—vii, 457,

Williams, J., Inspector, x, 284, 295.

Williams, Nathaniel, Indicted, vii, 457.

Williams, Samuel, ii, 129.

Williams, Thomas, vi, 245—vii, 436, 457.

Williams, William, Opinion of, on Elizabethtown Patent, i, 272.

Williamson, John, i, 134.

Williamson, Matthews, x, 536.

Williamson, William, v, 155—vi, 245—vii, 457.

Willis, Aaron, x, 717.

Willis, George, iv, 310.

Willis (Willes), John, ii, 129, 315, 325, 334, 396.

Willis, William, i, 269—ii, 396.

Wills, Daniel, i, 239, 268, 288, 291—iii, 164, One of the first commissioners to buy and lay out lands, 221.

Wills (Wells), John, iii, 221; Member of the Council of the West Jersey Proprietors, iv, 152; Affirmation of, 376; Referred to, 283, 284; Clerk, 290; Salary, 268, 369, 454; Moneys paid to, v, 133, 137, 141; Member of Governor Morris' Council, vi, 14; Discharged at own request, 106, 237.

Wills, Samuel, i, 421.

Willocks, George, i, 460, 499—ii, 32, 113, 171, 177; Authorized to collect quit-rents, 186; Notice of, 186; Rip Van Dam authorized to receive quit-rents from, 194; Instructions to Governor Basse concerning him, 209; Referred to, 237; Signs the surrender of the government, 456–460; Recommends Andrew Hamilton for Governor, 470; Objected to as a member of Council, 488.—Renders a service to Jeremiah Basse, iii, 25; Referred to, 154, 314; Complained of to Lord Lovelace by

the Council, 392, 398, 407; Referred to, 418, 423, 435, 446, 449, 450, 451; Refuses to take the oaths to the Queen, 454; Referred to, 455; Documents relative to, 476–496; Indicted, 481–486; Referred to, 489, 490, 494; Recommended for Council of Governor Hunter, 498.— Freeholder of Middlesex County, iv, 9; Statement of, respecting the conduct of Peter Sonmans at Woodbridge, 15; Referred to, 41, 74; Answer of J. Basse to him, 90-112; Referred to, 119, 124, 130; Signs as a Proprietor, 141; Letter from, to Governor Hunter, relative to Rev. Mr. Talbot, 290, 298; Deposition of, relative to Mr. Talbot, 301; Letter to, from James Logan, relative to the division line between the provinces, 377; Referred to. 390; One of the Commissioners for running partition line, 394; Referred. 416, 418, 429, 435—v, 11, 33, 34, 57, 59-63, 70, 101—vi, 352—vii, 37, 326—viii, Part I, 239, 264.

Willocks, James, ii, 186.

Willmot, Henry, List of New Jersey Commissioners named by, for running the boundaries between that Province and New York, ix, 447; Appointed agent of the Province of New Jersey, 571; Petition of, to alter the list of commissioners, 589, 623.—Referred to, x, 98; Letter from, on the paper currency and the bill for Septennial Elections, 142.

Wilson, James, i, 299—ii, 326, 396.

Wilson, John, ii, 396.

Wilson, John, Jr., ii, 366.

Wilson, John, of Morris County, x, 717.

Wilson, Joseph, ii, 326.

Wilson, Peter, ii, 396.

Wilson, Robert, ii, 148.

Wilson, Robert, of Morris County, x, 717.

Wilson, Stephen, iii, 165.

Winans, John, ii, 326.

Winans, Rade, ii, 339.

Winder (Window), Samuel, Secretary of West Jersey, i, 275; An East Jersey Proprietor, 529.—To confer with the Governor of West Jersey relative to the two Provinces, ii, 1; Signature and notice of, 2; Instructions from the Council of Proprietors to, 3; Desires to report, 24.

Winds, Colonel William, ix, 184.—Arrests Governor Franklin. x, 699, 703.

Winepress, Captain, ix, 365.

Wines, Barnabas, i, 50.

Wingett, Caleb, iv, 188.

Winins, Samuel, iii, 486.

Winne, Thomas, Appointed by Governor Penn a commissioner to treat with West Jersey, i, 415, 419.

Winslow, Colonel, Letter to, from Governor Belcher, vii, 65.

Winthrop, Colonel, Governor of Connecticut, dead, i, 153—iii, 271.

Winter, William, ii, 325, 397—iii, 212.

Wise, Richard, ii, 239, 240, 255.

Wisner, Henry, x, 530.

Wite, William, ii, 327.

Withers, Ralph, i, 394—ii, 63, 72.

Witherspoon, Rev. John, Petition of, x, 342, 345, 429.

Wolley, Charles, i, 157.

Wolley, John, ii, 326, 397.

Wollison, Woolley, i, 269.

Wolston, John, i, 288.

Wolverson, Peter, i, 50.

Wood, John, i, 269.

Wood, Jonas, i, 50—ii, 397.—Affidavit in support of the Assembly's remonstrance, iii, 202; Referred to, 211.

Woods, Joseph, Contributes to a supposed Cornbury Fund, iii, 199.

Wood, Richard, viii, Part II, 151—x, 530.

Wood, William, ii, 148, 327, 396.—Letter from, to the Lords of Trade,
relative to the issuing of paper money, vi, 51, 52.

Woodbridge, Oath of allegiance taken by the inhabitants, 1667-68, i, 50;
Order from Governor Carteret, enlarging the authority of the Court
at, 62; Letter from Governor Carteret to the people of, relative to
admitting persons to vote at town meetings who had not lands surveyed and patented to them, 63; Grant to the Freeholders of, from
Lords Berkeley and Carteret, 104; Notice to the inhabitants to take
out their patents, 120; Relations with the Council of New Netherlands, 122, 125, 126, 128, 129, 130, 131, 133, 134, 137, 144, 147; Differences between, and Piscataway, 154, 159; Election of Justices under
instruction of Governor Andros, objected to, 318.—Documents relating to the riots in, iii, 480–486.—Elections of, iv, 8, 15; Petition of
the inhabitants of, for a church, 189.

Woodcock, Henry, vii, 326, 327.

Wooden, Andrew, ii, 327.

Wooden, Josias, ii, 327.

Woodhouse, Anthony, 269.

Woodhouse, William, i, 288.

Woodrofe, Thomas, i, 268, 451.

Woodroffe, Benjamin, ii, 396.

Woodroof, Joseph, ii, 129, 146.

Woodruff, Benjamin, x, 345.

Woodruff, David, ii, 129.

Woodruff, Isaac, x, 364.

Woodruff (Woodroffe), John, i, 50, 65, 133, 177—ii, 129, 380, 397—iii,
199.

Woodruff, Joseph, vi, 213—x, 44.

Woodruff, Samuel, vii, 420.—Nominated for Council, viii, Part II, 236.
—Member of Council, ix, 274; Commissioner for trying pirates, 283;
   Referred to, 511.—Dead, x, 44; Notice of, 44; Referred to, 58, 59.
Woodward, Anthony, ii, 397—iii, 210—iv, 111, 377.
Wooley (Wolly), Robert, ii, 129, 326, 396.
Woolly, Edward, Contributes to the supposed Cornbury Fund, iii, 212.
Woolly, John, Contributes to the supposed Cornbury Fund, iii, 212, 218.
Woolman, John, iii, 165—ix, 346.
Woolsson, John, iv, 147.
Woolsson, John, Jr., iv, 147.
Woolsson, Samuel, iv, 147.
Woolston, John, ii, 148.
Woolton, John, iv, 277-285.
Woolverton, Thomas, viii, Part 11, 235.
Wooster, General, ix, 339.
Worledge, John, i, 269—ii, 146.
Worral, Joseph, x, 450.
Worth, John, ii, 337—iii, 486, 487—iv, 188.
Worth, Joseph, i. 186.
Worth, William, i, 413, 414.
Wraxall's Complaint, viii, Part 1, 116.
Wright, Benjamin, iv, 83.
Wright, James, ix, 622.
Wright, John, ii, 148—iv, 310—v, 133.
Wright, Jonathan, v, 141.
Wright, Joseph, i, 527—ii, 171, 177, 186-193—iii, 314.
Wright, Joshua, i, 268—v, 211.
Wright, Robert, iv, 10, 190.
Wright, Samuel, iv, 310—vii, 99.
Wright, Thomas, i, 51, 288—iv, 113, 310.
Wrightman, Philip, ii, 470.
Wrighton, William, ii, 481.
Wuoyt, One of the owners of Cape May, i, 1.
Wyat, Bartholomew, v, 133, 137.
Wyat, Justice, iv, 296, 299.
Wyckoff, Simon (Cornelius), vi, 455, 465, 469, 470—vii, 64, 403, 449, 450,
   451, 458.—Imprisonment of, viii, Part I, 37, 38, 39, 43, 45-52.
Wyllys, George, x, 642.
Wynd, Barnabas, i, 65.
Wynings, John, i, 65.
Wyth, George, x, 678, 691.
Wywannattamo, Indian murderer, i, 73.

Y.

Yard, Joseph, Inspector of the Press, viii, Part II, 70; Commissioner for procuring supplies for the troops, 140; Letter to, from Governor Belcher, 140; Warrants to, 151, 153, 230–233.

Yard, Secretary, ii, 420, 427.

Yearins, Erigge, i, 413.

Yorke, Charles, Attorney-General, Answers queries as to the validity of Governor Hardy's appointmens, ix, 380; Questioned respecting the holding of lands by aliens in America, 382.

Yorkshire, Name given to Long Island by Governor Nicolls, i, 47.

Young, Arthur, x, 718.

Young, Christopher, i, 50, 299.

Young, Henry, Surrogate, ix, 359—v, 718.

Young, Israel, x, 717.

Young, Martin, x, 718.

Young, Robert, vi, 245, 401—vii, 216, 457.

Young, Stephen, vi, 245—vii, 454.

Young, Captain Thomas, i, 50, 66.

Young, Walter, Commissioner of Customs, ii, 131, 254.

Z.

Zabriskie, See Sobrisco.

Zane, Robert, i, 269.

Zenger, Catherine, vii, 53.